EXPERIMENTS IN LIFE

EXPERIMENTS IN LIFE
GEORGE ELIOT'S QUEST FOR VALUES

Bernard J. Paris
Michigan State University

1965   WAYNE STATE UNIVERSITY PRESS   DETROIT

3 - 1303 - 00002 - 9208

3-31-80

FOR SHIRLEY

My writing is simply a set of experiments in life—an endeavour to see what our thought and emotion may be capable of—what stores of motive . . . give promise of a better after which we may strive—what gains from past revelations and discipline we must strive to keep hold of as something more sure than shifting theory. I become more and more timid—with less daring to adopt any formula which does not get itself clothed for me in some human figure and individual experience, and perhaps that is a sign that if I help others to see at all it must be through that medium of art.

—*George Eliot to Dr. Joseph Frank Payne, January 25, 1876*

PREFACE

Since F. R. Leavis included George Eliot within the Great Tradition, there have been a number of studies both of her life and of her works. None, however, attempts what I try to do here. For another book which examines her ideas in relation to her time, and her art in relation to her ideas, we must go back to George Willis Cooke's *George Eliot,* first published in 1883. I do not mean to say that there has been no interest in her ideas; critics continually cite her humanism as one of the main reasons why we find her so interesting. But recent students of George Eliot have been primarily concerned with her technique, with analyzing her formal qualities and establishing her greatness as an artist. My study of her intellectual development and of the ways in which she employed her novels in her quest for values in a Godless universe will, I hope, contribute to a more complete appreciation of her achievement.

This book, then, is complementary to the work of such recent critics as Barbara Hardy, Reva Stump, and W. J. Harvey. I did not design it to be so, for I had completed my own investigations before I read these critics. When their books appeared, I had the pleasant sense that we were all reading the same George Eliot; in a number of cases we had come to similar conclusions but by quite different routes.

If my approach to the novels is to be classified, it should be called thematic. The question that I am chiefly concerned with is: What comment do the works make upon human nature, the human condition, and human values? My approach is both historical and critical. I have tried to see George Eliot's thought in relation to her intellectual milieu and to see her novels in relation to her thought. At the same time, I have tried to avoid imposing an intellectual system upon the novels by allowing my close reading of the fiction and my study of the philosophic background gradually to illuminate each other. I began by carefully analyzing the novels, and this analysis has shaped my view of their ideological framework quite as much as my study of the philosophers has shaped my view of the novels.

For purposes of clarity and economy, however, I have more or less separated my discussions of the philosophic background and of the fiction. Chapters I through V deal with George Eliot's ideas as they were shaped by her intellectual milieu. They should interest the historian of ideas and of the Victorian age as well as the student of fiction. In the pivotal sixth chapter I argue that George Eliot hoped through her novels, which she spoke of as "experiments in life," to discover enduring truths which would ennoble human existence and replace the outmoded beliefs and institutions of the past. Because of her distrust of "shifting theory" and her reluctance to "adopt any formula which does not get itself clothed . . . in some human figure and individual experience," art was the only means she could confidently employ for the discovery, verification, and expression of these truths. Chapters VII through XI examine the novels. They consider first the three stages of moral development through which George Eliot's characters go, then the moral implications of the relation between the individual and his social medium, and finally the religious nature of interpersonal relationships. The final chapter attempts to synthesize what my study both of the intellectual milieu and of the novels themselves tells us, finally, about George Eliot's quest for values in a universe without God.

My purpose has been to explicate rather than to evaluate. There is one value judgment, however, which is implicit in my book as a whole; that is, that George Eliot is worth studying with the utmost seriousness. Mr. Leavis, Mrs. Hardy, and Mr. Harvey have made excellent cases for her greatness. The time has come in George Eliot criticism when she no longer needs to be defended as an important artist, when she can be studied as an acknowledged master; and it is in this spirit that I have studied her.

I first studied George Eliot with Professor Earl R. Wasserman, of the Johns Hopkins University, and I shall always be indebted to him for stimulating my interest in the novel and for teaching me how to read analytically. To Professor J. Hillis Miller, also of Johns Hopkins, I am thankful both for his inspiration and for his careful, yet sympathetic, criticism of the earliest versions of my manuscript. Professors Charles R. Anderson and Ludwig Edelstein of Johns Hopkins, J. Burke Severs and James R. Frakes of Lehigh University, and Sam S. Baskett of Michigan State University have also read my manuscript, and their advice and support has been most helpful to me. I am especially grateful to Jackson I. Cope for his continued encouragement and sustaining faith.

I am grateful for two Michigan State All University Research Grants, which have enabled me to put the manuscript in final shape for the Wayne State University Press, and to Mrs. John B. Friedman, who typed with care. The portions of my study which have appeared in *Studies in Philology, The Humanist,* and *ELH* are included here, much revised, with the kind permission of the editors of these journals.

My deepest debts are to my parents, without whose assistance this book may never have been written, and to my wife, without whose aid and insight I must have written a lesser work.

B. J. P.

CONTENTS

xi

EXPERIMENTS IN LIFE

FROM CHRISTIANITY TO POSITIVISM

I

George Eliot's personal experience recapitulated Auguste Comte's famous Law of the Three Stages of human development; her approach to reality was first theological, then metaphysical, and finally positivistic. The mature George Eliot sought to reconcile the satisfaction of the needs of the heart, which was the great strength of the old creeds, with the allegiance to empirically verifiable truth that was the foundation of modern thought. With Guildenstern in "A College Breakfast-Party," she demanded that the religion of the future "satisfy ideal man,/His utmost reason and his utmost love." George Eliot was both a realist and a moralist. Realism and moralism were the two strongest demands of her culture and of her nature, and her problem was to satisfy both by reconciling them. This problem was the matrix of her artistic impulse, and it determined both her technique and her subject matter; for her art was the means by which she pursued its solution.

Realism in art, which is usually connected with nominalism and empiricism in philosophy,[1] took its rise in the late Middle Ages. "It was," writes Alfred Whitehead, "the rise of interest in natural objects and in natural occurrences for their own sakes. The natural foliage of a district was sculptured in out-of-the-way spots of the later buildings, merely as exhibiting delight in those familiar objects. The whole atmosphere of every art exhibited a direct joy in the apprehension of the things which lie around us."[2] The rise of realism was an early sign of that shift in emphasis to the sensuous, the earthly, the immediate, which has been one of the major developments in Western civilization since the Middle Ages. Realism stresses the sensuous apprehension of reality at the expense of the metaphysical or the theological; it is concerned with the thisness rather than with the whatness of things. Concerning the Dutch *genre* painters, with whose art George Eliot compared her own in the famous statement of her esthetic theory in Chapter XVII of *Adam Bede,* Mario Praz writes:

> With the exclusion of all transcendental aims, the painter's attention could be devoted to the rendering of material objects with complete and sincere abandonment, to the enjoyment of their richness, their quality, their charm. Hence, in the greatest of these painters . . . the firm intensity of contemplation that charges the object represented with a fullness of energy undiverted by any metaphysical intention. . . . And so, in this school of painting, realism triumphs.[3]

George Eliot, a realist, took direct pleasure in the apprehension and representation of reality; her novels, in their specificity, reveal this. Her senses responded to the slightest impression: she was intensely alive to the qualities of things. In her essay on German wit she complains of the German's want of "delicate perception" and "sensibility to gradation":

> All his subtlety is reserved for the region of metaphysics. For *Identität,* in the abstract, no one can have an acuter vision; but in the concrete he is satisfied with a very loose approximation. He has the finest nose for *Empirismus* in philosophical doctrine, but the presence of more or less tobacco-smoke in the air he breathes is imperceptible to him. To the typical German—*Vetter Michel*—it is indifferent whether his door-lock will catch; whether his teacup be more or less than an inch thick; whether or not his book have every other leaf unstitched; whether his neighbor's conversation be more or less of a shout; whether he pronounced *b* or *p, t* or *d;* whether or not his adored one's teeth be few and far between.[4]

Although a spontaneous delight in concrete reality is his starting point, the sophisticated realist, like the scientist, wants to add to our knowledge of the nature of things. George Eliot tried to present a true picture of man and his environment; her novels can be read, from one point of view, as scientific case studies of specific social, political, economic, historical, psychological, and religious phenomena.

Like most of the other positivists, she wanted not only to describe, but also to relieve the human condition. G. H. Lewes proclaimed that "the Intellect is the servant, not the lord of the Heart; and Science is a futile, frivolous pursuit . . . unless it subserve some grand religious aim."[5] Lewes is here echoing Comte, who made the affections central in his system, as he said they had been in the theological stage of human development. "The intellect," said Comte, "should devote itself exclusively to the problems which the heart suggests, the ultimate object being to find proper satisfaction for our various wants."[6] The scientist's dispassionate study of the relations of things, it was hoped, would enable man to discern and submit to the unalterable and to strive effectively after the possible. Only through positive knowledge could man adapt himself to reality and reality to his needs. Realism was thus the servant of moralism.

To say that George Eliot was a moralist does not mean that she employed her art chiefly as a means of teaching ethical lessons; she frequently and explicitly repudiated didacticism in art. And the problem of developing a secular ethic, though important, was only one facet of her moralism. Basic in her moralism was her concern with religious experience. Her private experience had made her aware of the strength and insistence of man's religious need; she knew that, regardless of his rational estimate of reality, man has a demand, in Suzanne Langer's phrase, to orient himself religiously in the cosmos. One of man's most basic religious drives, and hence a central concern of George Eliot's moralism, is his urge to overcome his sense of loneliness, of apartness, of alienation from the world around him. He needs somehow to control and understand and humanize the indifferent, mysterious otherness outside of himself, to make it one with himself, to find a home in it.

The greatest mediators between the self and the world had been

the Christian church—with its revelation, its ritual, and its Redeemer
—and the Platonistic philosophic tradition; but for George Eliot and
her fellow positivists Christianity and Idealism no longer possessed
religious virtue, for while they served the purposes of moralism, they
failed to meet the demands of realism. They were felt to be merely
the projections of inner drives and experiences into the external
order; they tell us nothing of the world, though they give us deep
insight into the nature of man. Thus they could not provide the
realist with a sense of religious orientation in the cosmos. But the
need for such orientation remained; indeed it grew more intense
with the deprivation of the old satisfactions.

Insofar as she was a realist, Eliot's approach to life was scientific,
and she was committed to science's picture of man and the universe—
a picture that tended to undermine man's traditional sense of his own
dignity and purpose, to leave him without guidance or consolation.
Insofar as she was a moralist, she sought means of satisfying the
heart's needs and ways of redefining man's cherished conceptions of
life and of himself. She tried to bring together in and through her
art what Henry Myers calls the "two fundamentally different views
of life, two ways of looking at man and the universe, one from within,
the other from the outside." "The first view," writes Myers, "is personal
and insighted. . . . From the individual's own point of view, the world
begins and ends with his awareness of it. As long as he clings to this
point of view, and believes in its validity, man is at home in the universe. . . . It is a world of values. . . . The second view is impersonal
and external. . . . When man sees himself from within and the world
as his world, he is the measure of all things; when he insists upon
viewing himself from the outside only, he discovers that he is no
longer the measure of anything." The major artist, according to
Myers, is the tragic realist, who presents us with "a world which,
though it is not impersonal and dehumanized as is the world seen
from the outside only, is nevertheless a world common to all."[7] It was
precisely the balance that Myers describes—between involvement and
detachment, between subjectivity and objectivity, between a self-
mirroring dream world and a world impersonal and dehumanized—
that George Eliot sought.

George Eliot's problem, then, was to discover a means of mediation

4

between the individual and the alien cosmos which would be consonant with the teachings of science and would at the same time satisfy the individual's demand for a moral relation to the universe. To understand why she was confronted with this problem and how she attempted to solve it, we must know something of her intellectual and moral development. It was only after she had abandoned both Christianity and pantheism that the problem arose, and it was only because she had been a Christian and a pantheist that the need to solve it was so imperative.

II

Before her break with Christianity George Eliot (then Marian Evans) was an ardent, otherworldly Evangelical who suffered from constant inner conflict, for she was simultaneously pulled in opposite directions. Under the influence of her religious creed she sought to submit herself entirely to the will of God and to live for him alone. She tried to relate all things to God's plan for the world. She practiced asceticism, denying the flesh and living not for the present but for eternity. She wrote to her Evangelical friend, teacher, and spiritual confidant Maria Lewis:

> I was once told that there was nothing out of myself to prevent my becoming as eminently holy as St. Paul. . . . O that we could live only for Eternity, that we could realize its nearness! . . . if you do not distinctly remember it, do turn to the passage in Young's "Infidel reclaimed" beginning O vain vain vain all else, Eternity! and do love the lines for my sake.[8]

She felt guilty about her delight in nature; although she found much to admire in Wordsworth, she wished that there could be added to many of her "favorite morceaux . . . an indication of less satisfaction in terrene objects, a more frequent upturning of the soul's eye" (*Letters* I, 34; see also I, 66). She regarded the world of material things and human beings as a snare for the soul, a temptation away from that highest good which is to "live and delight in conscious union with Him who condescends to say, 'Ye shall no more call me Baali or Lord but ye shall call me Ishi, my husband'" (*Letters,* I, 46). She wrote to Miss Lewis:

5

... when I hear of the marrying and giving in marriage that is constantly being transacted I can only sigh for those who are multiplying earthly ties which though powerful enough to detach their heart and thoughts from heaven, are so brittle as to be liable to be snapped asunder at every breeze. . . . I must believe that those are happiest who are considering this life merely a pilgrimage, a scene calling for diligence and watchfulness, not for repose and amusement. (*Letters*, I, 6)

Her striving for a marriage with God precluded any thought of an earthly love. But she was attracted by men. In May, 1840, she wrote to Miss Lewis of Joseph Brezzi, her language teacher: "My pilot too is anything but uninteresting, all external grace and mental power, but 'Cease ye from man' is engraven on my amulet." A few months earlier she had adopted a similar posture of renunciation with regard to another attractive young man whose name we do not know: "the image now seldom arises in consequence of entire occupation and, I trust in some degree, desire and prayer to be free from rebelling against Him whose I am by right, whose I would be by adoption" (*Letters*, I, 46, 51; see also I, 48-49, 70).

Marian Evans' religious creed did not demand an entire renunciation of the world and its pleasures. And she chose renunciation not because she was naturally ascetic, but because her nature was strongly sensuous and she was enamoured of this world. She craved the world's recognition and acclaim; she hungered for enjoyment and love. She frequently spoke of her pride and ambition, of the difficulty of subduing the flesh and resisting the strong pull of her worldly desires.[9] Her religion taught her to regard the present moment as a droplet in the ocean of eternity, but she wished to fill it with the pleasures of nature and learning and love. She recognized her spiritual danger and strove to renounce the world completely, the completeness and intensity of her renunciation being indicative of how well she loved life.

I do not deny [she wrote Miss Lewis] that there may be many who can partake with a high degree of zest of all the lawful enjoyments the world can offer and yet live in near communion with their God; who can warmly love the creature, and yet be careful that the Creator maintains his supremity in their hearts; but I confess that in my short experience and narrow sphere of action I have never been able to attain this; I find, as Dr. Johnson said respecting his wine, total abstinence much easier than moderation. (*Letters,* I, 6)

Her first extant poem, written at the age of nineteen, was entitled "Farewell!"

> As o'er the fields by evening's light I stray,
> I hear a still, small whisper—"Come away!
> Thou must to this bright, lovely world soon say
>   Farewell!"
>
> The mandate I'd obey, my lamp prepare,
> Gird up my garments, give my soul to pray'r,
> And say to earth and all that breathe earth's air
>   Farewell!

She displays no contempt of the world, but she does manifest an extreme of spiritual discipline. In the succeeding stanzas she bids farewell to the heavenly bodies, to animate and inanimate nature, to books, and to the Bible and kindred (which she will meet again in heaven). The final stanza, speaking of heaven, leaves us in no doubt of her sensuousness:

> There shall my new born senses find new joy,
> New sounds, new sights my eyes and ears employ,
> Nor fear that word that here brings sad alloy,
>   Farewell![10]

The opposing tendencies that produced inner conflict and an unbalanced response to life in the young Marian Evans are best described in their relation to each other by the German painter Naumann's comments on Dorothea Casaubon in *Middlemarch*. During her honeymoon stay in Rome, just after her first open clash with Casaubon, Dorothea was observed by Naumann and Will Ladislaw while she paused in front of the statue of the reclining Ariadne in the Vatican. Naumann, struck by her rich beauty in combination with her Quakerish dress and her posture of "brooding abstraction," remarked

7

to Will: "What do you think of that for a fine bit of antithesis? . . . There lies antique beauty, not corpse-like even in death, but arrested in the complete contentment of its sensuous perfection: and here stands beauty in its breathing life, with the consciousness of Christian centuries in its bosom." A moment later he spoke of Dorothea as "antique form animated by Christian sentiment—a sort of Christian Antigone—sensuous force controlled by spiritual passion" (Chap. XIX).[11] Naumann's comments suggest a way of understanding Marian Evans' consciousness and her historical situation. As G. H. Lewes wrote to John Blackwood, Dorothea "is more like her creator than any one else and more so than any other of her creations" (*Letters,* V, 308). It is clear to anyone who knows both Dorothea and George Eliot that George Eliot called upon her recollections of her own youthful consciousness in creating the Dorothea of the early chapters of *Middlemarch* and that part of her picture of the early Dorothea represents her mature judgment of her own Evangelical personality.

In Dorothea Brooke and Marian Evans we find the same conflict between sensuous force and spiritual passion, produced by the same combination of a sensuous nature and a Christian consciousness. Dorothea, like Marian Evans, sought always for meaning and value; the here and now must be significantly related to the world at large, to the past, to the future, and to eternity. Will Ladislaw remonstrated with her for "her want of sturdy neutral delight in things as they were" (Chap. XXX). Dorothea's delight in physical activity and in beauty was strong; but she was a product of the Christian experience of the world, and she could not rest content in an immediate enjoyment of life. She loved the countryside and horseback riding, but "she felt that she enjoyed" riding "in a pagan sensuous way, and always looked forward to renouncing it" (Chap. I). Dorothea could not be persuaded by Celia to wear some of their mother's jewelry, yet she responded to the beauty of the gems with an intensity that was unknown to her worldly sister. The habit of her mind, her "consciousness of Christian centuries," impelled her to seek a larger meaning in her delight:

"How very beautiful these gems are! . . . It is strange how deeply colours seem to penetrate one, like scent. I suppose that is the reason

8

why gems are used as spiritual emblems in the Revelation of St. John. They look like fragments of heaven." . . . All the while her thought was trying to justify her delight in the colours by merging them in her mystic religious joy. (Chap. I)

In both Dorothea and Marian Evans, the consciousness of the Christian centuries inhibited a free appreciation of art. On the subject of novel reading, Marian wrote to Maria Lewis: "The weapons of the Christian warfare were never sharpened at the forge of romance. . . . For my part I am ready to sit down and weep at the impossibility of my understanding or barely knowing even a fraction of the sum of objects that present themselves for our contemplation in books and in life. Have I then any time to spend on things that never existed?" (*Letters*, I, 23)[12] Dorothea complained to Will Ladislaw that "all this immense expense of art, that seems somehow to lie outside life and make it no better for the world, pains one" (Chap. XXII). Dorothea's limited, narrowly directed education was partly responsible for her inability to see the value of art; but no amount of academic instruction in the arts could have enabled Dorothea to delight in the representation of reality for its own sake. Her sensuous force was dominated by her spiritual passion. Had she become conscious of the statue in front of her as she stood brooding in the Vatican she would have been disturbed by its "antique beauty . . . arrested in the complete contentment of its sensuous perfection."

Dorothea's response to life was unbalanced; her consuming search for personal and social significance and her pervading concern for the ends of life made her humorless and blind to much of the life around her. Though her nature was capable of intense sensuous pleasure, as is evidenced by her love of riding and her response to the gems, she practiced continual self-denial and self-restraint; she could not yield herself up to the experience of the moment. Her response to life lacked spontaneity. For all her high-mindedness and earnestness—indeed, because of them—Dorothea appears to us in the early chapters of *Middlemarch* as a slightly ludicrous and unappealingly Purtanic figure.

The conflict in Marian Evans between sensuous force and spiritual passion, which makes her appear such an uneasy, unattractive figure

9

through the first 120 pages of her letters, was partially resolved by her break with Christianity. If she had remained a Christian she would never have become a novelist; if she had never been a Christian her art would not have been so strongly moralistic. After the break with Christianity at the end of 1841 her sensuous force and spiritual passion were both directed towards the earthly and the human; she was now able to feel spontaneous delight in what she had formerly felt compelled to renounce. In 1847 she wrote to Sara Hennell of her trip to the Isle of Wight: "I heartily wish you *had* been with me to see all the beauties which have gladdened my soul and made me feel that this earth is as good a heaven as I ought to dream of" (*Letters,* I, 239). She experienced a joyous sense of liberation, which she expressed in a letter written in August 1842, to Francis Watts, a clergyman whom her pious neighbors the Sibrees had sent to bring her back into the fold:

> I confess to you that I feel it an inexpressible relief to be freed from the apprehension of what Finney well describes, that at each moment I tread on chords that will vibrate for weal or woe to all eternity. I could shed tears of joy to believe that in this lovely world I may lie on the grass and ruminate on possibilities without dreading lest my conclusions should be ever-lastingly fatal. It seems to me that the awful anticipations entailed by a reception of all the dogmas in the New Testament operate unfavourably on moral beauty by disturbing that spontaneity, that choice of the good for its own sake, that answers my ideal. (*Letters,* I, 143–144)

Marian Evans gained, then, both a moral liberation—which was to create as many problems as it solved—and that freedom to take a sturdy neutral delight in things as they are which is the foundation of her realistic art. The strong sensuousness of her nature was now free to express itself. That it had been present before her break with Christianity is clearly demonstrated by a letter written in March 1841, probably to Martha Jackson, headed "Letters [*sic*] from a Town Mouse to a Country Mouse." The writer, the town mouse, is imagining "that we are strolling together round your five acres":

> Towzer's nose pushes itself against my fingers, and then my fingers wander about his rough coat as I write. I am in the country, without

the trouble of packing up: I see the autumn berries, I snuff the peculiar freshness of the autumn air between the hedge rows in the green
lane, and the new soil the plough is turning over in the next field; or
I wrap my cloak about me and enjoy the December hoar frost that
defines every lingering brown leaf on the brambles or the young oaks;
or I please myself in detecting the very earliest spring buds, and the
delicate hints of colour on the bough tips; or I hear the swirl of the
scythe as I watch the delicate grasses trembling under the eager flight
and restless alighting of the humming insects; or I stand entranced
before the glory of form and colour in the ripe full-eared corn field.
(*Letters*, I, 85–86)

It must be kept in mind, however, that while Marian Evans' break
with Christianity resulted in a moral liberation that was also a freeing
of her sensuous force, it did not diminish her desire to experience life
religiously. The letter to Francis Watts indicates the prevailing moral
bias of her thought. She abandoned the dogmas of Christianity, but
she could not abandon the Christian habit of mind, "the consciousness
of Christian centuries in her bosom," that had become an integral
part of her being. Her Christian consciousness remained with her all
her life, shaping the way in which she addressed herself to reality.

III

After her break with Christianity, Marian Evans did not immediately arrive at the purely secular humanism that characterizes her
mature thought and art. Nor did she go from a Christian universe
in which every thought and action vibrated "for weal or woe to all
eternity" to a meaningless universe in which life is to be experienced
blindly and disconnectedly from moment to moment. From her
readings in such writers as Wordsworth, Carlyle, Spinoza, Bray, and
Hennell, she derived a pantheism which permitted her to retain many
of her old values despite her rejection of the authority of the Bible.
The Higher Criticism of Hennell and Strauss, while it attacked
orthodox conceptions of Christianity, attempted to show that the
Scriptures, despite their lack of historical authority, are a repository of
eternal spiritual truths. Christ remained an object of veneration: for
Hennell he was the hero endowed with unclouded right reason, and
for Strauss he bodied forth the profoundest teaching of the Hegelian

philosophy in that he symbolized the ultimate union of matter and spirit, phenomenal and noumenal, man and God.

Both Spinoza, whose *Tractatus Theologico-Politicus* Marian Evans began to translate in March 1843, and Charles Christian Hennell, whose *Inquiry Concerning the Origin of Christianity* was the immediate cause of her rejection of Christianity, replaced theology with metaphysics by affirming the inseparability of God from his creation. God is nature; whatever is, is one. He is immanent in the laws of nature and in the rational faculties of man. Everything that exists is fraught with divine significance. The pantheism of Spinoza and Hennell, along with the ideas propounded in Charles Bray's *The Philosophy of Necessity* (1841), enabled Marian Evans to accept the determinism of science without sacrificing her belief that a spiritual principle governs the universe. God exists. He is revealed to man not miraculously through a special collection of writings but through man's own mind contemplating itself and the course of nature.[13] Her break with Christianity did not, then, involve a complete revolution in her world view. Although some of her beliefs underwent radical change, many were simply cast into a new form.

Hennell concluded his *Inquiry* (1838) with a brief exposition of the new religion that was to supplant and improve upon the old, and in *Christian Theism* (1839) he developed his ideas more fully. In April 1842, Marian Evans wrote to Francis Watts: "I feel with Coleridge that, the notion of Revelation abandoned, there is ever a tendency towards Pantheism, and the personality of the Deity is not to be maintained quite satisfactorily apart from Christianity" (*Letters, I,* 136). Hennell's concern, too, in *Christian Theism* was to speculate "on the direction which the religious sentiments of men may be expected to take after the relinquishment of their belief in miraculous revelations." According to him, man will come to see nature as the source of his truth and the object of his veneration. Man's hope lies in the fact that nature's God-given law is progress, a movement towards that kingdom of heaven on earth that was at the center of Christ's teachings (hence Christian theism). God reveals himself and his purposes for man through nature: ". . . the hieroglyphics are ineffaceable; the tablet is continually within view; time, then, must ever bring men nearer to Nature's great revelation, the full knowledge of God." "Nature presents us with a magnificent and harmonious pattern. . . . The pattern makes its own declaration of a designing mind. . . ." Not only in the physical universe, but also in man, especially in the great man, do we find revealed the nature and purpose of the Deity. The universe has purpose and direction, and, like its maker, it is beneficent to man. The "Soul of the World" is "a principle bearing close relationship to man's heart, and beaming forth through all material things to the intellectual eye." Questions concerning happiness, the grounds of ethical action, and the meaning and purpose of life are answered by Nature: "The Natural Consequences of actions become . . . the Scripture of God's will concerning the conduct of man." It is at once man's purpose and salvation (happiness) to put himself in harmony with the will of God as it is revealed in the constitution of human and physical nature.[14]

Marian Evans must have greeted Hennell's reasoning eagerly, for now she could at once be liberated from the fears and restrictions of her Evangelicism and remain in possession of a belief that gave significance to life.[15] Pantheism, by identifying the material with the spiritual, the natural with the supernatural, permitted the intimate combination of sensuous force and spiritual passion, of realism and moralism. Thing and value, sensuous delight and moral relation were one. Thus, she wrote to Mrs. Pears, in March 1842:

> There are externals . . . that I could ill part with—the deep, blue, glorious heavens, bending as they do over all, presenting the same arch, emblem of a truer omnipresence, wherever we may be chased, and all the sweet, peace-breathing sights and sounds of this lovely Earth. These, and the thoughts of the good and great are an inexhaustible world of delights, and the felt desire to be one in will and design with the Great Mind that has laid open to us these treasures is the Sun that warms and fructifies it. (*Letters*, I, 133)

The reconciliation of sensuous force and spiritual passion which pantheism provided is even more clearly indicated in her letter to Martha Jackson in December, 1841, during or just after her intensive study of the Bible and her reading of Hennell. She wished that there were some way in which she could hasten the acquisition of knowledge, to "make up for girlish miseducation and idleness":

13

This is the fool's hectic of wishing, which must give place to a determination in the view of all past truant-playing, to enjoy and improve
to the utmost the treasures of earth, air, and sky through the rest of
our journey. This is true gratitude and its last expression. This beautiful world is given to us children of men as a trial-field indeed, a gym-
nasium wherein temperance and self-government are both means and
ends, but withal as an Eden to dress and to keep with songs of adoration to the Giver. Each little plant, the very lichens that clothe the
dead boughs, are lovely and useful, and a link that would be missed
in the chain of being. And so we, dear Martha, have our place of use-
fulness and fitness, and cannot fail if we are true to the indications of
His will who has originated and sustains our existence to be harmoniz-
ing notes in the great chorus of praise ever ascending from every part
of the universe. (*Letters*, I, 123)

It is difficult to say exactly how long Marian Evans was a pantheist.
Her letters through April 1849 contain scattered pantheistic utterances.[16] In February 1849, she wrote to John Sibree: ". . . to me even
the works of our own Stanfield and Roberts and Creswick [landscape
painters] bring a whole world of thought and bliss—'a sense of something far more deeply interfused.' The ocean and the sky and the
everlasting hills are spirit to me, and they will never be robbed of their
sublimity" (*Letters*, I, 248). And in the following month she asked
him: "Is not the universe itself a perpetual utterance of the One
Being?" (*Letters*, I, 253.)

By 1852, and probably before, she had rejected pantheism. In a letter
of July 1852, to John Chapman, she expressed her opposition to the
school of thought "that looks on manhood as a type of the godhead
and on Jesus as the Ideal Man" and contended that "a nobler presentation of humanity has yet to be given in resignation to individual
nothingness, than could ever be shown of a being who believes in the
phantasmagoria of hope unsustained by reason" (*Letters*, II, 48–49).
Instrumental in her rejection of pantheism, of course, was her contact
with the positivistic philosophies of Comte, Mill, Spencer, Feuerbach,
and Lewes. In March and April of 1849 she still spoke of "the divine-
human soul" and "the living soul—the breath of God within us"
(*Letters*, I, 278, 280). Five years later, in the "Literature" column of

14

the *Leader,* she was engaged in defending the materialist position against the attacks of the spiritualists. Her article is not easily accessible and is worth quoting at length:

> In an article on Locke in the *Edinburgh Review* the writer, while vindicating Locke from what he calls a "gross physiological bias," admits that there is a *"tang* of materialism" in him, and that there is too much truth in the accusation that "his philosophy smells of the earth, earthy." Of course, "gross materialist" and "grovelling material- ism" come to the lips or the pen of "lofty spiritualists" as inevitably as the "Venerable Bede" or the "admirable Crichton;" but those . . . who decline to accept any conclusions drawn from definitions of the "immaterial," who find no reason to think contemptuously of matter, and who hold that the "smell of the earth" is a very wholesome smell for human nostrils, may very fairly protest against this opprobrious christening as a begging of the question. To the theory that the mind of man has some kindred with that of the brutes, the spiritualist says, with the Mormon prophet, "The very idea lessens man in my estima- tion. I know better"; but cogent as this reasoning may be, the man of "gross physiological bias" may reply that in *his* estimation this theory does not lessen man. . . . He may say that the ill-name "grovelling" is most appropriately applied to what narrows sympathy and admiration, and that in elevating the material and the earthly to the height of his loving reverence he is so much the farther from that negative condi- tion,—that to raise "a mortal to the skies" evidences the same love of the angelic as to bring "an angel down."[17]

As this passage indicates, the forces which led to Marian Evans' abandonment of the old creed provided her at the same time with a basis for a new system of values. But the rejection of pantheism was a more serious and a more radical step than the break with Christi- anity—intellectually, if not psychologically—for there was no ready- made explanation of the universe and man's relation to it to take the place of pantheism as pantheism had taken the place of Christianity. The new philosophies provided facts about the human condition and methods of discovery and verification; but they were less successful in answering questions of meaning, end, and value, in giving man a sense of religious orientation in the cosmos.

IV

The basic problem that confronted the mature George Eliot first took shape with her rejection of pantheism. Its nature was determined not only by the loss of old values but also by the demand of her realism for objectivity, for irreducible stubborn facts. I have already suggested the sources of her realism; its epistemological basis I shall discuss in Chapter V. Here I shall be concerned with her realism as it was a habit of mind and a manifestation of the positivistic spirit of the age.

Even when truth clashes with deeply held beliefs, George Eliot felt, or is offensive to the desires of the ego, it must be faced and accepted. "It seems to me pre-eminently desirable," she wrote to Mrs. Peter Taylor, "that we should learn not to make our personal comfort a standard of truth" (*Letters,* IV, 367). George Eliot was often upset when the true state of affairs, even though painful, was kept from her. Upon hearing belatedly of the death of a mutual friend, she wrote to Sara Hennell: "I think you and I are alike in this, that we can get no good out of pretended comforts, which are the devices of self-love, but would rather, in spite of pain, grow into endurance of all naked truths" (*Letters,* IV, 201).

In his manuscript notebook, entitled "Thoughts of G. H. Lewes," Lewes expressed very well what was essentially George Eliot's attitude:

So little do men care for Truth, & so much for Flattery, that false doctrines are urged on our acceptance solely on the ground of their flattery of our self-love or our desires. When Science proved that man was organized like animals, and that his mental functions were dependent on his bodily structure, the proof was rejected not because it was seen to be invalid, but because it "degraded man to the level of the brute."[18]

Lewes elaborated upon this idea, again in a way that is completely parallel to George Eliot's position, in his editorial "Causeries" column in the *Fortnightly Review:*

The other day a critic avowed his opposition to Mr. John Mill's philosophy on the ground of its being "dreary and cheerless." This is indeed a common weakness. While every one loudly proclaims his earnest desire to arrive at the truth, many reject the truth if they imagine it is likely to be unpleasant. The fact is, truth is only the object of the intellect; and most men argue as much from the data of their feelings, as from the data of logic. They wish to ascertain *what is,* but they wish the result to accord with their preconception of what *ought to be.* Instead of loyally submitting their minds to the conclusions of research, they affix a condition to their submission, and withhold assent unless the conclusion is agreeable. Thus it is that certain theories are offered to us under the tempting guise of being lofty or consoling; and against others we are solemnly warned as being cheerless and degrading; whether they are true or false seems of much less moment; or rather their truth and falsehood are supposed to be involved in the assumption of their loftiness and cheerfulness. The answer to this is twofold. The facts of the universe have their own order, and this order, which we desire to ascertain, is quite irrespective of our feelings. Upon what ground can we claim that truth shall be cheerful and consolatory? and however we may wish the truth to be pleasant to us, how will our wishes affect the actual order of things? Suppose that the truth is such as rudely to shake our preconceptions, and painfully to press upon our sensibilities—as indeed truth often does—shall we not rather resign ourselves to this necessity, and shall we not be stronger from our clearer vision and our more patient resignation?[19]

Lewes' remarks constitute a classic expression and defense of the realistic spirit of the age.

George Eliot's demand for objectivity was more than a philosophic attitude brought into being by her contact with positivism; to a certain extent, it was an involuntary habit of mind, a part of her nature. (Like all of us, of course, she had a number of things about which she could not be objective and which she did not wish to face.) As we have seen, she could not bear to have news of suffering concealed from her. In 1862 she wrote to Mme. Bodichon:

Miss Allen, however, kept back the sad part of the news—poor Ellen's illness, which I would rather have known; for in this as in all other cases, I think the highest and best thing is rather to suffer with real suffering than to be happy in the imagination of an unreal good. I would rather know that the beings I love are in some trouble and suffer because of it, even though I can't help them, than be fancying them happy when they are not so, and making myself comfortable on the strength of this false belief. And so I am impatient of all ignorance and concealment: I don't say, "that is wise" but simply "that is my nature." (*Letters*, IV, 13)

George Eliot's unflinching examination of the human lot often gave rise to melancholy and pessimism. She consoled Mrs. Charles Bray on the death of her adopted child Nelly (1865) by asserting her belief that it is a blessing, a "salvation," to die young:

> Life, though a good to men on the whole, is a doubtful good to many, and to some not a good at all. To my thought it is a source of constant mental distortion to make the denial of this a part of religion, to go on pretending things are better than they are. (*Letters*, IV, 183)

There is seldom in George Eliot's work a glossing over of the hardness of the human condition in order to arrive at desired solutions to human problems. There is no facile optimism rearranging the nature of things to suit its own purposes. The facing of facts is perhaps the primary quality of her realism.

One of the clearest expressions of her concept of objectivity occurs in the semi-autobiographical first chapter of *The Impressions of Theophrastus Such*. Theophrastus is a sensitive, ineffectual man whose physical peculiarity and unattractiveness prevent him from receiving his due recognition in an unjust world. As a result, he early begins "to seek for some consoling point of view . . . some comfortable fanaticism which might supply the needed self-satisfaction." He fastens on to the doctrine of compensation, but ultimately rejects it because, while it allows him to shape the undefined future after his own desires, it obviously cannot apply to the "multitude with as bad a share as mine, who, instead of getting their corresponding compensation, were getting beyond the reach of it in old age":

> I dropped a form of consolation which seemed to be encouraging me in the persuasion that my discontent was the chief evil in the world, and my benefit the soul of good in that evil. May there not be at least a partial release from the imprisoning verdict that a man's

18

philosophy is the formula of his personality? In certain branches of science we can ascertain our personal equation, the measure of difference between our own judgments and an average standard: may there not be some corresponding correction of our personal partialities in moral theorising? . . . is there no remedy or corrective for that inward squint which consists in a dissatisfied egoism or other want of mental balance? In my conscience I saw that the bias of personal discontent was just as misleading and odious as the bias of self-satisfaction. Whether we look through the rose-coloured glass or the indigo, we are equally far from the hues which the healthy human eye beholds in heaven above and earth below. I began to dread ways of consoling which were really a flattering of native illusions, . . . to watch with peculiar alarm lest what I called my philosophic estimate of the human lot in general, should be a mere prose lyric expressing my own pain and consequent bad temper. The standing-ground worth striving after seemed to be some Delectable Mountain, whence I could see things in proportions as little as possible determined by that self-partiality which certainly plays a necessary part in our bodily sustenance, but has a starving effect on the mind. . . .

Objectivity—seeing the external world as it is in fact rather than as we wish it to be—is a leading motif in George Eliot's thought and art. Throughout her life, by means of her art, she sought to discover what in fact the human condition is. She was searching for an objective philosophy of action and values, the conditions of which Theophrastus clearly describes. The novel, as she practiced it, was an exercise in objectivity; the position she adopted towards her characters, as omniscient narrator, exactly corresponds to Theophrastus' Delectable Mountain. She strove for an objective but "passionately interested contemplation" of life, a combination of sympathetic insight and disinterestedness.

Objectivity, however, has its dangers. The egoist, the purely subjective man, exalts his selfhood by projecting it outward until it constitutes the cosmos; but in doing this he isolates himself from the true external world and completely loses contact with it. When the outer world impinges upon him, shattering the illusion, he is apt to be bewildered or destroyed, reduced to physical or psychic nothingness. The purely objective man, on the other hand, by detaching himself from his private lot and identifying himself completely with the non-self, is in danger of losing his selfhood, of dissolving his ego, and thus of also being reduced to nothingness. Both the complete egoist and the completely objective man fail as social beings, for they cannot establish relations with their fellow men, the one because he is entirely self-enclosed and the other because he has no self with which to relate. There must be a reconciliation, therefore, between objectivity and subjectivity, just as there must be a reconciliation between realism and moralism. Theophrastus states the problem for us:

> I am really at the point of finding that this world would be worth living in without any lot of one's own. Is it not possible for me to enjoy the scenery of the earth without saying to myself, I have a cabbage-garden in it? But this sounds like the lunacy of fancying oneself everybody else and being unable to play one's own part decently—another form of the disloyal attempt to be independent of the common lot, and to live without a sharing of pain.
>
> Perhaps I have made self-betrayals enough already to show that I have not arrived at that non-human independence.

The problem of adjusting the relation between objectivity and subjectivity in the way in which one addresses the world becomes, then, the problem of defining the self. Viewing the matter from a slightly different but complementary point of view, the world must be seen neither as completely other, alien to the self (an annihilating experience), nor as entirely identical with the self, a reflection of self. The latter view provides a religious orientation which is illusory, and the former makes a religious orientation impossible.

George Eliot placed her major emphasis, however, upon the need for objectivity. She believed that man is born a subjective creature and that objectivity is developed only through the painful education of experience. Those of her characters who yearn for a religious orientation in the cosmos often vainly seek satisfaction through illusion. Her novels are filled with egoists, with characters whose immaturity or desire to escape frustration leads them to confuse the internal and the external. Their divorce from external reality always results in their failure to find the satisfaction they are seeking, and it usually brings pain to others. In this respect George Eliot's insistence on objectivity is a product of her moralism. Subjectivity is destructive of morality; the egoist is as alien to his fellows as the non-moral, indifferent physical universe, and he causes them the same anguish.

George Eliot's realistic facing of the evils and limitations which were often explained away by traditional philosophy and religion touched her view of life with a melancholy pessimism; but she was not without the optimistic belief, so characteristic of her age, that painful truth would eventually lead man to a higher life and a nobler religion than any he had known. "I have faith," she wrote in 1860 to Mme. Bodichon, "in the working-out of higher possibilities than the Catholic or any other church has presented, and those who have strength to wait and endure, are bound to accept no formula which their whole souls—their intellect as well as their emotions—do not embrace with entire reverence. The highest 'calling and election' is to *do without opium* and live through all our pain with conscious, clear-eyed endurance" (*Letters*, III, 366).

V

After her rejection of Christianity Marian Evans still lived in a universe in which the natural and the supernatural orders interpenetrated each other; and although she no longer believed in personal immortality, she still felt that man's spiritual nature linked him to God. Her insistence on human mortality was very important, of course, for it was the basis of her new humanistic approach to life; it turned her attention from heaven and eternity to man's now all important earthly existence, and it liberated her sensuous force from the restraints which had been imposed by her otherworldly spiritual passion. But her new belief harmonized in many essentials with the one she had abandoned. By endowing all existence with a divine presence and purpose, pantheism satisfied her need for a sense of religious orientation in the cosmos. When she rejected pantheism, however, she found herself in a universe that was unrelated to any value-giving supernatural order. The old questions of purpose and value had to be grappled with all over again, and there was nothing built into the order of things to assure that there were any answers. The old systematic explanations of human life were gone, and there was no new systematic explanation, despite the efforts of Comte and Spencer, to take their place.

Marian Evans' mental condition in the early 1850's had much in common with that of the inexperienced Dorothea Brooke; both had a consciousness of Christian centuries in their bosoms but had no creed by which their consciousness could be satisfied. Dorothea has the Puritan's habit of incessant introspection and looking for signs; but the Puritan knew, as she does not, how to interpret his experience. Because she lacks a binding theory of life Dorothea has a perpetual fear that she may not be justified in her beliefs and actions. Plagued by uncertainty, she feels herself a slave to her own ignorance and has a militant desire for knowledge (see Chap. VII). The tenor of her mind is Christian, but in essence she is modern man looking for a creed where there is none to be found. In addition to being the product of centuries of Christian consciousness, Dorothea is, like her creator, also the product of an age basically secular in its orientation, an age of intellectual and social fragmentation. In Dorothea, George Eliot dramatized her own quest for values.

Her rejection of the old creeds left George Eliot with a need of new consolations for the hardship and injustice of the human lot. Both Christianity and pantheism had provided consolation for misfortune and apparent injustice through their conception of the universe as providentially ordered. Christianity, in addition, offered eternal bliss through belief in a God who had suffered so that man could be saved. With these consolations gone, what was to sustain man through a painful existence (his only one) in a blind, indifferent universe? Actually, George Eliot sought not consolations, but a means of reconciling man to the realities of his lot. She wrote to Sara Hennell: ". . . it seems to me that the conception of religion as chiefly valuable for the personal consolations that may be extracted from it, is among the most active sources of falsity. The test of a higher religion might be, that it should enable the believer to do without the consolations which his egoism would demand" (*Letters,* V, 68–69). The difficulty, the tragedy, of the human lot lies, in George Eliot's view, chiefly in the disparity between the inward and the outward, in the "irreparable collision between the individual and the general." "Tragedy consists," she argued, "in the terrible difficulty" of the "adjustment of our individual needs to the dire necessities of our lot."[20] She attributed the timelessness of Greek tragedy to its insistence upon the inevitability and universality of the collision between the individual and the general: "They had the same essential elements of life presented to them as we have, and their art symbolized these in grand schematic forms. The Prometheus represents the ineffectual struggle to redeem the small and miserable race of man, against the stronger adverse ordinances that govern the frame of things with a triumphant power" (Cross's *Life,* III, 37).

But she did not feel that man must accept the painful disparity between wish and reality with blind submission. Whereas the traditional religions had taught complete submission to the will of God and the vanity or sinfulness of attempting to alter the existing order, the positivist, with his Comtian motto of "resignation and activity," strove to resign himself to the unalterable and to mitigate or eliminate accidental evils. Thus, in addition to seeking a means of reconciling man to his fate, she hoped to see how the human condition could be improved.

The need for a way to accept and endure the painful disparity between the inward and the outward is vividly depicted in the plight of Maggie Tulliver in *The Mill on the Floss.* Although her nature had always been in disharmony with her environment, Maggie became painfully aware of the disparity between her inner impulses and outer facts only after the illness and financial ruin of her father, when she could no longer live in dream worlds and when all other opiates were denied her. She was desperately in need of succor, of some way of conceiving life which would give her soul a sense of being at home in the world and would make the pain of existence bearable. The pleasures of nature, of music, of family affection were gone. Her school books "were all barren of comfort" and "so were the hard dry questions on Christian Doctrine: There was no flavour in them—no strength." Maggie "wanted some explanation of this hard, real life . . . : she wanted some key that would enable her to understand, and, in understanding, endure, the heavy weight that had fallen on her young heart" (Book IV, Chap. III). "To the usual precocity of the girl," Maggie "added that early experience of struggle, of conflict between inward impulse and outward fact, which is the lot of every imaginative and passionate nature" (Book IV, Chap. II). "No wonder," George Eliot reflected, "when there is this contrast between the outward and the inward, that painful collisions come of it (Book III, Chap. V).

Both Maggie Tulliver and Dorothea Brooke are eager, passionate creatures whose natures are oppressed by the indifference, and sometimes the hostility, of external reality. Their plight typifies George Eliot's conception of human destiny; her novels show men and women grappling with the circumstances of their lives, seeking ways to escape frustration and despair, searching for a home for themselves in the world. Many of her characters do not experience the central problem of human existence—the "contrast between the outward and the inward"—in the same ways as Maggie and Dorothea; but it is there, built into the nature of things, for all.

George Eliot devoted the years of her maturity, after her rejection of pantheism, to the reconciliation of realism and moralism. She sought, for both personal and social reasons, to satisfy the demands of her Christian consciousness by arriving at a conception of life which would endow it with meaning and value; she searched for a way to reconcile man to the pain which is an inevitable consequence of his unequal struggle with the forces outside himself; and she strove to meliorate the harshness of life by reducing the disparity between the inward and the outward. Her problem was created by the fact that her Christian consciousness was severed from its historical sources by her adherence to the methods and data of realism. The forces of realism, however, played a dual role in her mental development; they both created her problems and contributed to their solution. Her conception of life was never in suspension; she constantly developed new points of view in the process of discarding the old ones. Her rejection of Christianity and pantheism was brought about by her knowledge of the cosmological and epistemological tenets of positive science; and, as the following chapters will show, the cosmology and epistemology of science were instrumental in leading George Eliot to a morality which, for her, met the needs of the heart and yet was independent of supernatural sources and sanctions.

THE NATURE OF THINGS

I

With her abandonment of pantheism George Eliot turned to empiricism for an understanding of man, nature, and society. From the positive philosophies of Auguste Comte, John Stuart Mill, Herbert Spencer, George Henry Lewes, and Ludwig Feuerbach, she derived the premises upon which her aesthetic theory, her representation of life, and her understanding of moral and religious phenomena are based. The principles of the positivistic cosmology and epistemology constitute the most general laws of her fictional worlds; they are the presuppositions which govern every phase of her thought.

In her article on W. E. H. Lecky's *History of Rationalism,* George Eliot spoke of the basic tenet of the scientific cosmology—"the great conception of universal regular sequence, without partiality and without caprice"—as "the conception which is the most potent force at work in the modification of our faith, and of the practical form given to our sentiments."[1] She was quick to see the moral implications of the scientific cosmology. In her review of Mackay's *The Progress of the Intellect,* she complained that the notion of undeviating law "is still perversely ignored in our social organization, our ethics and our religion." She felt that the regularity of nature is a boon to man, for it alone can "give value to experience and render education in the true sense possible." With man's new knowledge comes a new power which promises a continual improvement in the human condition. Further, the conception of invariability of sequence, which in the moral sphere is the "inexorable law of consequences," leads us to see the experience of past ages as part of the "education of the race": "every mistake, every absurdity into which poor human nature has fallen, may be looked on as an experiment of which we may reap the benefit."[2]

George Eliot was aware that nature's orderliness also has its darker issues. The order of things can be neither denied nor resisted without disastrous consequences; but submission to it will not necessarily avert calamity or suffering. The idea of a deity who orders phenomena for the benefit of the species or the individual, who responds to men's prayers, or who compensates for injustice is a waking dream of the human mind. There is no reprieve from death, and there is no forgiveness of sins; causes are invariably followed by their effects, and once a deed is done it is ineradicable. Man's desire for absolute, immediate power over the course of things can never be fulfilled. But she felt that once man devotes himself to the study of things as they are, his position is far from hopeless. The disparity between the inner and the outer can never be eliminated, but it can be diminished by scientific knowledge.

The epistemology of positivism was no less important for George Eliot than its cosmology. A satisfactory relation to external reality is impossible, she felt, without an accurate conception of how things are ordered. Felix Holt tells the workingmen that "the way to get rid of folly is to get rid of vain expectations, and of thoughts that don't agree with the nature of things" (Chap. XXX). In her review of Ruskin's *Modern Painters,* Vol. III, George Eliot advocated the application of science's objective approach to reality to every phase of life:

> The truth of infinite value that he teaches is *realism*—the doctrine that all truth and beauty are to be attained by a humble and faithful study of nature, and not by substituting vague forms, bred by imagination on the mists of feeling, in place of definite, substantial reality. The thorough acceptance of this doctrine would remould our life; and he who teaches its application to any one department of human activity with such power as Mr. Ruskin's, is a prophet for his generation.[3]

There is instance after instance, in her novels, of worldly failure and of moral error and frustration resulting from thoughts that don't agree with the nature of things.

George Eliot employed her novels as a means of envisioning the implications for human existence of the order of things and of the subjective and objective approaches to reality. As the next several chapters will show, her vision of human nature, the human condition, and human values was largely shaped by the cosmology, sociology, and psychology of science. All of her characters can be classified, and understood, in terms of their tendency towards egoism or objectivity. The novel was the means by which she experimentally brought into contact the dispassionate order of things and the passionate subjectivity of human beings in an effort to discover their true relation to each other and to explore the possibilities of a reconciliation between them.

II

The primary tenets of the positive cosmology were: (1) that *all* phenomena manifest the law of causation, and (2) that change results from the *interaction* of the laws of the entities involved. These conceptions illuminated every area of human inquiry, not only physical science, but also the sciences of biology, psychology, and sociology, and, through them, moral theory.

The Law of Causation, according to Mill, "is but the familiar truth, that invariability of succession is found by observation to obtain between every fact in nature and some other fact which has preceded it."[4] The great aim of the nineteenth-century positivists was to extend the realm of nature and to make science coextensive with it by demonstrating that social and psychic phenomena, which had hitherto been explained by metaphysical speculation, are subject to the universal law of natural causation. That which is beyond nature, if there is anything, is completely unknowable, and speculation about it and about the nature of things in themselves is fruitless. The primary purpose of Comte's *Cours de Philosophie Positive* was to make all of our fundamental conceptions homogeneous by establishing the science of social physics.[5] And in the concluding section of his *Logic* ("On the Logic of the Moral Sciences"), Mill endeavored to answer the question

27

"which the decay of old opinions, and the agitation that disturbs European society to its inmost depths" had rendered supremely important: namely,

> Whether moral and social phenomena are really exceptions to the general certainty and uniformity of the course of nature; and how far the methods by which so many of the laws of the physical world have been numbered among truths irrevocably acquired and universally assented to, can be made instrumental to the formation of a similar body of received doctrine in moral and political science. (*Logic*, p. v)

Man was no longer seen to be separate from nature; he is entirely a part of it, and all of his ideas and institutions are the result of natural processes. By studying their history and the conditions under which they occur, we can begin to understand, control, and predict social and psychic phenomena.

Change results from the interaction of the laws of the entities involved. The positivists rejected any conception of the laws of nature as imposed. Many theologians and metaphysicians contended that God had imposed laws upon nature, making that orderly and harmonious which would otherwise be chaotic. Metaphysicians held, as G. H. Lewes put it, that law has "not only an objective existence *in* the phenomena, but an objective existence independent of the phenomena; . . . that Law is independent of the phenomena which it rules."[6] Thus, laws are not the manifestations of phenomena, but phenomena are manifestations of the spiritual laws which govern them. For the positivists, on the other hand, the laws of nature are not separable from the phenomena which manifest them. Lewes argued that a law expresses *"the observed series of positions. It is the process of phenomena, not an agent apart from them, not an agency determining them,* but simply the ideal *summation of their position"* (*PLM,* I, 283). To make a law an entity in itself is to commit the error of reifying abstractions. There is no such thing as a deviation from the laws of nature: the process is the law. Nature has an overall order, in the sense that it frequently repeats itself, because identical conditions often recur.

The metaphysical tradition frequently presented a universe in which each object is causally independent of all other objects. Each object was endowed with its own nature by God, and, like Leibnitz's windowless monads, it could enter into relation with other objects only through a supernatural agency. The Cartesians, as Mill pointed out, "affirmed it to be impossible that a material and a mental fact could be causes of one another. They regarded them as mere Occasions on which the real agent, God, thought fit to exert his power as a Cause." The impossibility of conceiving mutual action between mind and matter led, Mill claims, to a denial of the possibility of action of matter upon matter: "*The deus ex machina* was ultimately called in to produce a spark on the occasion of a flint and steel coming together, or to break an egg on the occasion its falling on the ground" (*Logic,* p. 261).

The positivists, on the other hand, held that objects have direct contact with each other; that it is this contact which produces phenomena; and, very important, that the contact between objects results in a change in their physio-chemical properties or laws. The results of their interactions are a consequence of their laws, and their laws are, to a large degree, the embodied history of their previous interactions. Change is gradual, but it may result in the emergence of novelty. The present state of the universe is to be explained not in terms of an imposed divine plan, but by the concept of evolution. Lewes wrote: "Final causes are said to have made things for each other, when in point of fact, the things were evolved, one out of the other, or both out of a common ground."[7]

Natural sequences are the product not of noumenal agencies, nor simply of the direct action of one thing upon another, but of the interaction of the causes (i.e., groups of relations or properties) which constitute them. When a change occurs in an object, the object itself is not merely the theater of the change, but one of its causes. According to Mill, "things are never more active than in the production of those phenomena in which they are said to be acted upon . . . patients are always agents; in a great proportion, indeed, of all natural phenomena, they are so to such a degree as to react forcibly on the causes which acted upon them" (*Logic,* p. 242). It is impossible to explain why phenomena are determined by the laws of the objects which enter into them, but experience shows that this is and has been the case and is our warrant for believing that nature will continue to operate in this manner. The law of causation is simply a brute fact. The positivistic explanation of the why of things provides man with a power over nature which he can use to satisfy the desires of his heart, but it cannot satisfy his moral urge for a meaning in the order of things. Things are what they are. And they are what they are because they are what they are: because they have been what they have been, because they have been acted upon by what has acted upon them, because they act in accordance with their laws, their natures. The universe as a whole is orderly because the behavior of each of its components is determined by its properties. What are its properties? Its properties are its relations to other entities and to our consciousness; its properties are identical with its behavior, its laws. It acts the way it does because it is what it is; it is what it is because it acts the way it does.

III

Science pictured the universe as a vast network of relations: in the language of Comte and Lewes, as an organism composed of many smaller organisms which are related at once to each other and to the whole; or, to use Mill's metaphor, as a web composed of dynamically interwoven phenomena. George Eliot employed the metaphors of the organism and the web again and again. In *Romola,* for example, speaking, of the interdependence of individual and society, she wrote:

> Since that Easter a great change had come over the prospects of Florence; and as in the tree that bears a myriad of blossoms, each single bud with its fruit is dependent on the primary circulation of the sap, so the fortunes of Tito and Romola were dependent on certain grand political and social conditions which made an epoch in the history of Italy. (Chap. XXI)

In *Middlemarch* she explains that the modern author, unlike Fielding, has little time for pleasant digressions: "I at least have so much to do in unravelling certain human lots, and seeing how they were woven and interwoven, that all the light I can command must be concentrated on that particular web, and not dispersed over that tempting range of relevancies called the universe" (Chap. XV)[8]. The nature of the web which constitutes the cosmos of her novels is clearly described in Mill's *Logic*.

Mill emphasized that the regularity of the course of nature is the product not of one uniformity, but of the interconnection of a great number of less general uniformities. The various classes of phenomena, each having their own laws, are "much intermixed and entangled with one another," and hence, "the regularity which exists in nature is a web composed of distinct threads" (*Logic,* p. 231). The web of the present is the product of past interweavings; it has been formed by a process of evolution. The threads are only hypothetically distinct; they are in fact so intricately interwoven that we cannot account for any one without seeing it in relation to a great many others. The way in which the web is put together is explained in Mill's discussion of two subsidiary aspects of the law of universal causation: one, the plurality of causes and the intermixture of effects, and the other, the composition of causes.

Every phenomenon has a plurality of causes. In the physical sciences, under laboratory conditions, it is relatively easy to master all of the causes which produce a given effect. But the states of mind and actions of human beings and the structure and institutions of societies are the products of an immense number of causes, all of which must be taken into account. Some of these causes are of such a general nature that they may be taken for granted in explaining a specific event; but even so, the network of causes which must be envisaged to explain any human phenomenon is extremely complex.

Think, for example, of how many causes are operative in Mr. Tulliver's decision, in *The Mill on the Floss,* to have Tom educated by Mr. Stelling. Or note how many social, political, and economic conditions and personal motivations, each with its own complex history, George Eliot depicts in her explanation of the election day riot at Treby Magna and its consequences for Felix Holt. Not only does she show every situation and action as the product of natural causes; she also strives to give the whole picture, the whole network of relations, past and present, inner and outer, or as much of it as possible. What she does not present in detail, she suggests. A very large part of "Janet's Repentance" is devoted to depicting the numerous antecedent and co-existent causes and conditions of Janet's relation to

Mr. Tryan. If the Evangelical movement had not come to Milby, Mr. Tryan would not have been there; and if certain social, economic, and political changes had not occurred in the life of the nation and in the life of the town, the Evangelical movement would not have come to Milby. Mr. Tryan would not be in Milby as an Evangelical preacher if he had not had the experience which led him to devote himself to the religious life. Further, if Mr. Tryan had not had this experience he would not have the character and the sympathy which enable him to be an inspiration to Janet.

In the phenomena of politics and history, Mill writes, "Plurality of Causes exists in almost boundless excess, and effects are, for the most part, inextricably interwoven with one another." Such phenomena are "liable to be affected directly or indirectly either in *plus* or in *minus* by nearly every fact which exists, or event which occurs, in human society" (*Logic*, p. 324). The multiplicity of causes involved in human affairs endows them with a complexity which resists analysis. In expressing her agreement with Charles Bray's necessitarian doctrine that "mind presents itself under the same condition of invariableness of antecedent and consequent as all other phenomena," George Eliot noted that the difference between mental and physical phenomena is "that the true antecedent and consequent are proportionately difficult to discover as the phenomena are more complex" (*Letters*, II, 403). Mill points out that although it may be possible to reduce social and psychic phenomena to a few general laws (e.g., the law of association of ideas), or to discover the major causes which act upon men and societies as a whole, such knowledge does little to explain individual phenomena:

> Suppose that all which passes in the mind of man is determined by a few simple laws; still, if those laws be such that there is not one of the facts surrounding a human being, or of the events which happen to him, that does not influence in some mode or degree his subsequent mental history, and if the circumstances of different human beings are extremely different, it will be no wonder if very few propositions can be made respecting the details of their conduct or feelings, which will be true of mankind. (*Logic*, p. 598)

Such considerations led George Eliot to distrust all abstract approaches to human behavior and to try to represent life in all its concreteness and complexity.

"All laws of causation," Mill writes, "in consequence of their liability to be counteracted, require to be stated in words affirmative of tendencies only, and not of actual results" (*Logic*, p. 319). The effect that each cause *tends* to produce may be—in fact, usually is—thwarted or modified by the laws of the other entities with which it interacts. The effect of all the causes is "identical with the sum of their separate effects" (*Logic*, p. 267). But when a great many causes are in operation, it is difficult to ascertain or predict the effect of any one cause. "In social phenomena," Mill contends, "the Composition of Causes is the universal law" (*Logic*, p. 608). As phenomena become more complex, the web they weave becomes more tangled. Applied to the human situation, the composition of causes means, for one thing, that our intentions are seldom completely realized; our actions may, indeed, produce results which are quite alien to what we had anticipated or desired and which are entirely unforeseeable. Mill, like George Eliot, objects to the Benthamite school of political science because the Benthamites relied much too heavily upon the unimpeded effects of legislation, failing to recognize that legislation is but one among the many interacting causes which determine the structure and course of society.

The composition of causes is consistently operative in George Eliot's plots. Felix Holt's fate at the election riots is a striking example of how this principle manifests itself in human affairs. Felix' noble aims were again and again thwarted by the electioneering machinery which Mr. Johnson set in motion on behalf of Harold Transome. At his first encounter with Johnson, Felix' plan to get the workingmen to set up a school for their sons received a blow. As he returned home, Felix thought to himself: "Where's the good . . . of pulling at such a tangled skein as this electioneering trickery?" (Chap. XIII; see epigraph to Chap. XI.) When he attempted to avert serious trouble by leading the election day crowd out of town Felix knew that "he was in the midst of a tangled business" (Chap. XXXIII). His efforts were of no avail, for there were a number of "sharp-visaged men" in the crowd who wished the cover of a riot for private pillage: "While Felix was entertaining his ardent purpose, these other sons of Adam were entertaining another purpose of their peculiar sort, and the moment was come when they were to have their triumph" (Chap. XXXIII). And in pursuing his noble but fruitless plan Felix accidentally killed constable Tucker.

George Eliot's characters frequently find their aspirations and intentions thwarted by the retarding friction of circumstance, by the resistance which their will encounters in the will of others and in the pre-existing network of relations which constitutes their medium. Farebrother, himself a frustrated man, sums up the situation in his comment on Lydgate's ambitious and confident plans for medical reform and discovery: "You have not only got the old Adam in yourself against you, but you have got all those descendants of the original Adam who form the society around you. You see, I have paid twelve or thirteen years more than you for my knowledge of difficulties" (*Middlemarch,* Chap. XVII).

IV

The cosmology of science, then, presented George Eliot with a world that is characterized by universal regular sequence, slow but incessant evolutionary change, and enormous complexity. Above all, it is a world in which phenomena are extensively interrelated and interdependent. "Who having a practised vision may not see," she asks, "that ignorance of the true bond between events, and false conceit of means whereby sequences may be compelled—like that falsity of eyesight which overlooks the gradations of distance, seeing that which is afar off as if it were within a step or a grasp—precipitates the mistaken soul on destruction?"[9] She strove to enlighten her readers by presenting, in her novels, the connections of things. Even more important, she sought, by depicting the connected*ness* of things, to develop in her readers mental vision, the habit of mind that imaginatively surrounds every event with the network of relations, past, present, and prospective, in which it exists.

Herbert Spencer lays down the rule that "there can be no correct idea of a part without a correct idea of the correlative whole." If the part is not conceived in relation to the whole to which it belongs, "its relations to existence in general are misapprehended" and we cannot understand "the position which the part occupies in relation to other parts."[10] Observation, though the chief source and test of truth, cannot possibly furnish the comprehensive picture of reality which is necessary for a true understanding of any given phenomenon. Observation of the apparent relations of things must be supplemented by a vision or imagination of the existing but unapparent relations. Truth, scientific, moral, or artistic, is impossible without vision. After visiting George Eliot in June, 1861, John Blackwood wrote to his wife: "I never heard anything so good as her distinction between what is called the real and the imaginative. It amounted to this, That you could not have the former without the latter and greater quality. Any real observation of life and character must be limited, and the imagination must fill in and give life to the picture" (*Letters*, III, 427).

If it is impossible to have the real without the imaginative, it is likewise impossible to have a powerful and veracious imagination without a large store of accurately observed detail. The task of imagination is to find the hidden relations between these details, to construct the whole out of its visible fragments.

> Powerful imagination [George Eliot writes] is not false outward vision, but intense inward representation, and a creative energy constantly fed by susceptibility to the veriest minutiae of experience, which it reproduces and constructs in fresh and fresh wholes; not the habitual confusion of provable fact with the fictions of fancy and transient inclination, but a breadth of ideal association which informs every material object, every incidental fact with far-reaching memories and stored residues of passion, bringing into new light the less obvious relations of human existence.[11]

Truth lies in the combination of experience and vision.

The characteristics of imagination, or mental vision, are essentially the same whether the area of application be human behavior, astronomy, biology, or pathology. Both the artist and the scientist, for example, project from the known to the unknown, from the visible to the invisible, in order to approach the whole truth. George Eliot prefaces Chapter XVI of *Daniel Deronda,* in which she gives Deronda's psychological history, with the following epigraph:

35

Men, like planets, have both a visible and an invisible history. The astronomer threads the darkness with strict deduction, accounting so for every visible arc in the wanderer's orbit; and the narrator of human actions, if he did his work with the same completeness, would have to thread the hidden pathways of feeling and thought which lead up to every moment of action, and to those moments of intense suffering which take the quality of action.

Lydgate, in *Middlemarch,* hoped to discover the single primitive tissue which forms the common basis from which all else has developed by differentiation: "he longed to demonstrate the more intimate relations of living structure, and help to define men's thoughts more accurately after the true order" (Chap. XV).

Through Lydgate George Eliot presents her conception of the workings of the objective, scientific imagination. Lydgate was fascinated by Louis' new book on fever:

Fever had obscure conditions, and gave him that delightful labour of the imagination which is not mere arbitrariness, but the exercise of disciplined power—combining and constructing with the clearest eye for probabilities and the fullest obedience to knowledge; and then, in yet more energetic alliance with impartial Nature, standing aloof to invent tests by which to try its own work.

Many men have been praised as vividly imaginative on the strength of their own profuseness in indifferent drawing or cheap narration:— reports of very poor talk going on in distant orbs; or portraits of Lucifer coming down on his bad errands as a large ugly man with bat's wings and spurts of phosphorescence; or exaggerations of wantonness that seem to reflect life in a diseased dream. But these kinds of inspiration Lydgate regarded as rather vulgar and vinous compared with the imagination that reveals subtle actions inaccessible by any sort of lens, but tracked in that outer darkness through long pathways of necessary sequence by the inward light which is the last refinement of Energy, capable of bathing even the ethereal atoms in its ideally illuminated space. He . . . was enamoured of that arduous invention which is the very eye of research, provisionally framing its object and correcting it to more and more exactness of relation; he wanted to pierce the obscurity of those minute processes which prepare human

36

misery and joy, those invisible thoroughfares which are the first lurking-places of anguish, mania, and crime, that delicate poise and transition which determine the growth of happy or unhappy consciousness (Chap. XVI).

Unfortunately, Lydgate does not bring his vision of causes, consequences, and connections to bear upon his relations with his fellow men; he brought "a much more testing vision of details and relations into this pathological study than he had ever thought it necessary to apply to the complexities of love and marriage, these being subjects on which he felt himself amply informed by literature, and that traditional wisdom which is handed down in the genial conversation of men" (Chap. XVI). And his failure in human knowledge negates his great potentialities as a scientist.[12]

An extensive discussion of vision and its function in science and in art occurs in Chapters II and III of G. H. Lewes' *The Principles of Success in Literature*. Lewes' and George Eliot's views are, it will be clear, identical. Lewes argues that perception, inference, ratiocination, and imagination are all forms of mental vision; they all involve the "extension of the known to the unknown, of the apparent to the unapparent":

> The mental vision by which in Perception we see the unapparent details—i.e., by which sensations formerly co-existing with the one now affecting us are reinstated under the form of ideas which *represent* the objects—is a process implied in all Ratiocination, which also presents an *ideal series,* such as would be a series of sensations, if the objects themselves were before us. . . . Correct reasoning is . . . seeing with the mind's eye. False reasoning is . . . distorted or defective vision.

Lewes defines imagination as "the power of forming images; it reinstates, in a visible group, those objects which are invisible, either from absence or from imperfection of our senses." It supplies "the energy of Sense where Sense cannot reach."

Imagination is necessary in science because "the relations of sequence among phenomena must be seen; they are hidden; they can only be seen mentally." If all phenomena were available to the senses, "a glance would be science"; "it is because we see little, that we have to imagine much." From known facts the scientist infers unapparent facts: "he does so by an effort of imagination . . . : he makes a mental picture of the unapparent fact, and then sets about to prove that his picture does in some way correspond with the reality." Like George Eliot, Lewes objects to those who laud hypotheses "as imaginative in proportion as" they depart "from all suggestion of experience. . . . To imagine—to form an image—we must have the numerous relations of things present to the mind and see the objects in their actual order." Vision acts in two ways: it perceives objects of sense with great precision, and it forms ideal pictures of objects and relations beyond sense.

"All great authors," writes Lewes, "are seers." It is the purpose of literature "to show others what they failed to see." If we were to meet Shakespeare, "we should notice that he had an independent way of looking at things. He would constantly bring before us some latent fact, some unsuspected relation, some resemblance between dissimilar things." If we took a walk with him and he described that walk, he would "surprise us with revelations." We could "then and thereafter see all that he points out; but we needed his vision to direct our own. And it is one of the incalculable influences of poetry that each new revelation is an education of the eye and the feelings." When we are in contact with "an independent mind which *sees*" we discover "how servile we have been to habit and opinion, how blind to what we also might have seen, had we used our eyes. The link, so long hidden, has now been made visible to us."

Lewes vigorously opposed those who regard the scientific and artistic processes as radically different. "Philosophy and Art," he argued, "both render the invisible visible by imagination." The experimental process employed by the scientist to test his hypotheses is analogous to the novelist's invention of a story:

> The experiments by which the problem may be solved have to be imagined; and to imagine a good experiment is as difficult as to invent a good fable, for we must have distinctly *present*—in clear mental vision —the known qualities and relations of all the objects, and must *see* what will be the effect of introducing some new qualifying agent. . . . Easy enough, indeed, is the ordinary practice of experiment, which is

either a mere repetition or variation of experiments already devised (as ordinary story-tellers re-tell the stories of others), or else a haphazard, blundering way of bringing phenomena together, to see what will happen. To invent is another process. The discoverer and the poet are inventors; and they are so because their mental vision detects the unapparent, unsuspected facts, almost as vividly as ocular vision rests on the apparent and familiar.[13]

This is the best description I know of the process by which George Eliot conceived and developed the action of her novels; and it certainly defines one sense in which her novels are "experiments in life."[14]

George Eliot, whom Lewes referred to as "a very imaginative writer," was fond, as we have seen, of pointing to the similarities between the problems and techniques of the story teller and those of the scientist. Chapter I of *Daniel Deronda* has the following epigraph:

Men can do nothing without the make-believe of a beginning. Even Science, the strict measurer, is obliged to start with a make-believe unit, and must fix on a point in the star's unceasing journey when his sidereal clock shall pretend that time is at Nought. His less accurate grandmother Poetry has always been understood to start in the middle; but on reflection it appears that her proceeding is not very different from his; since Science, too, reckons backwards as well as forwards, divides his unit into billions, and with his clock-finger at Nought really sets off *in medias res*. No retrospect will take us to the true beginning; and whether our prologue be in heaven or on earth, it is but a fraction of that all-presupposing fact with which our story sets out.

Daniel Deronda opens in the middle of things, with the encounter between Deronda and Gwendolen in the casino at Leubronn; and the novel as a whole can be viewed as an elaboration of the web of relations which forms the context of the incidents and states of mind depicted in the first two chapters. The significance of these chapters is gradually unfolded as they are encompassed with a past and a future which give them meaning. It is only after we know Gwendolen's history that we can appreciate the impact upon her of the two crucial events with which the novel opens—her experience with Deronda and her reception of the news of financial disaster. As the story, after

Chapter XXV, moves in time beyond the events of the opening, the narrator and the characters again and again refer back to Deronda's glance which chilled Gwendolen when she was at the peak of her gambling success and to the necklace which Deronda redeemed for her. Gwendolen's financial difficulties, in combination with her character, lead to her morally degrading marriage to Grandcourt; and her relationship with Deronda, the tone of which is set in Chapters I and II, leads to her moral redemption. The full meaning of the opening chapters in relation to Gwendolen is available only at the end of the novel when we see the outcome of her relationship with Deronda. But this, of course, is an exaggeration; for not only can we never arrive at the true beginning, but also, as Eliot was fond of pointing out, "fruit and blossom hang together . . . harvest and spring-time are continually one."

In *Daniel Deronda*—and, in varying ways, in most of her novels—George Eliot makes signal use of the point of view of the omniscient narrator to impress upon the reader the fact of the connectedness of things and the need to envision the hidden relations of visible phenomena. The novel, by imaginatively transcending the limits of human perception, presents a truer, more complete picture of life than can be perceived by the actual participant in life situations. In life the individual has a very limited perception of the network of relations in which he exists and acts. He cannot directly experience, for example, the subjectivity of others. Further, his perspective is necessarily relative; he sees things in relation to himself or as they strike his consciousness. The omniscient narrator, on the other hand, sees the totality of the relations, internal as well as external, involved in a given situation. And the omniscient narrator views phenomena objectively, as they are in fact related to each other, rather than as they are related to a special subjectivity. The world of the novel, illuminated by the imagination of the author, is perfectly intelligible. The reader, having become identified with the narrator's objective viewpoint, and having been made aware of normally hidden relations, will be better able to imagine the order of things in which he lives and his relation to it. The real, he will have learned, cannot be grasped without the imaginative.[15]

The proper exercise of mental vision has extremely significant moral consequences for George Eliot. One of the greatest deterrents to wrongdoing and incentives to right behavior is a vision of the consequences of our deeds. Much evil is the result of stupidity, lack of vision, or faulty vision. But a truly accurate vision of consequences requires such a high degree of knowledge and imagination that Herbert Spencer, for example, felt that we can not yet effectively substitute a scientific conception of Nemesis for the more traditional incentives and deterrents.[16] In novel after novel George Eliot vividly presents the consequences of wrongdoing, leading the reader to become very much aware, at least, of the complexity and inevitability of the chain of consequences which good and evil deeds set in motion.

According to Comte, the application of the scientific intelligence to the study of society "may strengthen social feeling by diffusing juster views of the relations in which the various parts of society stand to each other; or it may guide its application by dwelling on the lessons which the past offers to the future."[17] In her notes on the "Historic Imagination," George Eliot advocates imaginative re-creation of great events in the past.

The exercise of a veracious imagination in historical picturing seems to be capable of a development that might help the judgment greatly with regard to present and future events. By veracious imagination, I mean the working out in detail of the various steps by which a political or social change was reached, using all extant evidence and supplying deficiencies by careful analogical creation. How triumphant opinions originally spread; how institutions arose; what were the conditions of great inventions, discoveries, or theoretic conceptions; what circumstances affecting individual lots are attendant on the decay of long-established systems—all these grand elements of history require the illumination of special imaginative treatment. . . . for want of such real, minute vision of how changes came about in the past, we fall into ridiculously inconsistent estimates of actual movements, condemning in the present what we belaud in the past, and pronouncing impossible processes that have been repeated again and again in the historical preparation of the very system under which we live.[18]

Her careful presentation of social, political, and religious movements in such novels as *Adam Bede, Felix Holt, Romola,* and *Middlemarch* clearly reflects the methods and aims which she assigns to the historic imagination.

Like Comte, she felt that a vision of social interconnectedness would strengthen social feeling; the individual would become aware of his solidarity with his fellows and of his own importance in the social order. In her "Notes on 'The Spanish Gypsy' " she expresses her conviction that "love, pity, constituting sympathy, and generous joy with regard to the lot of our fellow-men . . . has been growing since the beginning." And these moral sentiments have been "enormously enhanced by wider vision of results, by an imagination actively interested in the lot of mankind generally."[19]

In both the individual and the race, vision is the product of a long and painful evolution through the three stages of moral development. The child and the savage see all things in relation to themselves rather than in relation to each other. It is only after men have been made to realize the autonomy of the outer world and have experienced conscious suffering that they can come to the heightened awareness of the connections of things and of the inner states of others that for George Eliot is the chief characteristic of moral and intellectual maturity.

V

The positivists depicted society as an evolving organism composed of interacting organs which are themselves organisms. This conception of society appears to have originated with Comte's discussion of social statics, which is "the investigation of the laws of action and reaction of the different parts of the social system." Mill, Spencer, Lewes, and George Eliot agreed with Comte in opposing "the existing philosophical practice of contemplating social elements separately, as if they had an independent existence," and in insisting that the proper procedure is "to regard them as in mutual relation, and forming a whole which compels us to treat them in combination."[20] The positivistic conception of society as an organism profoundly influenced George Eliot's vision of the human condition and resulted in what she called a "social-political-conservatism."

Because of the dynamic interconnection of the social elements, the fate of each individual is largely determined by the state of the whole, and the state of the whole is modifiable by the actions of individuals.

Although the individual is but an organ in the social organism—subordinate to the whole, and helpless to defy it or to shape his individual lot independently of it—he is, nevertheless, capable of exerting a plastic force upon it. "A man," wrote Lewes, "although powerless *against* Society, becomes a power *with* Society" (*PLM,* I, 139). The individual initiates changes in the whole indirectly, by acting upon its parts. Action upon the parts is ultimately communicated to the whole, but often in a very diluted or altered form. Men are sharers of a common fate, and, at the same time, each man helps to determine the fate of his fellows.

"Society stands before us," wrote George Eliot, "like that wonderful piece of life, the human body, with all its various parts depending on one another." And "because the body is made up of so many various parts, all related to each other," all are likely "to feel the effect if any one of them goes wrong." It is only a lack of vision that can lead us to conclude that "there is no better rule needful for men than that each should tug and rive for what will please him, without caring how that tugging will act on the fine widespread network of society in which he is fast meshed."[21] Even a rudimentary understanding of the structure of the social organism convinces us of the identity of self-interest and social good. The order of things is such that we often contribute to the welfare of our fellows while pursuing our own ends. In *Impressions of Theophrastus Such,* George Eliot claims that "any molecule of the body politic working towards his own interest in an orderly way gets his understanding more or less penetrated with the fact that his interest is included in that of a large number."[22]

The connectedness of things does not always work for public and private good. Often the individual must suffer for the sins and blunders of others. Since the web of relations in which we act is so extensive and so entangled blunders are hard to avoid and are widespread in their effects. A recurrent theme in George Eliot is the evil which comes about through casual acts of thoughtlessness or through well-meaning incompetence. Spencer points out that as civilization has advanced and life has become more highly socialized, the extensiveness, heterogeneity, and intricacy of the human environment has rapidly increased; and while this has knit men together in closer fellowship, it has also made knowledge and adaptation extremely difficult. More often than not, in George Eliot's fiction, there is a painful disparity between the individual's nature and the circumstances in which he finds himself; the medium presents limitations, retarding friction, as well as possibilities. Altering the old proverb "into agreement with new formulas," she postulated that "the Internal Order proposes and the External Order disposes" (*Letters,* V, 102). "For a long while to come," she wrote to Mrs. Congreve, "I suppose human energy will be greatly taken up with resignation rather than action" (*Letters,* IV, 115).

We must accept the unalterable limitations of our lot and act within them in the best possible way. "The great division of our lot," George Eliot wrote in 1878, "is that between what is immodifiable and is the object of resignation and that which is modifiable by hopeful activity —by new conceptions and new deeds" (*Letters,* VII, 56). The formula is Comte's. In 1853, she had written to Mrs. Henry Houghton: "I enjoy life more than I ever did before, not only on account of outward things, but because I have better learned that as Comte and other wise men have said, 'Notre vraie destinée se compose de *resignation* et d'*activité*'" (*Letters,* II, 134). She did not underestimate the difficulty of resignation. In 1866 she wrote to Sara Hennell that she enjoyed study more than ever: "But that very fact makes me more in need of resignation to the certain approach of age and death. . . . Unfeigned, unselfish, cheerful resignation is difficult. But I strive to get it" (*Letters,* IV, 316). The previous year she had written to Bessie Rayner Parkes: "The calm acceptance of a lot and faithful devotedness to whatever may come, seems to me quite as noble as the energetic creating of a lot" (*Letters,* IV, 196).

Typical of resignation is Sethe Bede, who lives by Christ's words in the Sermon on the Mount—"Take therefore no thought for the morrow: for the morrow shall take thought for the things of itself." Seth's resignation is manifested in his generally acquiescent attitude and in his apparent lack of jealousy, resentment, and frustration when Dinah marries Adam, his brother. In Seth there is no balance between resignation and activity. His resignation is coupled with his day-dreaming and his other-worldliness, which serve him as means of compensation and escape. In contrast is Adam, whose motto is "God helps those who help themselves." Adam, a strong, determined, effective man, is initially wanting in resignation, as is indicated by his impatience with his father and mother. Adam—like Maggie Tulliver, Dorothea Brooke, Lydgate, Farebrother, Romola, and Felix Holt—must learn to bear frustration and to accept the weaknesses of human beings and the limitations of the human lot. Those—like Arthur Donnithorne, Mrs. Transome, Tito Melema, or Gwendolen Harleth—who rebel against the restraints and ties to which their life in society commits them bring painful consequences upon themselves and usually upon others.

The proper exercise both of resignation and of activity requires an informed vision of the web of relations in which we exist. George Eliot does not advocate an attitude of blind resignation any more than she favors impetuous activity. We should accept those evils only which cannot be altered. Our actions should always be governed by a sober awareness of realities. Concerning debate on colonial problems, she wrote to Mrs. Mark Pattison: "It is piteous to see men talking diffusely and to no purpose about what has been or what ought to have been when the only object of statesmanship should be to find the best course that *can be*" (*Letters,* VI, 343).

The interdependence of the various parts of the social organism works, as we have seen, for both good and ill. The individual is committed, without choice, to a social life. He cannot disengage his lot from that of his fellows; and, just as he cannot help being acted upon, he cannot act for himself alone—he cannot help shaping the lives of others. As a consequence of this dynamic relation of the individual to his fellows, moral responsibility, duty, is built into the order of things. Often this duty is onerous; but more often it is a precious source of moral direction and value. Not only does the individual have a moral responsibility towards those with whom he has an intimate bond; he is also a contributor to the proper or improper functioning of the organism as a whole, future as well as present. "The progress of the world," George Eliot wrote to Mrs. Ponsonby in December 1874, "which you say can only come at the right time—can certainly never come at all save by the modified action of the individual beings who compose the world" (*Letters,* VI, 99). In February 1875, she wrote to Mrs. Ponsonby of Herbert Spencer's anxiety to "vindicate himself from neglect of the logical necessity that the evolution of the abstraction 'society' is dependent on the modified action of the units; indeed he is very sensitive on the point of being supposed to teach an enervating fatalism" (*Letters,* VI, 124).

A vision of the connectedness of things provides man with a sense of religious orientation in the universe. When he relinquishes the conception of a loving, law-giving deity who grants his wishes, judges his actions, and exercises unceasing providence, the individual, confronted with the vastness, indifference, and seeming meaninglessness of the cosmos, often feels his own existence to be futile and insignificant. A vision of the connectedness of things, George Eliot felt, when it is combined with the recognition that human consciousness is the sole criterion of human worth, brings to the individual a sense of the importance of his life. For he sees that his actions affect not only his own well-being, but also that of his fellows. Through his relations with his fellows he gives definition and extended existence to his own being.

George Eliot was fond of pointing out that one man can influence a vast number of individuals whose sphere of activity is remote from his own. Since the effects he produces in others continue beyond his death, the individual has an impersonal immortality. He consciously experiences this immortality in that he enjoys it imaginatively in life, for the imagination makes the future live in the present. The cosmology of science would not permit George Eliot to imagine a personal existence beyond the grave, but it did enable her to imagine an impersonal existence, an existence in and through others. In place of the conventional heaven, she envisioned

> the choir invisible
> Of those immortal dead who live again
> In minds made better by their presence.

Each man's effort should be to live in such a way that his influence will likewise persist; for

> So to live is heaven:
> To make undying music in the world.[23]

Their conception of society as an organism produced in George Eliot and the positivists a profound distrust of abstract theories and a marked tendency towards conservatism—not in principles so much as in methods and expectations. In *Comte's Philosophy of the Sciences* (p. 33) Lewes, echoing Comte, complains that men's thinking about society is still so metaphysical that "they almost universally believe in the absurd notion of a political *change* being wrought by an alteration in the Government, or by the adoption of some scheme." Lewes objects to forms of government being "*given* to a nation, instead of *growing out* of the national tendencies and ideas." We must replace "the old theological, *mechanical* conception" of society "by a dynamical conception, and understand that the social organism has its laws of growth and development, like the human organism."

As Lewes' remarks suggest, the conservatism of the positivists was heightened by their perception of the role of the past in shaping the present. Defending Comte against the accusation that he slights the importance of history, Lewes wrote to Sara Hennell: "no one has more clearly seen and expressed that truth, that the past rules the present, lives in it, and that we are but the growth and outcome of the past" (*Letters,* III, 320). Mill, citing Comte, pointed out that "what we now are and do" is the result "mainly of the qualities produced in us by the whole previous history of humanity" (*Logic,* p. 633). Society is not merely an organism, it is an evolved organism; its present state is its embodied history. It is impossible successfully to institute a change in society which is at variance with the characters of the individuals who compose it, or which would defy the relations already existing in the social organism. Change must be gradually evolved from the interaction of man and his medium. In an article in the *Leader,* George Eliot wrote: "There is a perpetual action and reaction between individuals and institutions; we must try and mend by little and little—the only way in which human things can be mended."[24]

Her exposition of Riehl's "social-political-conservatism" exactly describes her own position:

He sees in European society *incarnate history,* and any attempt to disengage it from its historical elements must, he believes, be simply destructive of social vitality. What has grown up historically can only die out historically, by the gradual operation of necessary laws. The external conditions which society has inherited from the past are but the manifestation of inherited conditions in the human beings who compose it; the internal conditions and the external are related to each other as the organism and its medium, and development can take place only by the gradual consentaneous development of both.

"The nature of European men," she continues, "has its roots intertwined with the past, and can only be developed by allowing those roots to remain undisturbed while the process of development is going on, until that perfect ripeness of the seed which carries with it a life independent of the root."[25] George Eliot was, to use her own word, a meliorist. Improvement is possible because of the gradual action of the parts of society upon the whole, but it is bound to be very slow because present conditions are deeply rooted in the past—we will not understand how deeply until we have examined her belief in the inheritance of acquired characteristics. In the 1840's she was in sympathy with radical measures; the Revolution of 1848 aroused great hopes in her. Her contact with positivism quickly revised her attitudes, which from the early 1850's underwent little change. In August 1878, she wrote to D'Albert-Durade: "You remember me as much less of a conservative than I have now become. I care as much or more for the interests of the people, but I believe less in the help they will get from democrats" (*Letters,* VII, 47).

The more we know of society in its details, she contended in her essay on Riehl, "the more thoroughly we shall be convinced that *a universal social policy has no validity except on paper,* and can never be carried into successful practice." "A wise social policy must be based not simply on abstract social science, but on the natural history of social bodies." Riehl shows that the mechanical procedures of the German bureaucracy, failing to recognize the community as "an organism the conditions of which are bound up with the historical characteristics of the peasant," have been "disintegrating and ruinous to the peasant character." What Riehl has done for our understanding of the German peasantry makes clear the need for similar studies of English life:

If any man of sufficient moral and intellectual breadth, whose observations would not be vitiated by a foregone conclusion, or by a professional point of view, would devote himself to studying the natural history of our social classes, especially of the small shopkeepers, artisans, and peasantry, the degree in which they are influenced by local conditions, their maxims and habits, the points of view from which they regard their religious teachers, and the degree in which they are influenced by religious doctrines, the interactions of the various classes on each other, and what are the tendencies in their position towards disintegration or towards development; and if, after all this study, he would give us the results of his observations in a book well nourished with specific facts, his work would be a valuable aid to the social and political reformer.[26]

This program was very likely in her mind when she wrote *Scenes of Clerical Life, Adam Bede, The Mill on the Floss, Silas Marner,* and *Felix Holt.* These works are contributions to the data of sociology.

VI

The principle that change results from the interaction of the laws of the agencies involved was basic to George Eliot's understanding of human thought and behavior. The fates of the men and women who people her novels are determined by the interaction of character and circumstance. The individual exists in a medium the nature of which largely determines his character and his fate. But the way in which his environment affects him is the consequence of his own nature. Mr. Irwine tells Arthur Donnithorne: "A man can never do anything at variance with his own nature. He carries within him the germ of his most exceptional action" (*Adam Bede,* Chap. XVI). Circumstances, however, are responsible for bringing the germs of character to their good or bad fruition. Arthur's flaws of character, for example, might never have disclosed themselves under a different set of conditions. "Ships," George Eliot comments, "certainly, are liable to casualties, which sometimes make terribly evident some flaw in their construction, that would never have been discoverable in smooth water; and many a 'good fellow,' through a disastrous combination of circumstances, has undergone a like betrayal" (Chap. XII). Our fate, then, is both determined by us and determined for us. This is succinctly expressed in her epigraph to Chapter IV of *Middlemarch:*

1st Gent. Our deeds are fetters that we forge ourselves.
2nd Gent. Ay, truly: but I think it is the world
   That brings the iron.

Character, for George Eliot, is neither immutable nor imposed; it is evolved. It would be risky, she remarks early in *Middlemarch* (Chap. XV), to bet on Lydgate's future, even with a close knowledge of his character; "for character too is a process and an unfolding. The man was still in the making, as much as the Middlemarch doctor and immortal discoverer, and there were both virtues and faults capable of shrinking or expanding." An individual's inherited organization initially determines how he will be affected by external stimuli. But as he reacts to external agencies according to the laws of his nature and of theirs, his nature is altered. Each new experience modifies the experiencing subject, and each new modification is at once the product of all previous modifications and a determinant of all subsequent experiences and modifications. Lewes writes: "Although an organ can only respond to a stimulus according to its own modes, which depend on its structure, and which vary with the variations of structure, yet the very reaction itself tends to establish a modification which will alter subsequent reactions" (*PLM,* I, 117). An individual's character at any given moment is not the sum of all preceding experiences but the evolved resultant of them; it is embodied history. Change takes place slowly but continuously. One's past self is inescapable; it is immanent in the present self. The individual's earlier experiences tend to exert a profound influence upon the total development of his character. (See the epigraph to Chap. VIII of *Felix Holt.*) Character, then, is the evolved and evolving product of hereditary organization and experience.

The positivists derive not only character but also knowledge from the interaction of the conscious subject and his medium. They reject the metaphysical conceptions of innate ideas, imposed categories of perception, and intuitive knowledge of noumena. Experience is the source and limit of knowledge, and experience is the product of the interaction of subject and object. It is, says Lewes, "the sum of the modifications which arise from the relations of the Sensitive Organism to its environment."[27] Experience includes ratiocination as well as sensation; it involves "not only the direct presentations to Sense, but the indirect representations—the verifiable inferences from Sense" (*PLM*, I, 29).

Our knowing faculties respond to the external world in accordance with the laws of their organization. The response produces modifications in organization which determine the nature of subsequent responses, and so on. In the act of knowing, consciousness is an active agency contributing to the nature of its impressions. According to Lewes, the great point at issue between the positivists and the metaphysicians is whether "the Laws of Consciousness evolved out of the relations between the Sensitive Organism and its environment" or are "pre-existent, and independent of any such relations." Lewes argues that the relation of consciousness to its medium is not one of pure passivity, as is supposed by the extreme Sensationalists, and that consciousness does not have "a pure spontaneity, undetermined by the conditions of the Organism and its environment" as the a priori school holds. Consciousness is not "absolved from the universal law of action and reaction." "Mind," says Lewes, "is a successive evolution from experiences, and its laws are the action of results. The Forms of Thought are developed just as the Forms of an Organism are developed."[28]

Like character, the forms of thought are based upon organization; and organization is the product not only of the experience of the individual, but also, to a far greater degree, of the experience of the race. George Eliot, Lewes, and Spencer attribute man's apparently innate moral sentiments and modes of cognition to the biological transmission of the structural modifications produced in organisms by their experience. As the following chapter will show, George Eliot's belief in the inheritance of acquired characteristics is an important aspect of her conception of the nature of things: the biological transmission of the results of experience is one of the several aspects of the cosmic order of things which contribute to the evolution of a moral order which is at once a part of and in opposition to the amoral cosmic process.

THE MORAL ORDER

George Eliot held the cosmos to be composed of two disparate, yet interrelated orders: the moral order and the non-moral order, or the human order and the cosmic order. Man—being at once a social, sympathetic being and an individual, self-regarding being—is a part of both orders. His inward nature and the outward conditions of his existence are the products partly of the social and psychic evolution of the race and partly of the cosmic evolutionary process. The moral progress of the race and the virtue and satisfaction of the individual depend upon the predominance of the human over the nonhuman, upon the ability of social man to triumph over the unconscious forces which oppress him from without and the egoistic impulses which drive him from within. Human life has true meaning and value, George Eliot insisted, only when the human order is recognized to be supreme in its own sphere, when it is seen to be the sole source and sufficient sanction of moral values.

The moral order is manifested in love and fellow-feeling between individuals, in the products and traditions of human culture, in the laws and institutions of society, in the creeds, symbols, and ceremonies of religion; in general, in any human institution or activity which by interposing itself between the individual and the unhuman otherness of the order of things lessens the disparity between the inward and the outward and humanizes the world. The moral order is not independent of the non-moral order but exists within it and is in some respects a product of it. Moral phenomena, like the phenomena of physics and biology, are the necessary products of antecedent natural causes and coexistent natural conditions; and change results from the interaction of the laws of the agencies involved. Because of this social science is possible.

The moral order is an evolved order, but its evolution differs from that found in the non-moral order in that it is produced and directed in some degree by human feeling and conscious purpose, causal agencies which are entirely absent in non-moral evolution. Hence moral evolution is often in conflict with the tendencies of non-moral evolution; the function of the moral order, in fact, is to ameliorate the suffering caused by the non-moral conditions of life. In a letter to John Morley in which she attempted to clarify her views on woman suffrage and the proper position of women in society, George Eliot attacked "the 'intention of Nature' argument, which is to me a pitiable fallacy." Not nature, not biological evolution which is indifferent to human suffering, but human feeling is the proper source of social goals. "As a fact of mere zoological evolution," she argued, woman has "the worse share in existence. But for that very reason I would the more contend that in the moral evolution we have 'an art which does mend nature.' It is the function of love in the largest sense, to mitigate the harshness of all fatalities." She contended that "the goal towards which we are proceeding is . . . as near an approach to equivalence of good for woman and for man as can be secured by the effort of growing moral force to lighten the pressure of hard non-moral outward conditions" (*Letters,* IV, 364–65).

The distinction between the moral and the non-moral orders was not a product of her personal world-view; it was thoroughly elaborated by her fellow positivists. A useful discussion of several aspects of this distinction occurs in T. H. Huxley's famous essays entitled "Evolution and Ethics." Since these appeared in 1894, they did not, of course, influence George Eliot, but their terminology is convenient and most of the ideas they express were current in the 1860's and 1870's.

In order properly to determine "whether there is, or is not, a sanction for morality in the ways of the cosmos," it is necessary, Huxley argues, that we recognize the essential dissimilarities between the "cosmic process" and the "ethical process." The ethical process, which is manifested in the development of civilization, is artificial in the sense that its products, like all products of art, "could not be brought about in the state of nature"—that is, without the interposition of human energy and intelligence. Huxley recognizes that the ethical process "is, strictly speaking, part and parcel of the cosmic process," but he holds that there is, nevertheless, a constant antagonism between the cosmic process and the artificial process which is a part of it.

In its early forms human society was "as much a product of organic necessity as that of the bees." Social union aided survival in the conflict with surrounding forces, and those societies whose members were most devoted to the common welfare were naturally selected. Thus the cosmic process, whose "characteristic feature . . . is the intense and unceasing competition of the struggle for existence," gave birth to the ethical process, which attempts to eliminate "that struggle, by the removal of the conditions which gave rise to it." The cosmic process, however, also produced man's aggressive, selfish qualities. This is man's "inheritance (the reality at the bottom of the doctrine of original sin) from the long series of ancestors, human and semi-human and brutal, in whom the strength of this innate tendency to self-assertion was the condition of victory in the struggle for existence." Although self-assertiveness is "one of the essential conditions of success in the war with the state of nature outside," it is "the sure agent of the destruction of society if allowed free play within." Since the ethical process tends more and more, in the course of its development, to place "restraints upon the struggle for existence between men in society," it is "in opposition to the principle of the cosmic process."

Huxley concludes that "cosmic nature is no school of virtue but the headquarters of the enemy of ethical nature"; that "the ethical progress of society depends not on imitating the cosmic process, still less in running away from it, but in combating it." "In place of ruthless self-assertion" the ethical process "demands self-restraint; in place of thrusting aside, or treading down all competitors, it requires that the individual shall not merely respect but shall help his fellows; its influence is directed, not so much to the survival of the fittest, as to the fitting of as many as possible to survive." In the moral order natural selection is resisted, and artificial selection (employed by the gardener and the breeder) is unthinkable. The moral order works at "the creation of conditions more favorable than those of the state of nature; to the end of facilitating the free expansion of the innate faculties of the citizen, so far as it is consistent with the general good." With his energy and intelligence providing the means, and his socially developed sympathy and conscience dictating the ends, man has "succeeded in building up an artificial world within the cosmos"; and it is to this world, not to cosmic nature, that his moral life belongs.

George Eliot's conception of the moral order was, as the letter to Morley makes clear, very similar to Huxley's version of the ethical process. It is quite possible that she was influenced by Herbert Spencer's distinction between inorganic, organic, and super-organic evolution. Spencer spoke of social evolution as super-organic, though, like Huxley, he made no absolute separation between the organic and the super-organic processes. Super-organic evolution "must have arisen by insensible steps out of the organic," and it is at every point subject to the influence of the physical environment and the cosmic process. In its initial stages social evolution depends almost entirely upon environmental conditions and upon the qualities of the individual members of the social group. In time, however, these original factors are eclipsed in importance by "the secondary or derived sets of factors, which social evolution itself brings into play." Spencer recognized the immense influence on the course of social development of such super-organic products as tools, language, scientific knowledge, traditions, laws, religious creeds and institutions, codes of behavior, and works of art. Super-organic products and influences "gradually form . . . an additional environment, which eventually becomes even more important than the original environments—so much more important that there arises the possibility of carrying on a high type of social life under inorganic and organic conditions which originally would have prevented it."[2]

We find similar ideas developed by G. H. Lewes. Man, says Lewes, is a product of both the animal kingdom and the social organism—"the soul of man has thus a double root, a double history" (*PLM*, I, 125). Man's egoistic impulses, his concern for himself at the expense of others, are manifestations of his animal nature; but his moral life, his desire for the welfare of others, is the consequence of his relation to society. The moral education of the individual is the process by which his animal egoism is subdued and transformed into altruism by his social experience. Civilization, not primitive nature, is the source of our highest life and greatest good: "Culture transforms Nature physically and morally, fashioning the forest and the swamp into garden and meadow-lands, the selfish savage into the sympathetic citizen." As an animal organism man merely adjusts himself to the conditions in his external medium. As a moral being he "creates, and is in turn modified by, the social medium, for Society is the product of human feelings, and its existence is *pari passu* developed with the feelings which in turn it modifies and enlarges at each stage."[3]

George Eliot's conception of the moral order was crucial in the resolution of two major problems which she confronted in her effort to construct a realistic morality. She needed to explain, without recourse to a supernatural agency, the source of man's moral virtues and his consciousness of right and wrong; and she had to establish an empirical sanction for social values and for the dignity of the individual.

II

The fact that man is, even though imperfectly, a moral being, with a conception of right and wrong, a sense of guilt, and a feeling of duty and love towards his fellows was one of the chief supports of theology and idealistic philosophy. Man's moral qualities, the idealists contended, can be explained only by the existence of a God. Since man's moral conceptions have a divine parentage, they are absolutely valid. Theologians tended to emphasize the revealed teachings of the church as the chief source, guide, and impetus of ethical action. They contended that moral virtue and a belief in Christian doctrine are inseparably connected; that a rejection of Christian dogma was almost sure to result in moral chaos. Mrs. Elma Stuart confided to George Eliot that she was "troubled in mind" by the arguments of W. H. Mallock in his article "Modern Atheism: Its Attitude towards Morality," which appeared in the January, 1877, issue of *Contemporary Review*. Mallock contended, as George Eliot put it, that apart from the central dogmas of Christianity "there is nothing in the constitution of things to produce, to favour, or to demand a course of action called right." George Eliot advised Mrs. Stuart to "put the words 'cleanliness' and 'uncleanliness' for 'virtue' and 'vice,' and consider how fully you have come not only to regard cleanliness as a duty, but to shudder at uncleanliness"; and to ask "what are the doctrines which, if taken from you, would make you at once sink into uncleanly habits yourself, and think it indifferent to the health of mankind whether such a habit as that of cleanliness existed in the world or not" (*Letters,* VI, 338–339).

As her letter to Mrs. Stuart suggests, George Eliot held moral attitudes to be the products chiefly of deeply ingrained feelings, feelings which do not depend for either their existence or their continuance upon doctrines of any kind. The presence of these feelings she attributed to the natural operation of the human ethical process, a process which itself produced the religious and philosophic conceptions by which supernaturalists explain it. She wrote to Mrs. Ponsonby that her novels

> have for their main bearing . . . a conclusion without which I could not have cared to write any representation of life—namely, that the fellowship between man and man which has been the principle of development, social and moral, is not dependent on conceptions of what is not man: and that the idea of God, so far as it has been a high spiritual influence, is the ideal of a goodness entirely human (i.e., an exaltation of the human). (*Letters,* VI, 98)

She felt that man's social virtues have become historically and psychologically allied with doctrines, like those concerning the nature and existence of God and of an after-life, which the findings of science show to be unfounded and very probably false. But she was convinced that the denial of these doctrines need not have a deleterious effect upon morality if we understand the true source, nature, and sanction of moral values and actions.

In June 1879, George Eliot wrote to Frederick Harrison in reference to G. H. Lewes' *The Study of Psychology:* "It is melancholy enough that to most of our polite readers the Social Factor in Psychology would be a dull subject. For it is certainly no conceit of ours which pronounces it to be the supremely interesting element in the thinking of our time" (*Letters,* VII, 161). According to Lewes, human psychic phenomena cannot be fully explained unless they are regarded as the products of our interaction with the super-organically evolved social medium and of our organic inheritance from the past—of the "psychological evolution of sociological material" (*PLM,* I, 134).

There has evolved in man, and in man alone, consciousness, the ability to separate "Self from Not-self," "objects from feelings." Consciousness is "that Inner Sense which Kant marks as the distinguishing attribute of man when it makes its own affections objects of thought." Consciousness is the primary source of the moral order; it produces that awareness of species, of others as different from yet like ourselves, which is the basis of all ethical action, of the sense of solidarity with our kind which leads us to sacrifice our own immediate gratification for the good of others. "The law of animal action," writes Lewes, "is Individualism; its motto is 'Each for himself against all.' The ideal of human action is Altruism; its motto is 'Each *with* others, all for each.' "

By its ability to organize and transmit experience and to raise "personal relations . . . into impersonal conceptions," consciousness creates society. Between the individual man and the cosmos there is interposed the social medium. The higher animals have structures much like our own; but they are separated from us by an impassable barrier due to the fact that they have no social medium with which to interact. In the social medium, with its product, the general mind, we find

the impersonal experiences of Tradition accumulating for each individual a fund of knowledge, an instrument of Power which magnifies his existence. The experiences of many become the guide of each; they do not all perish with the individual; much survives, takes form in opinion, precept, and law, in prejudice and superstition. The feelings of each are blended into a general consciousness, which in turn reacts upon the individual consciousness. And this mighty impersonality is at once the product and the factor of social evolution.[4]

The social experience of the race is organized, transmitted, and impressed upon the individual not only by means of impersonal tradition, but also through the agency of biological evolution. George Eliot, Spencer, Lewes, and Darwin (somewhat hesitantly) believed that habit modifies organic structure, and that acquired structural modifications are biologically transmitted. Spencer and Lewes invoked the inheritance of acquired characteristics to explain the presence of a priori forms of thought as well as the existence of innate moral predispositions. They felt that in this way they could reconcile the empiricism of Locke and Hume with the idealism of Kant. The laws of consciousness, they granted, cannot be derived from the experience of the individual; but they are, nevertheless, the products of experience— of the accumulated, organized, and biologically transmitted experience of the race. The individual is endowed with modes of perception which are antecedent to and independent of *his* experience; "but this is *historical,* not *transcendental;* it is itself the product of Experience, though not of the individual" (*PLM,* I, 150). The term "experience," Lewes argued, includes "not only the individual experiences, slowly acquired, but the accumulated Experience of the race, organised in Language, condensed in Instruments and Axioms, and in what may be called the *inherited Intuitions*" (*PLM,* I, 29). We do not inherit the specific experiences of our ancestors; we inherit tendencies to respond coherently and sensitively to the stimuli which modified their organic structures. Without the appropriate stimuli, our inherited tendencies either never become actualized or are modified.

"What is conspicuous in the case of Intellect," Lewes wrote, "may also be discerned in Conscience. Both are social products. The hereditary transmission of organized tendencies . . . enables us to reconcile the *a priori* intuitional with the experiential theory." Man's innate moral sense, he insisted, does not bring with it definite conceptions of what is right and what is wrong: "What it carries are certain organized predispositions that spontaneously or docilely issue in the beneficent forms of action which the experience of society has classed as right."[5] The individual's own experiences play an important role in determining his moral and intellectual life; but they are not, as the associationists had argued, the sole causes.

As Herbert Spencer puts it, man is to a large degree "organically moral." Harald Höffding remarks that the importance of Spencer's *Principles of Psychology* (1855) "lies in the fact that, although based on empirical philosophy, it emphasizes the impossibility of explaining individual consciousness by the experiences of the individual himself."[6] To understand the conscious life of the individual, we must take into account the experiences of the race as they are embodied in society and in our psychological organizations. George Eliot, Spencer, Lewes, and Darwin all agree that conscious consideration of self-interest, pleasure and pain, reward and punishment, the general good, etc., is less important than instinctive or habitual feeling as an impetus to moral action. Darwin observes that "man seems often to act impulsively, that is from instinct or long habit, without any consciousness of pleasure." "In many instances," he feels, "it is probable that instincts are persistently followed from the mere force of inheritance, without stimulus of either pleasure or pain. . . . Hence the common assumption that men must be impelled to every action by experiencing some pleasure or pain may be erroneous."[7]

Spencer did not put aside entirely the principle of utility. He felt that man's inherited tendencies and traditions are the result of slowly, often unconsciously, accumulated and organized racial experiences of utility. His position is succinctly set forth in a famous letter to Mill, in which he denies that he is anti-utilitarian:

To make my position fully understood, it seems needful to add that, corresponding to the fundamental propositions of a developed Moral Science, there have been, and still are, developing in the race, certain fundamental moral intuitions; and that, though these moral intuitions are the results of accumulated experiences of Utility, gradually organized and inherited, they have come to be quite independent of conscious experience. Just in the same way that I believe the intuition of space, possessed by any living individual, to have arisen from organized and consolidated experiences of all antecedent individuals who bequeathed to him their slowly-developed nervous organizations —just as I believe that this intuition, requiring only to be made definite and complete by personal experiences, has practically become a form of thought, apparently quite independent of experience; so do I believe that the experiences of utility organized and consolidated through all past generations of the human race, have been producing corresponding nervous modifications, which, by continued transmission and accumulation, have become in us certain faculties of moral intuition—certain emotions responding to right and wrong conduct, which have no apparent basis in the individual experiences of utility.[8]

George Eliot employed Spencer's and Lewes' theory of the inheritance of racial experience directly in *The Spanish Gypsy* and *Daniel Deronda*.[9] She praised Sara Hennell's *Thoughts in Aid of Faith* because of "the largeness and insight with which it estimates Christianity as an 'organized experience,' a grand advance in the moral development of the race" (*Letters,* III, 315–16). Two passages in it in which the influence of Herbert Spencer is apparent, received particular approbation.[10] Sara Hennell argued that it is surely erroneous to regard Christianity as "a mere excrescence, the product of morbid, fanatical humors," as something which can be cast aside once its doctrines are seen to be fallacious; for the Christian experience of past ages has "moulded actually anew" our internal constitutions. Christianity has become "an integral part of the organic life of humanity." In the second passage she described the sentiments of Christianity which are born within us as the product "of the whole of previous human existence"; they are "slumbering as it were in our nature, ready to be awakened into action immediately they are roused by hint of corresponding circumstances." All men of Christian parentage are born with the consciousness of the Christian centuries in their bosoms, and no view of life is satisfactory which does not make provision for that consciousness.

Although George Eliot attacked the efforts of theologians to derive all moral dispositions and values from Christianity, she by no means denied the cultural and ethical importance of Christian tradition. Indeed, she felt that many Christian doctrines embody, either in precepts or in symbols, profound moral truths. But instead of morality being initially inspired and sanctioned by religious creeds, religious creeds, in her view, were originally inspired and sanctioned by the moral emotions and perceptions of mankind. "I look at it," says Adam Bede, "as if the doctrines was like finding names for your feelings." To find that which is universally valuable in religious creeds, we must discover the feelings which they name.

George Eliot strove to discover the enduring truth in Christianity by putting aside speculation and turning to experience. As early as October 1843, she wrote to Sara Hennell: "Speculative truth begins to appear but a shadow of individual minds, agreement between intellects seems unattainable, and we turn to the *truth of feeling* as the only universal bond of union" (*Letters*, I, 162). In 1859 she wrote to D'Albert-Durade:

> I have no longer any antagonism towards any faith in which human sorrow and human longing for purity have expressed themselves; on the contrary, I have a sympathy with it that predominates over all argumentative tendencies. I have not returned to dogmatic Christianity . . . but I see in it the highest expression of the religious sentiment that has yet found its place in the history of mankind, and I have the profoundest interest in the inward life of sincere Christians in all ages. . . . on many points where I used to delight in expressing intellectual difference, I now delight in feeling an emotional agreement. (*Letters*, III, 231)

The intellectual differences between man and man, between past and present, give way to emotional accord when we recognize all systems of value and belief to be expressions of human experience. "All the great religions of the world historically considered," George Eliot wrote in 1873, "are rightly the objects of deep reverence and sympathy—they are the record of spiritual struggles which are the types of our own" (*Letters*, V, 447–48).

The beneficial influence of *The Imitation of Christ* upon Maggie Tulliver is an excellent example of how Christian experience of the past can be living truth in the present, despite the fact that the form in which it was cast is now alien. In her bewilderment and discontent with her lot, Maggie sought a vision of life which would enable her to understand and endure her pain. *The Imitation of Christ* had significance for Maggie because it presented self-renunciation more as an experience than as a theological doctrine. The inner life of Thomas à Kempis spoke directly to the inner life of Maggie Tulliver: "She knew nothing of doctrines and systems—of mysticism or quietism; but this voice out of the far-off Middle Ages was the direct communication of a human soul's belief and experience, and came to Maggie as an unquestioned message" (Book IV, Chap. III). It is because Thomas à Kempis has deeply felt the doctrines he is teaching that *The Imitation of Christ* has a profound meaning for men of every age and belief:

I suppose that is the reason why the small old-fashioned book, for which you need only pay six-pence at a book-stall, works miracles to this day, turning bitter waters into sweetness: while expensive sermons and treatises, newly issued, leave all things as they were before. It was written down by a hand that waited for the heart's prompting; it is the chronicle of a solitary, hidden anguish, struggle, trust and triumph —not written on velvet cushions to teach endurance to those who are treading with bleeding feet on the stones. And so it remains to all time a lasting record of human needs and human consolations: the voice of a brother who, ages ago, felt and suffered and renounced—in the cloister, perhaps, with serge gown and tonsured head, with much chanting and long fasts, and with a fashion of speech different from ours—but under the same silent far-off heavens, and with the same passionate desires, the same strivings, the same failures, the same weariness. (Book IV, Chap. III)

George Eliot died, we are told, with a copy of *The Imitation of Christ* by her bed.[11]

George Eliot's awareness of the truths of experience which underlie creeds was partly the result of her own history. As a positivist, she was highly conscious of the disparity between her old and new world-views; but she was also aware of an emotional continuity between her old and new selves, between her old and new experiences of life. In 1875 she wrote to Mrs. Ponsonby: "I should urge you to consider your early religious experience as a portion of valid knowledge, and to cherish its emotional results in relation to objects and ideas which are either substitutes or metamorphoses of the earlier" (*Letters,* VI, 120). The truth of feeling was not only the bond of union between past and present and between men of differing philosophies; it was also the bond of union between the Evangelical Marian Evans and the positivistic George Eliot.

Christianity, then, is not the source of the moral order for George Eliot, but, as a form of organized experience, it is certainly an important part of the ethical process. Under the influence of the positivists, she came to feel that all of the traditions, creeds, institutions, laws, and ceremonials of society contribute to the moral order, along with the sentiments which their social heritage and identification inspire in the breasts of individuals. Tradition, she felt, is "the basis of our best life"; moral life is based on sentiment, and "our sentiments may be called organized traditions" (*Essays*, p. 181). Sentiment saves existence from absurdity, for it hallows and sanctifies that which reason finds meaningless or relative. Sentiment moves us to acts of goodness, of unselfishness, of reverence, for which reason provides no motivation or rationale: The only check to turning the bones of our ancestors into spoons "is a sentiment, which will coerce none who do not hold that sentiments are the better part of the world's wealth" (*Daniel Deronda,* epigraph to Chap. XXXIII).

George Eliot placed great emphasis upon the importance, for the individual, of having "that sense of special belonging which is the root of human virtues, both public and private." "The effective bond of human action is feeling"; and one of the most morally valuable of feelings is the sense of identification with a racial, political, social, or religious group, or with an historical tradition—the feeling of being part of a worthy corporate body: "The pride which identifies us with a great historic body is a humanising, elevating habit of mind, inspiring sacrifices of individual comfort, gain, or other selfish ambition, for the sake of the ideal whole; and no man swayed by such a sentiment can become completely abject."[12] Their devotion to the cause of their people inspires self-sacrifice and heroic effort in men like Mordecai, Savonarola, and Zarca, and in women like Romola and Fedalma. Through identification with the social group it is possible to gain spiritual independence of the accidents of one's own lot and a sense of the enduring significance of one's life and deeds.

In Mirah's purity in the midst of evil and in the Cohens' kindliness in the midst of their crass commercialism, we have examples of the moral power of sensed racial identity and of inherited racial characteristics. According to George Eliot, it is because the Jews have "a feeling of race, a sense of corporate existence, unique in its intensity" that they have retained many virtues and a surprising vitality despite the fact that they have lived many centuries under extremely demoralizing conditions. The vigor and intensity of Jewish life, like the vigor and intensity of Florentine life in *Romola*, is largely due to the richness of inherited tradition. In *Romola*, Francesco Cei, a man who has shaken off old prejudices, finds many objects for jest in the pageant celebrating the Nativity of St. John the Baptist, patron saint of Florence. "Life," he remarks, "was never anything but a perpetual see-saw between gravity and jest." Pietro Cennini, a worshipper of the ancients and a public-spirited man, replies:

> Keep your jest then till your end of the pole is uppermost . . . and that is not when the great bond of our Republic is expressing itself in ancient symbols, without which the vulgar would be conscious of nothing beyond their own petty wants of back and stomach, and never rise to the sense of community in religion and law. There has been no great people without processions, and the man who thinks himself too wise to be moved by them to anything but contempt, is like the puddle that was proud of standing alone while the river rushed by. (Chap. VIII)

George Eliot recognized that tradition frequently sanctions erroneous ideas and harmful practices; but insofar as it is a potent force for order and fellowship, tradition should be maintained; and insofar as it embodies our best wisdom, our noblest sentiments and ideals, and is the chief cause of that moral life which is the distinction and the glory of man, it should be venerated.

In Tito Melema Eliot presented the moral consequences which occur when tradition and a sense of social loyalty fail to take root in a basically selfish nature. Tito's selfishness alone cannot explain his complete lack of trustworthiness; it is re-enforced by his rationalistic hedonism, by his lack of hereditary ties in Florence, and by his sceptical attitude toward the usages, codes, and religious creeds of society. When Romola tells Bernardo del Nero that he will soon forget that Tito is not a Florentine, her godfather replies: "It seems to me he is one of the *demoni*, who are of no particular country. . . . His mind is a little too nimble to be weighted with all the stuff we men carry about in our hearts" (Chap. XIX). Tito recognizes no higher law of action than his own interests; he has no sense of that moral order, that doctrine of consequences, which tradition holds over the heads of wrongdoers. He had been "nurtured . . . in erudite familiarity with disputes concerning the Chief Good, which had after all, he considered, left it a matter of taste" (Chap. XLVI). In morality, reason is the servant of desire; socially inspired sentiments and feelings of immediate love and sympathy are far more trustworthy as guides and effective as sources of ethical action.

Even Tito is not entirely immune to the influence of traditional moral standards, especially when they are vigorously supported by public opinion. After he has convinced himself that he has amply repaid Baldassare for his care and kindness, that his chief duty is now to himself, that Baldassare is dead, he experiences a private sense of shame at what he knows all would hold to be the violation of a sacred trust:

> he had avowed to himself a choice which he would have been ashamed to avow to others, and which would have made him ashamed in the resurgent presence of his father. But the inward shame, the reflex of that outward law which the great heart of mankind makes for every individual man, a reflex which will exist even in the absence of the sympathetic impulses that need no law, but rush to the deed of fidelity and pity as inevitably as the brute mother shields her young from the attack of the hereditary enemy—that inward shame was showing its blushes in Tito's determined assertion to himself that his father was dead, or that at least search was hopeless. (Chap IX)

Social law has wrought itself into Tito's inner nature, but not deeply and powerfully enough to triumph in the conflict of motivations.

There are, then, apart from the dogmas of Christianity, a number of forces in the constitution of things which, in George Eliot's view, produce, favor, and demand a course of action called right. In addition to the "outward law which the great heart of mankind makes for every individual man" and its inward reflex in conscience, there is fellow feeling which springs from "the sympathetic impulses that need no law." The noblest and most enduring parts of tradition are objectifications of sympathetic experience, and sympathy is important in rendering the individual sensitive to the beliefs and codes of his society. Darwin points out that "however great weight we may attribute to public opinion, our regard for the approbation and disapprobation of our fellows depends on sympathy, which . . . forms an essential part of the social instinct and is indeed its foundation-stone"; and he cites with approval Bain's contention that "the love of praise and the strong feeling of glory, and the still stronger horror of scorn and infamy, 'are due to the workings of sympathy.' "[13]

The sympathetic tendencies may be encouraged by tradition, but sympathy is antecedent to tradition and potentially superior to it. The individual who has a strongly sympathetic nature combined with profound personal experience and the ability to imagine the inward states of others has a moral life independent of tradition; he has a truer sense of good and evil and a more highly developed conscience than tradition could supply. Lewes remarks that in the lower stages of moral development remorse is connected chiefly with fear of punishment; "but in a mind where the educated tracing of hurtful consequences to others is associated with a sympathetic imagination of their suffering, Remorse . . . is the agonised sense, the contrite contemplation, of the wound inflicted on another. . . . The sanction which was once the outside whip has become the inward sympathetic pang."[14] The internalization of tradition also produces a private sense of remorse, but the remorse is independent of the actual goodness or badness of the violation which causes it. When they are strong enough, the sympathetic tendencies can lead an individual to rebel against the harsh usages of tradition, even when such rebellion involves great personal sacrifice.

According to Darwin, Spencer, and Lewes, man is innately social and sympathetic; he has a strong desire for the company of his fellows, and he feels for and with them. Sympathy and sociality were initially products of the cosmic process; they arose through random variation and were naturally selected because of their survival value. They were instrumental in the formation and strengthening of social groups, and they have been strengthened and developed by habit and by the encouraging influence of the social medium. Even so, the development of these moral qualities in man has been very slow because, as Spencer points out, "this moral evolution" has at each stage been "negatively restrained . . . by defect of intelligence" and "positively restrained by the predatory activities . . . necessitated by the antagonisms of societies." The competition between societies has contributed to an increase of fellow feeling among the members of each group, but it has prevented the giving of sympathy to members of other groups. In order for the society to survive, the natures of its members have "to continue such that . . . destructive activities are not painful to them but on the whole pleasurable." Spencer concluded that "only when the struggle for existence has ceased to go on under the form of war" can those "highest social sentiments which have sympathy for their root . . . attain their fullest development."[15]

Lack of intelligence is also an obstacle to sympathy. "The egoistic impulses," Lewes explains, "are directed towards objects simply so far as these are the *means* of satisfying a desire. The altruistic impulses, on the contrary, have greater need of Intelligence to understand the object itself in all its relations" (*PLM*, I, 153). A sympathetic feeling is one which is excited by the signs of that feeling in another person; intelligence, that is, mental vision, is needed to read the signs. Without vision there is little or no sympathy. An increase in vision usually produces an increase in sympathy. Sympathy and vision are both dependent upon experience. Unless we have had an experience much like that which another person is undergoing, we cannot perceive and share the states of feeling signified by that person's behavior. "Suffering," says Lewes, "humanizes." Experience and vision unite to produce sympathy. Spencer is careful to insist that "higher representative power does not involve greater commiseration, unless there have been received painful experiences like, or akin to, those which are witnessed. . . . since unless a sensation or emotion has been felt, it cannot be sympathetically excited." Spencer's next remark succinctly explains the situation of Adam Bede at the beginning of the novel: "For this reason strong persons, though they may be essentially sympathetic in their natures, cannot adequately enter into the feelings of the weak."[16]

It would be difficult to overestimate the importance of the experience-vision-sympathy pattern in George Eliot's understanding of the moral process; it pervades her letters, essays, novels, and poems. When Mrs. Ponsonby complained that science's rejection of immortality made her regard human existence as unimportant and human actions and values, therefore, as insignificant, George Eliot replied that surely she had not lost

all keen sense of what is cruel and injurious—all belief that your conduct (and therefore the conduct of others) can have any difference of
effect on the wellbeing of those immediately about you (and therefore
on those afar off), whether you carelessly follow your selfish moods or
encourage that vision of others' needs which is the source of justice,
tenderness, sympathy in the fullest sense? . . .

With regard to the pains and limitations of one's personal lot, I
suppose that there is not a single man, or woman, who has not more
or less need of that stoical resignation which is often a hidden heroism,
or who, in considering his or her past history is not aware that it has
been cruelly affected by the ignorance or selfish action of some fellow-
being in a more or less close relation of life. And to my mind, there
can be no stronger motive, than this perception, to an energetic effort
that the lives nearest to us shall not suffer in a like manner from *us*.
(*Letters*, VI, 98–99)

Our own suffering, if it does not simply embitter, leads us to be sympathetic with the suffering of others, and our sympathy leads us to
behave so that others will not suffer as we have. The moral action of
sympathy is independent of law or creed; and George Eliot implies
that it is quite independent of the supposedly demoralizing effects of
the scientific picture of man and the cosmos.

George Eliot opposed those who felt that the sole basis of morality
is man's selfish desire for reward and fear of punishment. Edward
Young, whose religion, she contended, was nothing but "egoism
turned heavenward," had made the fear of future punishment man's
sole inducement to ethical action: "If it were not for the prospect of
immortality, he considers, it would be wise and agreeable to be in-
decent . . . ; and, heaven apart, it would be extremely irrational in
any man not to be a knave." In the person of an hypothetical un-
believer, she attributes Young's position to his "utter want of moral
emotion":

I am just and honest, not because I expect to live in another world,
but, because, having felt the pain of injustice and dishonesty towards
myself, I have a fellow-feeling with other men, who would suffer the
same pain if I were unjust or dishonest towards them. . . . The fact
is, I do *not* love myself alone, whatever logical necessity there may be

for that conclusion in your mind. . . . It is a pang to me to witness the suffering of a fellow-being, and I feel his suffering the more acutely because he is *mortal*—because his life is so short, and I would have it, if possible, filled with happiness and not misery. Through my union and fellowship with the men and women I *have* seen, I feel a like, though a fainter, sympathy with those I have *not* seen; and I am able so to live in imagination with the generations to come, that their good is not alien to me, and is a stimulus to me to labour for ends which may not benefit myself, but will benefit them.[17]

George Eliot viewed suffering as a part of man's education which leads him from his innate subjectivity to objectivity—that is, to an awareness of the interior life of others.

This is emphatic in her novels and I devote three chapters to it later under the heading of "The Three Stages of Moral Development." Suffering shocks us out of the first stage, in which self is seen as the center of the world and the world as an extension of self, into the second stage, in which the world is seen as alien and the self as insignificant. It can, if it promotes vision and sympathy, nurture us to moral maturity, the third stage. Vision and sympathy unite us with others, reducing the disparity between inner and outer for ourselves, and prompting us to function as mediator for others. A concern for future rewards and punishments tends to enmesh us in our egoism by encouraging us to regard others as means to our own ends.

George Eliot felt that although abstract theories exert a powerful influence upon attitudes and actions, morally pernicious beliefs are often ignored in practice when the individual's sympathetic emotions are sufficiently powerful. In *Adam Bede,* speaking of Methodism, she exclaims: "it is possible, thank Heaven! to have very erroneous theories and very sublime feelings" (Chap. III). The best morality she argues, is that which is based upon feeling and exhibits "itself in direct sympathetic feeling and action, and not as the recognition of a rule. Love does not say, 'I ought to love!'—it loves." "It is only where moral emotion is comparatively weak that the contemplation of a rule or theory habitually mingles with its action; . . . the minds which are predominantly didactic are deficient in sympathetic emotion" (*Essays,* p. 59).

* * *

70

The ethical process, George Eliot held, though productive of creeds and dogmas, is not dependent for its origin or continuance upon them. Its chief agent is human feeling—the sympathetic feeling that is the product of experience and vision, and the social sentiment that is produced by the interaction of the individual and the social order. George Eliot, Spencer, Darwin, and Lewes not only disagreed with those thinkers who held conscience and the moral sentiments to be entirely innate and a priori—God-given; but they also opposed empiricists like Mill and Alexander Bain who denied that moral virtues and judgments were in any sense innate and attempted to derive them solely from painful and pleasurable associations in the experience of the individual.[18] Man's moral impulses and judgments, they contended, are partly innate and partly acquired; partly the result of the organic evolution of the race and the super-organic evolution of society, and partly the result of the individual's experience. The individual's experience, moreover, is determined not only by external stimuli, but also by his inherited psychic organization which responds to these stimuli in accordance with its innate laws. Man is not simply an animal endowed with a very highly developed nervous system; he is a social being with social feelings. He is different from other social animals by virtue of the fact that his social feelings have become embodied in an on-going society replete with codes and institutions and traditions. Man's social feelings have thus created an ethical process which constantly modifies and is modified by the social experience of successive generations of individuals.

The moral order, then, has both an inward existence in individuals and an outward existence in society. The interactions of man and his medium result in moral progress: society exerts an ever increasing influence upon its individual members, thus strengthening the inward moral tendencies; and socially-oriented individuals, who are growing more numerous, work for the betterment of society.

THE OBJECTIVE AND SUBJECTIVE APPROACHES TO REALITY

The truth of infinite value that he teaches is *realism*—the doctrine that all truth and beauty are to be attained by a humble and faithful study of nature, and not by substituting vague forms, bred by imagination on the mists of feeling, in place of definite, substantial reality. The thorough acceptance of this doctrine would remould our life; and he who teaches its application to any one department of human activity with such power as Mr. Ruskin's is a prophet for his generation.[1]

For George Eliot and her fellow positivists almost all issues—scientific, moral, aesthetic, political, or economic—were phases of the problem of knowledge. The primary goal of positivism was to secure the triumph of empirical methodology by demonstrating its applicability to all areas of human interest and by attacking metaphysical thinking wherever it was found.

The positivists branded as metaphysical any philosophy which displayed the following characteristics: (1) a concern with ontology and teleology; (2) a belief either in innate ideas or in laws of thought and categories of perception that do not have their origin in experience; (3) a belief in the possibility of an immediate, intuitive knowledge of the existence and nature of a reality which transcends experience; and (4) a method and test of knowledge which relies upon introspection, or upon a dialectic which, assuming a built-in correspondence between the internal and the external, bypasses or slights sensory experience and works from the inward to the outward. The basic epistemological conceptions of the positivists were: (1) that experience is the limit of knowledge, and hence that consideration of first and final causes, or of any realm beyond experience, is fruitless and misleading; (2) that we have neither divinely implanted innate ideas nor imposed categories of perception—that the contents and modes of consciousness are entirely the product of evolution and experience; (3) that all knowledge of the external world is relative, *i.e.,* that things cannot be known as they are in themselves, but only as they appear to human consciousness; and (4) that no conception of external reality can be accepted as true without verification, that experience or consonance with experience and not logical consistency or belief is the test of truth, and that the objective method—which bends the mind to the outward shows of things instead of ordering external existence according to the preconceptions or wishes of the mind—is the only path to truth.

The aims of the empiricists are clearly set forth in George Eliot's review of O. F. Gruppe's *Gegenwart und Zukunft der Philosophie in Deutschland.* Gruppe's chief concern is, according to her,

the rectification of the method of philosophical inquiry, which, as he justly insists, is the essential preliminary to all true progress. It is, he says, simply to a reform in method that we owe all the splendid achievements of modern natural science, and it is only by the extension of that reform to every department of philosophical inquiry that here also any of what Bacon calls "fruit" can be obtained.

To achieve its proper end philosophy must, in the future, "renounce metaphysics: it must renounce the ambitious attempt to form a theory of the universe, to know things in their causes and first principles." Its real task is the application of the empirical methodology "to the investigation of Psychology, with its subordinate department Aesthetics; to Ethics; and to the principles of Jurisprudence." George Eliot's closing remarks identify her as a militant empiricist: she finds great interest "in the fact that a German professor of philosophy renounces the attempt to climb to a heaven by the rainbow bridge of 'the high *priori* road,' and is content humbly to use his muscles in treading the uphill *a posteriori* path which will lead, not indeed to heaven, but to an eminence whence we may see very bright and blessed things on earth."[2]

George Eliot's chief criticism of Gruppe is that he fails to give adequate recognition to the work of John Stuart Mill. In Mill's *Logic,* she contends, the reformation and extension of method that Gruppe calls for have been largely achieved. Like Gruppe, Mill sees the empirical epistemology as the crucial factor in all efforts to improve man's intellectual and social state. In his *Autobiography,* Mill explains that his chief purpose in writing the *Logic* was to clear the way for social and political reforms. The cause of liberalism was impeded, he felt, by the support which the metaphysical epistemology gave to conservative tendencies and existing institutions. The *Logic* was designed to counter "the German, or a priori view of human knowledge, and of the knowing faculties" by supplying a "text-book of the opposite doctrine—that which derives all knowledge from experience." The idea that "truths external to the mind may be known by intuition or consciousness, independently of observation and experience" is, Mill contends, the chief support of "false doctrines and bad institutions," and results in a "false philosophy in morals, politics, and religion":

> By the aid of this theory, every inveterate belief and every intense feeling, of which the origin is not remembered, is enabled to dispense with the obligation of justifying itself by reason, and is erected into its own all-sufficient voucher and justification. There never was such an instrument devised for consecrating all deep-seated prejudices.

In recounting his motives for writing the *Examination of Sir William Hamilton's Philosophy,* Mill again stresses the fact that the difference between the intuitional and experimental schools "lies at the foundation of all the greatest differences of practical opinion in an age of progress." If conservative interests are to be overcome, there must be a "hand-to-hand fight" between the empirical and the metaphysical epistemologies. In the *Examination of Sir William Hamilton's Philosophy* Mill engaged in such a fight; and it was this book, which appeared one hundred and one years after Reid's first attack on Hume, that finally gave British empiricism a decisive victory over the Scottish Common Sense School.[3]

Although Mill took exception to many aspects of the philosophical system of Auguste Comte, his recognition of the conflict between the metaphysical and the empirical epistemologies as the crucial issue of the day is partly attributable to Comte's influence. Comte interpreted the history of human culture and the contemporary fragmentation of beliefs in terms of the conflict between theology, metaphysics, and positivism. His own philosophy, Comte contended, marked the emergence of positivism as the sole and ultimate program for knowledge and action. Traditional social, political, economic, and religious theories and institutions were, in Comte's view, largely the products of the theological and metaphysical habits of mind. Comte's view of history is succinctly embodied in his Law of the Three Stages. Basing his argument upon an empirical study of the "development of human intelligence" as it is manifested in the history of the species and in the psychological evolution of the individual, Comte contended "that each of our leading conceptions,—each branch of our knowledge,—passes successively through three different theoretical conditions: the Theological or fictitious; the Metaphysical, or abstract; and the Scientific, or positive." That the human mind successively employs these three modes of thought is a consequence of its nature: "the first is the necessary point of departure of the human understanding; and the third is its fixed and definitive state." In philosophy the final state of development is reached when the mind turns away from "the vain search after Absolute notions . . . and applies itself to the study of . . . laws,— that is, . . . invariable relations of succession and resemblance. Reasoning and observation, duly combined, are the means of this knowledge."[4]

George Henry Lewes, in his *History of Philosophy from Thales to Comte* follows the lead of Comte, presenting the development of Western thought in classical antiquity from theology to metaphysics. He then examines the medieval subjugation of metaphysics by theology, and the emergence of positive science and the emancipation of metaphysics from theology at the close of the Middle Ages. About sixty years after Bacon endeavored to turn the attention of philosophy to positive science, the subjective method, as it was defined for modern thought by Descartes, was carried to its extreme results in the pantheistic idealism of Spinoza. This, Lewes contends, brought about the first crisis in modern philosophy. Philosophers were led by Spinoza's demonstration of the conclusions which their premises logically involved to question the validity of the premises:

> Spinozism or Scepticism? There seemed no third alternative. Nor was there a third alternative, so long as Philosophy persisted in its ontological and absolute claims—persisted in the metaphysical method, in the search for truths lying beyond the sphere of relativity. A new conception of Philosophy was needed to restore the shattered confidence of philosophers.

The new conception came in the form of the proposition that all knowledge is relative. Inquiries into teleology and ontology must be held in abeyance until the nature and limits of knowledge are established: "the hopeless failures of so many generations suggested that the seekers had begun their search at the wrong end."

The second crisis in modern philosophy occurred with the reaction of Kant and the Scottish Common Sense School to the Scepticism of Hume and the Sensationalism of Locke and his followers in the Sensational School—Condillac, Hartley, Erasmus Darwin, de Tracy, and Cabanis. The major issue was the status of the mind: Is it an autonomous entity or an integral part of the body? The Sensational School, which, says Lewes, was the chief object of the reaction, brought philosophy to the point where it must either accept psychology as a branch of biology or fall "back upon Metaphysics which modern Science gloried in having escaped forever":

> The first issue was too repulsive for the majority of philosophers. It was repulsive because it disturbed the sacred associations of awe which surrounded the mystery of Mind, and because it was said by antagonists to lead to degrading and immoral conclusions; which it did *not,* and which it could not lead to, if true; though antagonists chose to affirm that it was not true, because they assumed that it led to the immoral conclusions.

Lewes' account of the German Idealists—Fichte, Schelling, and Hegel—who in claiming the possibility of absolute intuitive knowledge had returned to the assumptions and methods of Spinoza, is more polemical than expository. Lewes concludes his history triumphantly, however, with a laudatory discussion of Comte, who has, he feels, assured the ultimate victory of positivism and the defeat of metaphysics by establishing the scientific basis of all disciplines, including psychology and Comte's special contribution, sociology.

> Hitherto the History of Philosophy has been that of a long period of preparation. A new era dawns with the transformation of Science into Philosophy. Henceforward History will record development, not revolution—convergence of effort, not conflict. . . . The constitution of the Positive Philosophy closes the period of preparation, and opens the period of evolution.[5]

Like Gruppe, Mill, and Comte, Lewes saw the conflict between the metaphysical and empirical approaches to reality as centrally important in almost all areas of human activity. He endeavored systematically to apply the principles of the empirical epistemology to the problems of literary criticism and aesthetic creation in *Principles of Success in Literature*. A single passage from his *Life of Goethe* will clearly illustrate his concern with the moral and aesthetic implications of the objective methodology. By way of defining Goethe's mental characteristics, he cited the contention of Frederick Schlegel and S. T. Coleridge that every man is born either a Platonist or an Aristotelian. This distinction, said Lewes, is between two types of intellect, the subjective and the objective. The subjective intellect is "eminently *personal*," while the objective is "eminently *impersonal*." The objective intellect disengages "itself as much as possible from its own prepossessions, striving to see and represent objects as they exist"; the subjective views "all objects in the light of its own feelings and preconceptions." In philosophy the contrast is between the realist and the idealist: "The realist argues from Nature upwards. . . . The idealist argues from an Idea downwards."

Not only in philosophy and art, but also in morals there is "a constant antagonism" between the objective and subjective, or the realistic and idealistic, modes of thought:

> Thus in Morals the Platonists are those who seek the highest morality *out* of human nature, instead of in the healthy development of all

77

human tendencies, and their due coordination; they hope, in the *suppression* of integral faculties, to attain some super-human standard. They call that Ideal which no Reality can reach, but for which we should strive. . . . They draw from their own minds, or from the dogmas handed to them by tradition, an arbitrary mould, into which they attempt to fuse the organic activity of Nature.

The idealistic conceptions of human nature and human destiny owe their power over the minds of men to the fact that they satisfy man's craving for a glorified existence, a craving so powerful that it easily leads to self-delusion.

Goethe's intellect, Lewes tells us, belongs to the objective class. As an artist, as a philosopher, as a moralist, and as a scientist he invariably confronted his ideas with concrete reality. His characters are real men and women; his art, the material of which is drawn largely from his own experience, represents life and not an idea of life; his works do not have their moral evaluations arbitrarily superimposed upon them but "carry their moral *with* them, *in* them." He sought in morality not something out of nature, but "the high and harmonious action of all human tendencies."

> In every page of his works [says Lewes] may be read a strong feeling for the real, the concrete, the living; and a repugnance as strong for the vague, the abstract, or the supersensuous. His constant striving was to study Nature, so as to see her *directly,* and not through the mists of fancy, or through the distortions of prejudice,—to look at men, and *into* them,—to apprehend things as they were. . . . If we look through his works with critical attention, *we shall observe the concrete tendency determining—first, his choice of subjects; secondly, his handling of character; and, thirdly, his style.*[6]

As the comment on Ruskin which introduced this chapter indicates, George Eliot ascribed to realism an importance equal to that given it by Comte, Mill, and Lewes. "The thorough acceptance" of realism, she felt, "would remould our life." The position enunciated in her review of *Modern Painters* encourages an approach to her mind and art similar to that employed by Lewes in his study of Goethe. Many of her views on life and art, and much of her fiction, can be explained in terms of her adherence to the empirical epistemology. Equally important is her familiarity with the conflict between the objective and subjective approaches to reality, a conflict which she experienced in her own intellectual and moral development. She is concerned in her novels not only with exploring the implications for human life of empiricism, but also with portraying the nature and consequences of the subjective approach to reality. Her aim is to define the proper sphere of each approach to reality, to show the good or evil consequences of each when properly or improperly used, and to effect a reconciliation between the conflicting claims of realism and moralism. Let us now examine more closely the views of George Eliot and those of her fellow positivists concerning the opposing characteristics of the objective and subjective approaches to reality.

As the positivists see it, the essential characteristic of the metaphysical method is that it confuses the objective with the subjective. It converts the internal into the external, thereby making the subjective and the objective orders identical. There is no clear distinction between self and non-self; the world is an extension of the ego. The desires of the heart, the preconceptions of the intellect, and the qualities of human nature are projected into outer phenomena and are then assumed to have an objective existence. For Comte, both the theological and the metaphysical stages of thought are examples of subjective thinking. "In the theological stage," wrote Comte, "the human mind . . . supposes all phenomena to be produced by the immediate action of supernatural beings." In the metaphysical stage, "the mind supposes, instead of supernatural beings, abstract forces, veritable entities (that is, personified abstractions) inherent in all beings, and capable of producing all phenomena."[7] Feuerbach contended that the conceptions of both religion and traditional philosophy are products of the projection and reification of some element of human experience. The difference between them, for him, was, as Sidney Hook observed, "that in religion the hypostasis found its expression in concrete objects of sense and imagination while in philosophy the hypostasis was abstract and conceptual."[8]

Lewes attributed the creation of metaphysical entities to the mind's tendency to reify abstractions. The mind, having made generalizations from particular experiences, considers these generalizations as universals which have an autonomous existence. The tendency of the subjective method "is to confound concepts with percepts, ideas with objects, conjectures with realities." The tendency to explain the objective by the subjective, to transpose the internal into the external, accounts, according to Lewes, for the fetichism of children, the polytheism of primitive cultures, and the metaphysics and physics of the idealistic philosophers.

The primary object of philosophical inquiry, according to Lewes, is to ascertain the state of affairs which exists in the external world so that we can adapt internal to external relations. That the non-self has a real existence he holds to be as ultimate and irrefutable a datum of consciousness as that the thinking self exists (see *PLM,* I, 157, 163). The external world not only exists; it also exhibits an autonomous order which does not necessarily correspond to the order of thought. Truth, he says, lies "in the correspondence between the order of ideas and the order of phenomena, so that the one becomes a reflection of the other." He identifies the chief source of error as "*the Subjective current determining the direction of the thought.*" When, "instead of the movement of Thought being controlled by the movement of Things," the subjective current dominates the mind's activity, it disturbs "the clear reflection of the objective order," and results in "concepts and judgments which have no corresponding objects."[9]

The difference between the objective and subjective approaches is not that the one is inductive and the other deductive; science, as Mill argued at great length, can accomplish little without deduction. George Eliot defended Mill against Gruppe's criticism of the importance which he gives to deduction in the *Logic:* "Deduction, as Mill shows, . . . is a means of registering and using the results of induction, indispensible to any great progress in science."[10] "The true antithesis," writes Lewes, "is between verified and unverified cases of Induction and Deduction."[11] One can form a theory on the basis of little or no evidence and remain a positive thinker if the theory is then tested by seeing if it coincides or is consonant with sensory experience. Goethe, according to Lewes, "was a positive thinker on the *a priori* Method; a Method vicious only when the seeker rests contented with his own assumptions, or seeks only a *partial* hasty confrontation with facts . . .; a Method eminently philosophic when it merely *goes before* the facts, anticipating what will be the tardy conclusions of experience." Goethe "everywhere sought in the order of Nature for verification of the ideas which he had conceived *a priori*."[12]

The metaphysician, however, even if his starting point is derived from observation, does not test his speculations by confrontation with external reality. He often pursues knowledge of the objective order by introspection or by deduction from the premises which introspection yields. The method of metaphysics, writes Lewes, "is the determination of the external order according to *analogies drawn from within*. The culmination of this method is seen in the fundamental axiom of Des Cartes and Spinoza: *all clear ideas are true*."[13] The accuracy of our conceptions is determined by their logical consistency and their harmony with our preconceptions rather than by their agreement with external facts. Traditional beliefs, imaginative constructions, and egoistic prepossessions play a larger role in the formation of our idea of the world than do sense-data.

The method of metaphysics, which is identical with that of theology, is clearly illustrated by Mr. Casaubon's procedure in his proposed Key to All Mythologies. Casaubon's method is exactly the opposite of that employed by Lydgate in his medical research. Lydgate, we remember, worked by the objective method, employing observation, induction, mental vision (leading to the formation of hypotheses), and experiential verification.[14] Casaubon began with the a priori assumption "that all the mythical systems or erratic mythical fragments in the world were corruptions of a tradition originally revealed." He did not arrive at this conception after research, by envisioning the probable state of affairs on the basis of partial evidence; he began with his thesis and interpreted all evidence in the light of it. And, quite naturally, he found what he had anticipated: "Having once mastered the true position and taken a firm footing there, the vast field of mythical constructions became intelligible, nay, luminous with the reflected light of correspondences" (*Middlemarch*, Chap. III). What Casaubon found was the reflection of his own premise. He was further prevented from arriving at the truth by the fact that his work was not undertaken in the spirit of disinterested research, but as a means of satisfying the claims of his ego. He was concerned less with truth than with gaining personal glory and smiting his enemies. Dorothea could evaluate his work better than he: "It was not wonderful that, in spite of her small instruction, her judgment in this matter was truer than his: for she looked with unbiassed comparison and healthy sense at probabilities on which he had risked all his egoism" (Chap. XLVIII).

Theory and egoism, forming a powerful subjective current, stood between Casaubon and the facts. The external world lost its solidity for him, and he existed in a subjective world of his own construction, a world which he could mold as he pleased. His theory "was not likely to bruise itself unawares against discoveries: it floated among flexible conjectures . . .: it was a method of interpretation which was not tested by the necessity of forming anything which had sharper collisions than an elaborate notion of Gog and Magog: it was as free from interruptions as a plan for threading the stars together" (Chap. XLVIII). The mind in which the subjective current is dominant, instead of seeing things as they are, often sees them as it wants them to be, as it feels they ought to be. George Eliot objected to the eclecticism of Victor Cousin because "the investigator under this system does not appear to us to be working by what Lord Bacon calls a 'dry light,' but to be rather seeking for something that he himself wants."[15]

George Eliot vigorously attacked the subjective approach as it appears in religious thought in her essay "Evangelical Teaching: Dr. Cumming." This, like the essay on Young, is a biting satire on the moral deficiency of a widely-respected teacher of Christian theology. Like Bulstrode in *Middlemarch,* Cumming treats external facts in a subjective way, rationalizing, twisting them about to make them fit into a preconceived notion of God's plan. Cumming unscrupulously manipulates evidence in order to make the Scriptures support his brand of Calvinistic Protestantism and in order to defend his conception of Scriptural authority. George Eliot does not, however, accuse him of hypocrisy or conscious dishonesty. His "unscrupulosity of statement" stems from his subjective habit of thought. Insofar as a defense of Christian theology requires the distortion of evidence, which she feels that it almost necessarily must in modern times, that theology is a cause of immorality. She does not doubt the genuineness of Cumming's zeal for Christianity, or the sincerity of his conviction that the doctrines he preaches are necessary to salvation; on the contrary, we regard the flagrant unveracity found on his pages as an indirect result of that conviction— as a result, namely, of the intellectual and moral distortion of view which is inevitably produced by assigning to dogmas, based on a very complex structure of evidence, the place and authority of first truths. A distinct appreciation of the value of evidence—in other words the intellectual perception of truth—is more closely allied to truthfulness of statement, or the moral quality of veracity, than is generally admitted. That highest moral habit, the constant preference of truth, both theoretically and practically, pre-eminently demands the co-operation of the intellect with the impulses. . . . And it is commonly seen that, in proportion as religious sects believe themselves to be guided by direct inspiration rather than by a spontaneous exertion of their faculties, their sense of truthfulness is misty and confused. . . . Minds fettered by this doctrine no longer inquire concerning a proposition whether it is attested by sufficient evidence, but whether it accords with Scripture; they do not search for facts, as such, but for facts that will bear out their doctrine. . . . It is easy to see that this mental habit blunts not only the perception of truth, but the sense of truthfulness, and that the man whose faith drives him into fallacies treads close upon the precipice of falsehood.

"The fundamental faith for man," George Eliot writes, "is faith in the result of a brave, honest, and steady use of all his faculties."[16]

In George Eliot's view, we are all born egoists. Both the individual and the race, in their childhood, regard the world almost entirely from the subjective point of view. Maturation is the process of recognizing the independent existence of outer phenomena, of yielding up the absolute supremacy of the self. In defining "the initial stage of all speculation," Lewes quotes Goethe's essay on "Experiment as the Mediator between the Object and the Subject": "Man regards at first all external objects with reference to himself; and rightly so, for his whole fate depends on them, on the pleasure or pain which they cause him, on their utility or danger to him." In many respects, however, this approach to reality defeats its own ends, for it cannot possibly arrive at the truth of things, and man remains powerless to control the conditions of his existence. By a long series of defeats and a gradual accumulation of experience, mankind has finally been brought to the positive stage of thought. The objective method is not easy to accept and employ, for it requires rigorous self-restraint: Goethe remarks how much more difficult is the task of discerning objects according to this Method, *i.e.,* not as related to *us,* but as related to one another. Our touchstone of pleasure or pain is given up. With godlike indifference we become *spectators* and seek that which *is,* not that which touches *us.*"[17]

The great division among George Eliot's characters is between egoists and those who approach reality objectively. The complications of her plots frequently stem from the egoism of central characters; and the development of the action often hinges upon or produces the education of the protagonist from egoism to objectivity. The role of the subjective and the objective approaches to reality in the moral lives of George Eliot's characters I shall examine at length in my discussion of the three stages of moral development in Chapter VII.[18]

Perhaps the most extreme form of the subjective approach to external reality, the positivists felt, is found in religion. "The religious mind," Feuerbach proclaimed in *The Essence of Christianity,* "does not distinguish between subjective and objective,—it has no doubts; it has the faculty, not of discerning other things than itself, but of seeing its own conceptions out of itself as distinct beings." The real external order is supplanted by an illusory external order which is simply the subjectivity of the individual made into an object: "the religious mind . . . has the immediate certainty that all its involuntary, spontaneous affections are impressions from without, manifestations of another being."[19]

Thus Bulstrode justifies his lust for personal power and dominance and excuses the injuries he inflicts upon others by seeing himself as the chosen servant of God and referring all of his actions to the divine plan. He believes that what he wants to do is actually what God wants him to do; that every opportunity for gain which comes his way, even when it involves what the world would call crime or injustice, is providentially arranged, is a sign, a directive, from God. Dinah Morris, too, guides her actions by heaven-sent signs and directives which are really her own "spontaneous affections" seen as "impressions from without, manifestations of another being." Dinah desires the welfare of others; hence God always "leads" her to acts of self-sacrifice and altruism. When she falls in love with Adam she is afraid to marry him because their love might lead her away from God's service. She finds, however, that her love for Adam is the strongest drive of her nature; and when she accepts him she says, "Adam . . . it is the Divine Will" (Chap. LIV).

Feuerbach tries to show that almost all of religion's conceptions of God and the world are in reality unconscious objectifications of man's own nature, needs, and desires. According to him, the autonomous existence of physical nature and the teachings of science are inimical to religion. The religious doctrines of creation out of nothing, providence, prayer, and faith, he argues, are all objectifications of man's desires for the obliteration of physical nature and the supremacy of his own subjectivity.

In the inmost depths of his soul, Feuerbach asserts, man would prefer that the world did not exist. Since the world and matter do in fact exist, there is a contradiction between subjective desires and objective reality. How can man expel the world from his consciousness, so that it will not disturb him in "the beatitude of the unlimited soul"? Only "by making the world itself a product of will, by giving it an arbitrary existence always hovering between existence and non-existence, always awaiting its annihilation." In the doctrine of creation out of nothing man affirms "the non-essentiality, the nothingness of the world" and the omnipotence, the independence, the unlimitedness of the will. "The culminating point of the principle of subjectivity is creation out of nothing." The objective world arose from nothingness at the command of the will and is doomed by the will to annihilation; only subjectivity is underived and enduring. In God the Creator man conceives his own subjective nature when the limiting world is separated from it. By the doctrine of creation out of nothing man subjectively triumphs over the external order, characterized by ineluctable, impersonal causal sequences, that stands between himself and the absolute.

By his belief in Providence and miracle, which are merely versions of the doctrine of creation out of nothing, man exempts himself from any connection with the physical world, denies "the reality of external things," and asserts "the infinite value of his existence." In a world governed by a supernatural Providence, the individual need not be concerned with achieving his ends by material means, for material circumstances are entirely subservient to the will of God, which is, of course, really man's own will projected into objectivity. Things should happen as he wants them to precisely because it is *he* who wants them so to happen. Fred Vincy, for example, expects that his Uncle Featherstone will give him a sum of money large enough to cover all of his debts. When he counts the bills he gets he discovers that "they actually presented the absurdity of being less than his hopefulness had decided that they must be. What can the fitness of things mean, if not their fitness to a man's expectations? Failing this, absurdity and atheism gape behind him" (*Middlemarch,* Chap. XIV). Fred, like so many of George Eliot's egoists, sees all the world in relation to himself and cannot conceive that things will turn out differently than he wishes them to. "Having ample funds at disposal in his own hopefulness," Fred is confident that he will be able to meet the bill for which Caleb Garth has assumed responsibility:

> You will hardly demand that his confidence should have a basis in external facts; such confidence, we know, is something less coarse and materialistic: it is a comfortable disposition leading us to expect that the wisdom of providence or the folly of our friends, the mysteries of luck or the still greater mystery of our high individual value in the universe, will bring about agreeable issues, such as are consistent with our good taste in costume, and our general preference for the best style of thing. (Ch. XXIII)

"The essence of faith," says Feuerbach, "is the idea that that which man wishes actually is." Hope, in the theological sense, is belief in the fulfillment of those wishes which are not yet realized. The object of faith and hope is miracle, for faith and hope are "nothing else than confidence in the reality of the subjective in opposition to the limitations or laws of Nature and reason." Faith and hope are directed not only towards sensible miracles, but also, and more and more frequently as science gains in power, towards the complete realization of man's subjective desires in heaven. Prayer is "the wish of the heart," the desire for miracle, "expressed with confidence in its fulfillment." Prayer expresses not the dependence of man on external things but the supremacy of human needs and wishes over all else: ". . . prayer is the unconditional confidence of human feeling in the absolute identity of the subjective and objective, the certainty that the power of the heart is greater than the power of Nature, that the heart's need is absolute necessity, the fate of the world." The man of science does not pray:

> The man who does not exclude from his mind the idea of the world, the idea that everything here must be sought intermediately, that every effect has its natural cause, that a wish is only to be attained when it is made an end and the corresponding means are put into operation—such a man does not pray: he only works; he transforms his attainable wishes into objects of real activity; other wishes which he recognizes as purely subjective he denies, or regards as simply subjective, pious aspirations. In other words, he limits, he conditionates his being by the world, as a member of which he conceives himself; he bounds his wishes by the idea of necessity.

The appeal of miracle is not simply that it accomplishes man's wishes, but that it does this in opposition to the laws of nature and without material means. While miracle is the principle of religion, labor is the instrument of science, of the objective intellect.

Feuerbach opposes the subjective spirit of religion to the objective spirit of science, or, as he terms it, of culture, in several other ways. Religion is primarily the expression of man's emotional, personal, subjective nature; science is the product of his rational, impersonal, objective nature. Reason is aware of the existence of a non-self; feeling knows only itself:

> The element of culture, the Northern principle of self-renunciation, is wanting to the emotional nature. . . . Culture, in general, is nothing else than the exaltation of the individual above his subjectivity to objective universal ideas, to the contemplation of the world. . . . The decline of culture was identical with the victory of Christianity. The classic spirit, the spirit of culture, limits itself by laws . . . it is determined by the necessity, the truth of the nature of things. . . . With

Christianity man lost the capability of conceiving himself as a part of Nature, of the universe.

George Eliot's problem was to strike a balance between the two approaches to reality which I have just described; to reconcile self and nature, heart and head, subjectivity and objectivity, moralism and realism.

THE ESSENCE OF CHRISTIANITY

I

George Eliot sought an approach to Christianity which would en-able her at once to discover the enduring human truths it contained and to isolate those of its dogmas which were harmful and untrue. She did not feel that a morality which bypassed Christianity, and with it much of the past and present culture of the race, could be adequate to the demands of the age. Her own Christian experience had so profoundly impressed itself upon her nature that unless she could reconcile her past and present selves she would always suffer from a sense of self-alienation. In the culture as a whole the situation was even more critical. She viewed society as incarnate history, as the product of centuries of organic growth; and she feared that an entire abandonment of Christianity would destroy the vitality of the social organism—it would be like pulling a plant up by its roots. She saw the conflict between science and religion as one between two principles both of which have their validity. Christianity, regardless of its truth or falsity, was a living force in the minds and hearts of men.

George Eliot's attitude toward religious systems was, for the most part, very sympathetic. In reference to the *Vie de Jesus,* she wrote to François D'Albert-Durade: "I am surprised to hear that there is anything 'cavalier' in Renan's treatment of religious belief: he has always seemed to me remarkable as a French mind that is at once 'scientific' (in the German sense) and eminently tender and reverent towards the forms in which the religious sentiment has incarnated itself" (*Letters*, IV, 94). She quieted Sara Hennell's fears that she would object to the "undue preponderance" that Sara had given to "the Christian argument" in her *Christianity and Infidelity* by writing: "I have a growing conviction that we may measure true moral and intellectual culture by the comprehension and veneration given to all forms of thought and feeling which have influenced large masses of mankind—and of all intolerance, the intolerance calling itself philosophical is the most odious to me" (*Letters*, II, 301). To Mme. Bodichon she wrote: "I care only to know, if possible, the lasting meaning that lies in all religious doctrine from the beginning till now" (*Letters*, IV, 65).

That George Eliot had resolved the conflict between scientific culture and Christian tradition to her own satisfaction by the time she began to write fiction is evidenced by the fact that in *Scenes of Clerical Life,* especially in "Janet's Repentance," and in *Adam Bede* she drew much of her material from recollections of the experiences, people, and religious forms which were associated with the Evangelicism of her youth. She could not have made the religious experience so central in the lives of Mr. Tryan, Janet Dempster, and Dinah Morris unless she had arrived at a perspective which enabled her to see this experience as a valid solution to moral problems. Anyone who reads her novels with a knowledge of her intellectual development must ask how this earnest positivist and agnostic could treat traditional religion so sympathetically, why she made the religious experience the subject of so much of her fiction, and what moral truth she found religion to embody.

Shortly after she revealed her authorship of *Adam Bede* to the Brays and the Hennells, George Eliot wrote to Charles Bray: "I can't tell you how much melancholy it causes me that people are, for the most part, so incapable of comprehending the state of mind which cares for that which is essentially human in all forms of belief, and desires to exhibit it under all forms with loving truthfulness" (*Letters,* III, 111). In her view the higher criticism of the Bible and the teach-

90

ings of positive science had discredited organized religion as a source of information concerning the external order; but, by showing that religious records, beliefs, and institutions are human in origin, they converted religion into a source of profound truth about the subjective order. Herbert Spencer, for example, wrote that

> the universality of religious ideas, their independent evolution among different primitive races, and their great vitality, unite in showing that their source must be deep-seated instead of superficial. In other words, we are obliged to admit that if not super-naturally derived as the majority contend, they must be derived out of human experience accumulated and organized.[1]

Hennell and Strauss had argued that although the Scriptures do not contain an accurate account of history and of the order of things, they nevertheless are an immensely important expression of subjective states. "Many of the finer thoughts and feelings of mankind," Hennell pointed out, "find a vent in fiction, expressed either by painting, poetry, or the poetic tale; and the perception of historical inaccuracy does not prevent our sharing the thoughts and feelings which have embodied themselves in this manner." The religion of the ancient Greeks and the Catholic worship of images and relics of saints, martyrs, and the Virgin Mary can become meaningful for us if we see them as expressions of basic human feelings. "In like manner, whilst recognizing the true character of the evangelic fables, we may still discover in them and share the feelings from which, for the most part, they sprung,—respect and attachment towards a character of unwonted power and excellence."[2] Strauss identified the unhistorical elements in the Gospel accounts of Jesus as the product of the mythic consciousness of the race. Since the Gospels embody "the vivid impression of the original idea which the first Christian community had of their founder," they are "a faithful representation of the idea of the Christ." Strauss claimed that his method "leaves the substance of the narrative unassailed; and instead of venturing to explain details, accepts the whole, not indeed as true history, but as sacred legend."[3]

Both Hennell and Strauss, however, had introduced metaphysical speculations into their analyses of the enduring truths contained in

Christianity. Hennell was a believer in right reason and in revelation through great men and through nature. Christianity, when purified of the errors which mark it as in part the product of a specific time and place, turned out to be the purest form yet available of natural religion. Strauss employed the Hegelian dialectic to show that the mythic consciousness of the race, rather than a special revelation or miracles, is the means by which the Absolute reveals to the finite mind of man the ultimate inseparability of the phenomenal and the noumenal. For Hennell, Christ is the hero whose unclouded right reason grasps universal moral and metaphysical truths; for Strauss, he is a symbol of the union of the divine and the human, God and man —a union which has total reality not in a single man, a messiah, but in the race. As a result of their metaphysical orientations, neither Hennell nor Strauss had probed very deeply into the specific psychological sources of basic Christian beliefs; and thus, though they contributed to George Eliot's understanding of religion, they did not satisfy her, especially after she became a thorough-going positivist, in her effort to grasp concretely "that which is essentially human in all forms of belief." It was her study of Ludwig Feuerbach, combined with her own experience, that led George Eliot to her final interpretation of the essence of Christianity.

The influence of Ludwig Feuerbach's *The Essence of Christianity* upon George Eliot's understanding of religious experience cannot be overestimated. The task of translating Strauss's *Life of Jesus,* undertaken at the request of others, had proved wearisome, for she often found Strauss's ideas uncongenial (see *Letters,* I, 206–207). The translation of Feuerbach was a labor of love which left his conceptions deeply imprinted upon her consciousness. She objected to Feuerbach's stylistic excesses, but she wrote to Sara Hennell: "With the ideas of Feuerbach I everywhere agree" (*Letters,* II, 153). A month later, May 1854, she wrote: "The proof-reading of Feuerbach is really a pleasure to me and opens up afresh to me what there is of truth and beauty in the book" (*Letters,* II, 155).

Hennell and Strauss were of limited value to the mature George Eliot because their work contained a mixture of the empirical and the metaphysical epistemologies; as historical critics they were positivistic, but as speculative thinkers they were, in varying ways, idealists. Feuerbach was consistently empirical. George Eliot asked Sara Hennell, who was correcting her translation of Feuerbach, to pay especial attention to the style and accuracy of the preface, "as it is very important that this preface *should be read*" (*Letters,* II, 141). In the preface, Feuerbach, who was at one time a follower of Hegel, vigorously proclaims his opposition to the idealistic tradition in philosophy and asserts the empirical basis of his own methodology. His philosophy has for its principle, he asserts, "not the Substance of Spinoza, not the *ego* of Kant and Fichte, not the Absolute Identity of Schelling, not the Absolute Mind of Hegel, in short, no abstract, merely conceptual being, but a *real* being, the true *Ens realissimum*— man; its principle therefore is in the highest degree positive and real." His concern with concrete existence, he says, makes his philosophy appear "to all dull and pedantic minds" to be no philosophy at all. His method, in fact, "places philosophy in *the negation of philosophy, i.e.,* it declares *that* alone to be the true philosophy which is converted *in succum et sanguinem,* which is incarnate in Man." This last remark, as we shall see, does much to explain why George Eliot regarded the novel as the most potent of instruments for the discovery of moral truths and the verification of moral theories.

The "true object and substance" of religion, according to Feuerbach, is "*man,—anthropology.*" What religion posits about God is true of and has existence in no other being than man. "Man—this is the mystery of religion—projects his being into objectivity, and then again makes himself an object to this projected image of himself thus converted into a subject; he thinks of himself as an object to himself, but as the object of an object, of another being than himself." The objective existence of God is an illusion insofar as God is considered to exist as a being apart from the species. The real existence of God is nothing but the real existence of the divine predicates in man. God exists objectively, from the point of view of the individual, in the species; the species is God.

Feuerbach grounds his religious subjectivism, his reduction of theology to anthropology and exaltation of anthropology into theology, partly upon an analysis of the nature of consciousness. For the brute the internal and the external are one, but man is conscious both of the self and the non-self. Man's consciousness of physical nature as a non-self makes science possible. His consciousness of his species results in his religious conceptions of deity and in his longing to unite his individual nature with the Absolute, which he imagines to be God but which is in reality mankind. "Man," says Feuerbach, "is himself at once I and thou; he can put himself in the place of another, for this reason, that to him his species, his essential nature, and not merely his individuality, is an object of thought."

The foundation of Feuerbach's argument for the identity of the divine and human predicates, and hence of the divine and human subjects, is the proposition, familiar to all proponents of the relativity of knowledge, that "the limit of the nature is also the limit of the consciousness." Theologians argue that since man, a finite imperfect being, is conscious of the infinite and the perfect, there must exist outside of man an infinite and perfect being, a God, who has placed these ideas in the human mind. Feuerbach, denying any source of knowledge other than experience and holding that the objects of which the subject is conscious indicate the nature of the subject, argues that since man is conscious of the infinite and perfect, man must himself be an infinite and perfect being. That the individual feels his own finiteness and imperfection is no obstacle to Feuerbach. He feels his own limitation only because he is conscious of the unlimited; he is conscious of infinity and perfection not in himself but in his species. The individual may feel the species to be limited, but this is the consequence of his regarding the species egoistically rather than objectively and thereby making his own limitations the limitations of the species.

"The *absolute* to man is his own nature." Feuerbach means here, of course, man's essential nature, which is the nature of the species. The nature of the species is the absolute limit of human consciousness; therefore, to human consciousness, the nature of the species is absolute, infinite, perfect:

> Every being is sufficient to itself. No being can deny itself, *i.e.,* its own nature; no being is a limited one to itself. Rather, every being is in and by itself infinite—has its God, its highest conceivable being, in itself. . . . to a limited being its limited understanding is not felt to

be a limitation; on the contrary, it is perfectly happy and contented with this understanding; it regards it, praises and values it, as a glorious, divine power; and the limited understanding, on its part, values the limited nature whose understanding it is. . . . As far as thou seest, so far extends thy nature; . . . And so far as thy nature reaches, so far reaches thy unlimited self-consciousness, so far art thou God.

To think of the species as finite and imperfect we must regard it from the point of view of a higher nature; but this is impossible, for then we would ourselves have to have this higher nature.

"In religion," Feuerbach proclaims, "consciousness of the object and self-consciousness coincide. . . . here may be applied, without any limitation, the proposition: the object of any subject is nothing else than the subject's own nature taken objectively." When we view religion objectively we see that "the antithesis of divine and human is altogether illusory, that it is nothing else than the antithesis between the human nature in general and the human individual; that, consequently, the object and contents of the Christian religion are altogether human." Thus Christianity for Feuerbach, and for George Eliot, is no absurdity, no record of meaningless fantasies or mistakes of thought; rather it is the repository of real human experience; it is the key to man's subjective, moral nature.[4]

II

Feuerbach divides his empirical analysis of Christianity into two parts. The first part seeks to discover what Christianity veritably is, what it reveals about its creator, man. The second part attempts to show "that the distinction which is made, or rather supposed to be made, between the theological and anthropological predicates resolves itself into an absurdity." Feuerbach stresses the fact that he seeks not to destroy Christianity, but to explain it, to show its human origin and thus to render it humanly meaningful. His method is to "analyse speculation, *i.e.*, reduce theology to anthropology"; "to show that metaphysics is resolvable into psychology."

Many Christian doctrines are the expression of man's egoistic desire that his consciousness have unlimited freedom and power. The personal God of the Christian religion "is nothing else than the personal nature of man positing itself out of all connection with the world, making itself free from all dependence on nature." Christianity is "the dream of waking consciousness"; "the fundamental dogmas of Christianity are realised wishes of the heart." In Christianity "the requirements of human feeling" are "the absolute powers and laws of the world." The supreme dictum of Christianity, "God is love," expresses, among other things, man's certainty "that the inmost wishes of the heart have objective validity and reality, . . . That the whole world, with all its pomp and glory, is nothing weighed against human feeling." The belief in Christ's resurrection is "the satisfied desire of man for an immediate certainty of his personal existence after death." Christ as redeemer is man's fulfilled wish for happiness, and for virtue which is the means to happiness. The future life, the Christian heaven, "is nothing else than life in unison with the feeling, with the idea, which the present life contradicts. The whole import of the future life is the abolition of this discordance, and the realization of a state which corresponds to the feelings, in which man is in unison with himself."

Christianity is not only wish-fulfillment; it is also self-contemplation, man's contemplation of his highest, his essential nature. "God," says Feuerbach, "is the mirror of man." "God is for man the commonplace book where he registers his highest feelings and thoughts." There are important differences between those aspects of Christianity which objectify and venerate the highest qualities of human nature and of human relationships and those which are the reflection of man's needs and wishes. The latter reveal man's attitude toward nature and the extent of his self-love; they are not objectively true. The former contain religious truths which are transformed but not destroyed by empirical analysis. By viewing the old religion objectively, Feuerbach hopes to arrive at a new, objectively true religion, which is different in form from the old, but similar to it in essence. "The new philosophy," he writes, "being evolved from the nature of religion, . . . has in itself the true essence of religion,—is, in its very quality as a philosophy, a religion also." As Christianity was unconsciously, the new religion is consciously a religion of man.

The secret of religion, for Feuerbach, is atheism, the worship of man as God and the denial of any God who is not man. "Christ alone," he insists, "is the personal God; he is the real God of the Christians." The true atheist, according to Feuerbach, is he "to whom the predicates of the Divine Being,—for example, love, wisdom, justice,—are nothing; not he to whom merely the subject of these predicates is nothing."[5] A God who is denied the predicates of human nature has no real, positive being whatever. The distinction between the meaning of predicates (such as love, justice, mercy) when assigned to man and the same predicates when assigned to God is a fallacious, meaningless distinction.[6] Feuerbach argues that the distinction between what God is for me and what he is in himself is likewise untenable: "I cannot know whether God is something else in himself or for himself than he is for me; what he is to me is to me all that he is."

God has the divine predicates not because he is God but because the predicates are, in the eyes of man, Godly. Therefore, the "rank of godhead is due not to the subject, but to the predicate." When Christianity says that God is love, what is really meant is that love is God. Religion is man's evaluation of the qualities of the species: "What man praises and approves, that is God to him; what he blames, condemns, is the non-divine. Religion is a *judgment*."[7] Carlyle's *Life of Sterling,* wrote George Eliot, "is a touching monument of the capability human nature possesses of the highest love, the love of the good and beautiful in character, which is, after all, the essence of piety."[8] The true object of veneration, then, is man. Mankind is the God of man. The idea of God, she felt, "so far as it has been a high spiritual influence, is the idea of a goodness entirely human (*i.e.,* an exaltation of the human" (*Letters,* VI, 98).

Man becomes aware of the species and partakes in its life through his relationship with another human being, with a thou. To the individual, another human being "is the representative of the species, even though he is only one, for he supplies to me the want of many others, has for me a universal significance, is the deputy of mankind, in whose name he speaks to me, an isolated individual, so that, when united only with one, I have a participated, a human life." My fellow man is "my objective conscience; . . . he is my personified feeling of shame. The consciousness of the moral law, of right, of propriety, of truth itself, is indissolubly united with my consciousness of another than myself." In love the reality of the species, otherwise an abstract conception, becomes "a matter of feeling, a truth of feeling; for in love, a man declares himself unsatisfied in his individuality taken by itself; . . . he declares the life which he has through love to be the truly human life."[9] Religion consists preeminently in the love, admiration, sympathy, and sacrifice of man for man. George Eliot felt that Tennyson's "In Memoriam" "enshrines the highest tendency of this age" because whatever was its immediate prompting and "whatever the form under which the author represented his aim to himself, the deepest significance of the poem is the sanctification of human love as a religion."[10]

In an essay entitled "George Eliot as a Religious Teacher" (1881), Josiah Royce describes her religion of humanity in the following way:

> Religious knowledge and life come to us then, our author teaches, through the influence of individual souls, whose sympathy and counsel awaken us to a new sense of the value of life, and to a new earnestness to work henceforth not for self, but for the Other than self. This Other, as you see, is always at least negatively infinite; it takes in this philosophy the place of the supernatural. You know not its boundaries. This grand ocean of life stretches out before you without discovered shore. . . . To embark and to lose yourself is religion; to wait on the shore is moral starvation. . . . The infinite is conceived as known only in this world of fellow-beings.[11]

Royce makes these remarks in his discussion of the relation between Janet Dempster and Mr. Tryan in "Janet's Repentance." Brought to despair by her husband's cruelty, her sense of her own weakness in taking to drink, and the absence of human comfort and hope for the future, Janet loses faith in the existence of the divine love, "and if there was any Divine Pity, she could not feel it; it kept aloof from her . . ." (Chap. XV). Struck by Mr. Tryan's sympathetic nature and apparent understanding of deep experience, Janet reveals her problem to him. "I feel," she tells him, "as if there must be goodness and right above us, but I can't see it, I can't trust in it." Mr. Tryan is able to help Janet move from the second to the third stage of moral development (see Chapter VII below) because his own experience enables him to understand her plight and to offer the sympathy and direction she needs. George Eliot comments that "the tale of the Divine Pity was never yet believed from lips that were not felt to be moved by human pity" (Chap. XVIII). Royce analyses the situation very well: "He sees in this woman his own old despairing self. He speaks to her out of the fullness of an experience of torture. He uses the conventional terms of orthodoxy, to be sure; but we feel, as we read, that the force is not intended by the author to be in them." Janet accepts Tryan's message "not because of the essential might of the orthodox formula" but because of "the force of direct present sympathy. Janet feels that here is another, with like nature, tried, tempted, fallen also, but enabled to rise by seeing the vast world of human life about him in which there is so much to be done, in which there is such a mass of suffering and sin, to which his life is but a drop, and for which, as he sees, he must work."[12]

After her talk with Mr. Tryan Janet felt that a door had been opened in her "cold dark prison of self despair. . . . There was sunlight in the world; there was a divine love caring for her" (Chap. XXI). She was hopeful about the future: "The Divine Love that had already shone upon her would be with her; she would lift up her soul continually for help; Mr. Tryan, she knew, would pray for her" (Chap. XXIV). Near the end of the story Janet experienced a momentary weakening of resolve and was tempted to drink once more. In her fear she hastened to see Mr. Tryan, and almost immediately her strength returned. She felt once again that the divine presence was close to her, that "Infinite Love was caring for her" (Chap. XXV).

Mr. Tryan is God to Janet; his speech comes to her "charged with a divine power such as she had never found in human words before." Mr. Tryan is the representative of the species; through him Janet becomes aware of the universal existence of the divine predicates: "The act of confiding in human sympathy, the consciousness that a fellow-being was listening to her with patient pity, prepared her soul for that stronger leap by which faith grasps the idea of the Divine sympathy" (Chap. XXV). Tryan's words strike Janet with divine power because they are not mere formulae, but the utterances of profound experience; his theology has moral efficacy because he himself is a living embodiment of the divine renunciation, the divine suffering, the divine love. He speaks of Christ not as a miraculous redeemer, but as a compassionate friend who understands our troubles because he has shared the human lot. Christ, he tells Janet, "enters into your struggles; he has drunk the cup of our suffering to the dregs; he knows the hard wrestling it costs us to say, 'Not my will but Thine be done'" (Chap. XVIII). Tryan himself is at once Christ-like and very human. George Eliot's aim is to show us the human being beneath the Evangelical preacher and the human experiences of sin, suffering, repentance, and renunciation which give life to religious doctrines.

There are a number of relationships in her novels similar to that between Mr. Tryan and Janet Dempster: namely, the relationships between Felix Holt and Esther Lyon, Savonarola and Romola, Daniel Deronda and Gwendolen Harleth, and (in some ways) Thomas à Kempis and Maggie Tulliver. In each of these relationships one of the partners is morally superior and serves as a mentor to the other; the male (as the case is) leads the female away from egoism and sometimes despair to an awareness of the larger, higher life of love and service to one's fellow men. These relationships, which are fraught for George Eliot and for the characters themselves with religious significance, I shall discuss in Chapter XI. In general, the relations of man to man in her novels are religious in their nature and import. "The relations of child and parent," writes Feuerbach, "of husband and wife, of brother and friend—in general, of man to man —in short, all the moral relations are *per se* religious."[13]

The religious nature of interpersonal relationships can be seen in *Adam Bede:* in Dinah Morris' relations with almost all who know her, in Seth's love for Dinah, in Adam's relation to Arthur Donnithorne, and in Adam's love for Hetty and then for Dinah. Of Seth's feeling for Dinah, for example, George Eliot writes: "He was but three-and-twenty, and had only just learned what it is to love—to love with that adoration which a young man gives to a woman whom he feels to be greater and better than himself. Love of this sort is hardly distinguishable from religious feeling. What deep and worthy love is so? whether of woman or child, or art or music" (Chap. III).

When Adam tells Arthur of his feeling for Hetty, he distinguishes his love from mere sexual passion. The religious nature of Adam's

THE ESSENCE OF CHRISTIANITY

feeling for Hetty stems partly from the fact that his love is directed not chiefly toward Hetty as Hetty, but toward Hetty as a representative and embodiment of the divine qualities of the species. "I think," George Eliot writes, "the deep love he had for that sweet, rounded, blossom-like, dark-eyed Hetty, of whose inward self he was really very ignorant, came out of the very strength of his nature." It is no more a weakness to love a woman for her beauty than it is to be "wrought on by exquisite music":

> For the beauty of a lovely woman is like music: what can one say more? Beauty has an expression beyond and far above the one woman's soul that it clothes . . . : it is more than a woman's love that moves us in a woman's eyes—it seems to be a far-off mighty love that has come near to us, and made speech for itself there. . . . The noblest nature sees the most of this *impersonal* expression in beauty . . . , and for this reason, the noblest nature is often the most blinded to the character of the one woman's soul that the beauty clothes.

Adam "called his love frankly a mystery. . . . He only knew that the sight and memory of her moved him deeply, touching the spring of all love and tenderness, all faith and courage within him" (Chap. XXXIII).

Adam's religious nature manifests itself also in his relation with Arthur Donnithorne and in his attitude towards his work. Adam loved to dwell on Arthur's good qualities, which he had a pride in. "A nature like Adam's," George Eliot explains, "with a great need of love and reverence in it, depends for so much of its happiness on what it can believe and feel about others! And he had no ideal world of dead heroes; he knew little of the life of men in the past; he must find the beings to whom he could cling with loving admiration among those who came within speech of him" (Chap. XXVII).

One of Adam's heroes from the past was Moses, whose example strengthened Adam's belief in the nobility of honest, self-forgetful labor: "He carried a hard business well through, and died when other folks were going to reap the fruits: a man must have courage to look at his life so, and think what'll come of it after he's dead and gone. A good solid bit o' work lasts: if it's only laying a floor down, somebody's the better for it being done well, besides the man

101

as does it" (Chap. L). Adam, like Caleb Garth, finds a religious significance in his work, for through it he serves his fellows and gains, with the aid of vision, an impersonal immortality. "His work," we are told, "had always been part of his religion" (Chap. L). "Work," proclaims Feuerbach, "is worship." "Every man," he contends, "must place before himself a God, *i.e.,* an aim, a purpose. . . . He who has an aim, an aim which is in itself true and essential, has, *eo ipso,* a religion. . . ." (p. 64)

> Through the activity in which he realises this aim man is not only something for himself, but also something for others, for the general life, the species. He therefore who lives in the consciousness of the species as a reality, regards his existence for others, his relation to society, his utility to the public, as that existence which is one with the existence of his own essence—as his immortal existence. (p. 171)

One cannot speak of work as worship without thinking of Carlyle, especially since he exerted a powerful influence upon George Eliot in the 1840's. It is Feuerbach, however, rather than Carlyle, who best helps us to understand the role of work in her "Religion of Humanity." Adam, especially in his hymn to work in the first chapter of the novel, in some ways sounds like Carlyle, but he is unconsciously a Feuerbachian, a worshipper of man.

Adam's religion of work sustains him when his faith in those human beings whom he had loved and reverenced is shattered. Arthur and Hetty both prove to be false and ignoble, and Adam experiences, for a time, a bewildering sense of disillusionment in his fellow men. He ultimately finds another, more worthy, object of veneration in Dinah Morris. Even before he was conscious of loving Dinah, Adam frequently visited Hall Farm and "had become used . . . to listen for her voice as for a recurrent music; to think everything she said and did was just right, and could not have been better" (Chap. I). Adam regards Dinah as his moral superior, as his guide, protector, and setter of standards. He revels in her love as the Christian rejoices in the love and felt presence of God. Just before their encounter on the hill when Dinah agrees to marry him, Adam thinks to himself: "It's like as if it was a new strength to me . . . to love her, and know as she loves me. I shall look t' her to help me to see things right. For she's better than I am—there's less o' self in her, and pride. And it's a feeling as gives you a sort o' liberty, as if you could walk more fearless, when you've more trust in another than y' have in yourself" (Chap. LIX).

The religious admiration and reverence that Adam feels towards Dinah is matched in Dinah's feelings toward Adam. Dinah's fear, as she expresses it to Adam, that she will "forget the Divine presence, and seek no love but yours" (Chap. LII), is in reality her fear that she will become absorbed in the satisfactions of her love for Adam and will therefore cease to suffer for and serve all her fellow men. Dinah, of course, believes in God as an objectively-existing, individual, supernatural being. George Eliot, however, views Dinah's religious experience from a Feuerbachian perspective—only hinted at in the novel— which the present analysis tries to make explicit. George Eliot's object, in *Adam Bede,* is to present sympathetically those forms of traditional religious experience which have enduring meaning and virtue.

The central figure in Dinah's religion, as in Mr. Tryan's, is Jesus, the Man of Sorrows. Dinah models her life after her conception of the sympathetic, loving, suffering Christ, the Christ who is one with the Infinite Love, and she brings Christ's message to her fellows largely by being herself Christ-like. Blessedness, for Dinah, lies in sharing the Redeemer's cross and thereby partaking in the divine love and the divine sorrow. The Christ about whom Dinah tells her hearers is, like Mr. Tryan's Christ, that very human Christ who is claimed by Feuerbach to be the real God of the Christian religion. It is through Jesus, Dinah teaches, that man comes to know and feel God's love: "So then, all the love that Jesus showed to the poor is the same love that God has for us. We can understand what Jesus felt, because he came in a body like ours, and spoke words such as we speak to each other" (Chap. II).

Dinah herself, by the power of her love and of her subtle sympathy with suffering, produces in others a sense of the divine presence which she feels so strongly. The potency of Dinah's sympathy is clearly seen in the way in which she soothes Lisbeth Bede after Thias' death. George Eliot observes that Dinah's reliance, "in her smallest words and deeds, on a divine guidance, always issued in that finest woman's tact which proceeds from acute and ready sympathy." "And do we not all agree," George Eliot asks, "to call rapid thought and noble impulse by the name of inspiration?" As a result of Dinah's ministrations, "poor aged fretful Lisbeth, without grasping any distinct idea, without going through any course of religious emotions, felt a vague sense of goodness and love, and of something right lying underneath and beyond all this sorrowing life" (Chap. X). In Lisbeth's mind Dinah is connected with the picture in her Bible "of the angel seated on the great stone that has been rolled away from the sepulchre" (Chap. LI).

Dinah's love rescues Hetty from the black despair into which her crime and punishment have led her. Before Dinah's arrival Hetty had refused to speak with anyone and had refused to admit her guilt; Mr. Irwine tells Adam that "some fatal influence seems to have shut up her heart against her fellow-creatures" (Chap. XLI). Even after Dinah comes to her, Hetty's despair is at first unrelieved. Dinah does not, however, lose faith in the power of love to save Hetty: "she felt the Divine presence more and more,—nay, as if she herself were a part of it, and it was the Divine pity that was breathing in her heart, and was willing the rescue of this helpless one" (Chap. XLV). Dinah, by virtue of her characteristically religious mode of thought and feeling, experiences her own love and pity at first as something apart from herself and then as something with which she is united. But it is not only her own love and pity that she feels; her own feeling (in the terms of our Feuerbachian analysis) is partly the product of her consciousness of love and pity as divine qualities existing in the species. Dinah here is to Hetty the representative of the species; through her, Hetty becomes conscious of the divine love, that is, of love as it is a predicate of the species.

Dinah feels the source of her love to be Christ, and she feels Christ to be the power which will open Hetty's heart. Christ, according to Feuerbach, is an image of the species, the species conceived of as an individual. Dinah is inspired with love by her consciousness of Christ (i.e., of the species); and through her love she becomes Christ, and acts upon Hetty not only with the force of her individuality but also with the divine power of mankind. "It is the species," writes Feuerbach, "which infuses love into me. A loving heart is the heart of the

THE ESSENCE OF CHRISTIANITY

species throbbing in the individual. Thus Christ, as the consciousness of love, is the consciousness of the species. . . . He therefore who loves man for the sake of man, who rises to the love of the species, to universal love, adequate to the nature of the species, he is a Christian, is Christ himself. He does what Christ did, what made Christ Christ." Feuerbach adds that although our love is always directed to individuals, rather than to the species, "it is yet in its nature universal, since it loves man for man's sake, in the name of the race."[15]

Dinah's love, expressed through prayer, through invocation of the divine love, brings Hetty Sorrel to confess, to repent, and to seek the forgiveness of those she has injured. Arthur Donnithorne, when Adam forgives him, says of Dinah, in reference to her ministrations to Hetty: "I could worship that woman; I don't know what I should do if she were not there" (Chap. XLVIII).

Both Dinah Morris and Mr. Tryan teach that through Christ man can be saved from sin and suffering, and both Hetty Sorrel and Janet Dempster derive comfort and strength from this belief. Of course, the doctrine owes its efficacy in these instances largely to the fact that in Dinah and Tryan, Hetty and Janet find human beings who are not hard and condemning, but who are loving, understanding, and forgiving. As she wanders homeward in despair, after having failed to find Arthur, Hetty thinks of going to Dinah: "She couldn't imagine Dinah's face turning away from her in dark reproof or scorn, Dinah's voice willingly speaking ill of her, or rejoicing in her misery as a punishment. Dinah did not seem to belong to that world of Hetty's, whose glance she dreaded like scorching fire" (Chap. XXXVII). The truth in the doctrine of Christ as savior from sin and suffering is, according to Feuerbach, that love, for man, is a higher power than moral law, that through love man is saved from that soul-destroying sense of worthlessness and alienation from his kind which is the concomitant of a sense of sinfulness.

Feuerbach carefully distinguishes between God as the objective nature of the understanding and God as the objective nature of the feelings. The God of metaphysics is "the intelligence, satisfied in itself, thinking itself as the absolute being. . . . Hence all metaphysical predicates of God are *real* predicates only when they are recognised as belonging to thought, to intelligence, to the understanding." God as a being of the understanding is God as the giver of moral law, God as the judge of man. The understanding is objective, untender, indifferent; "the understanding knows nothing of the sufferings of the heart; it has no desires, no passions, no wants, and, for that reason, no deficiencies and weaknesses, as the heart has." The God which the understanding posits as a morally perfect being "is nothing else than the realised idea, the fulfilled law of morality, the moral nature of man [*i.e.,* of the species] posited as the absolute being." In his consciousness of God as a law-giver, as a morally perfect being, the individual experiences a painful sense of distance from God, of disparity between his own nature and the divine nature. Man is delivered from "this state of disunion between himself and the perfect being, from the painful consciousness of sin, from the distressing sense of his own nothingness" by virtue of the fact "that he is conscious of *love* as the highest, the absolute power and truth, that he regards the Divine Being not only as a law, as a moral being, as a being of the understanding; but also as a loving, tender, even subjective human being (that is, as having sympathy with individual man)." Through his consciousness of love, man "reconciles himself with God, or rather with his own nature as represented in the moral law."

The mystery of the incarnation, according to Feuerbach, is the consciousness of the divine love, of God, as human. Since out of love for man God renounced his divinity and became human, "love is a higher power and truth than deity. Love conquers God." The divine love, the suffering, self-sacrificing love of Christ, is identical with the highest human love: "the true human love, which is alone worthy of this name, is that which impels the sacrifice of self to another. Who then is our Saviour and Redeemer? God or Love? Love; for God as God has not saved us, but Love, which transcends the difference between the divine and human personality." The statement that God loves man, which is the very central point of religion, means, in actuality, "the highest is the love of man." The highest, truest teaching of Christianity, then, is that man's love for man is divine, that to love, pity, and suffer for others is to be as God: "God suffers . . . for men, for others, not for himself. What does that mean in plain speech? Nothing else than this: to suffer for others is divine; he who suffers for others, who lays down his life for them, acts divinely, is a God to men."[16]

III

The truth, the virtue of Christianity lies in the fact that the divine naure is human nature made objective to itself; the untruth, the evil of Christianity lies in the illusion that the divine nature is different from human nature and that God is a personal being who exists independently of mankind. "When this projected image of human nature is made an object of reflection, of theology," writes Feuerbach, "it becomes an inexhaustible mine of falsehoods, illusions, contradictions, and sophisms." The illusions of religion are by no means harmless; the doctrines and attitudes to which they give rise are, to use George Eliot's description of the teachings of Dr. Cumming, "subversive of true moral development, and therefore positively noxious." "As God has renounced himself out of love," Feuerbach preaches, "so we, out of love, should renounce God; for if we do not sacrifice God to love, we sacrifice love to God. . . ."

God is in truth the species conceived as an individual, but because it conceives of God as an independent being, Christianity ignores the species. "My fellow man," writes Feuerbach, "is *per se* the mediator between me and the sacred idea of the species. *Homo homini Deus est.*" Christianity weakens this religious relation of man to man. In Christianity "man has all in himself, all in his God, consequently he has no need to supply his own deficiencies by others as the representatives of the species, or by the contemplation of the world generally. . . . God fills to me the place of the species, of my fellow men. . . ." Faith in the existence of God is faith in the separateness of God and man; "the separation of God from man is . . . the separation of man from man, the unloosening of the social bond."

One of the most injurious of Christianity's teachings is that the source, end, and arbiter of moral action is God. Feuerbach points out, to begin with, that "what is done is done not because it is good and right, but because it is commanded by God. . . . whatever God commands is right." Of course, when actions are sanctioned or damned solely by God's command, actions which are in human terms bad are frequently condoned and good actions are called evil. Moreover, "the belief that God is the necessary condition of virtue is the belief in the nothingness of virtue in itself." For the religious man "good works do not proceed from essentially virtuous dispositions. It is not love, not the object of love, man, the basis of all morality, which is the motive of his good works. No! he does good not for the sake of . . . man, but for the sake of God." In and for themselves, other men are unimportant; Christianity "sacrifices the love of man to the honour of God" (p. 261). The God of theology is jealous of man; the illusion of religion "sucks away the best forces of morality."

> Above morality hovers God, as a being distinct from man, a being to whom the best is due, while the remnants only fall to the share of man. All those dispositions which ought to be devoted to life, to man —all the best powers of humanity, are lavished on the being who wants nothing. . . . Man thanks God for those benefits which have been rendered to him even at the cost of sacrifice by his fellow man. . . . He is thankful, grateful to God, but unthankful to man. Thus is the moral sentiment subverted into religion! Thus does man sacrifice to God!

Christianity claims to promote human love by enjoining man, in the name of the love and glory of God, to love his fellows. But a love for man which is based on Christ's love "does not rest on the proper ground of love. Are we to love each other because Christ loved us? Such love would be an affected, imitative love. Can we truly love each other only if we love Christ? Is Christ the cause of love? . . . Is not the ground of his love the unity of human nature?" Man must be loved, can only be loved, not for the sake of God, but for the sake of man. If I interpose God between myself and my fellow, "I annihilate the very soul of love."[17]

Feuerbach's criticisms of Christian doctrine are echoed in George Eliot's essay "Evangelical Teaching: Dr. Cumming."[18] We have seen that she attacked Cumming for his unscrupulosity of statement, for his subjectivity and sophistry. "Religion apart," she writes, Dr. Cumming "probably appreciates and practises veracity." Feuerbach contends that the belief in revelation "not only injures the moral sense and taste . . . ; it poisons, nay, it destroys, the divinest feeling in man—the sense of truth, the perception and sentiment of truth." The necessary consequence, for modern man, of faith in the documents and dogmas of religion is "superstition and sophistry." Feuerbach lays down the rule that, in general *"wherever religion places itself in contradiction with reason, it places itself also in contradiction with the moral sense.* Only with the sense of truth coexists the sense of the right and good. Depravity of understanding is always depravity of heart . . . ; sophistry corrupts the whole man."[19]

A conspicuous characteristic of Dr. Cumming's teachings, according to George Eliot, is "the *absence of genuine charity.*" The absence of "truly human sympathies" in Dr. Cumming's faith "is exhibited in the way he treats the doctrine of Eternal Punishment," for Cumming denies that "mercy will ultimately triumph, that God—*i.e.,* Love— will be all in all." Cumming preaches the necessity and virtue of Christian love:

> But the love thus taught is love of the *clan,* which is the correlative of antagonism to the rest of mankind. It is not sympathy and helpfulness towards men as men, but towards men as Christians, and as Christians in the sense of a small minority. Dr. Cumming's religion may demand a tribute of love, but it gives a charter to hatred; it may enjoin charity, but it fosters all uncharitableness. If I believe that God tells me to love my enemies, but at the same time hates His own enemies and requires me to have one will with Him, which has the larger scope, love or hatred?

The doubter, to Cumming, is "hardened, conceited, consciously shutting his eyes to the light." Cumming fixes his hearer's mind "on the conception of his fellow men, not as fellow sinners, but as agents of hell." For the Christian, writes Feuerbach, "to believe, is synonymous with goodness; not to believe, with wickedness. Faith, narrow and prejudiced, refers all unbelief to the moral disposition. . . . It is well-disposed towards believers, but ill-disposed towards unbelievers. *In faith there lies a malignant principle.*" "To love the man who does not believe in Christ, is a sin against Christ, is to love the enemy of Christ." Christianity preaches both faith and love, but "love is only the *morality,* faith the *religion* of the Christian religion." Faith is superior to love, for faith "makes salvation dependent on itself, not on the fulfilment of common human duties."[20] Faith destroys love, for faith is the source of religious hatred and persecution. In order for love to triumph, to be God, it is necessary to give up faith, to sacrifice God as a supernatural being.

The teaching of Dr. Cumming to which George Eliot chiefly objects is his insistence that good works are to be done in order to contribute to the glory of God; "he rarely represents them as the spontaneous, necessary outflow of a soul filled with Divine Love." This doctrine is a manifestation of Cumming's *"perverted moral judgment,"* a perversion which "belongs to the dogmatic system which he shares with all evangelical believers." The kindest, most upright men are evil, says Cumming (George Eliot quotes him), if their actions are not motivated solely by the desire to make God's name more known, his being more loved, and his praise more sung. This "positively noxious" doctrine represses, condemns as evil, fellow feeling and the love of good to man for its own sake, and substitutes for these a motivation that makes every deed "one of deference, of obedience, of self-interest, or vanity":

> The sweet charities of domestic life—the ready hand and the soothing word in sickness, the forbearance towards frailties, the prompt helpfulness in all efforts and sympathy in all joys—are simply evil if they result from a "constitutional tendency," or from dispositions disciplined by the experience of suffering and the perception of moral loveliness. A wife is not to devote herself to her husband out of love to him and a sense of the duties implied by a close relation—she is to be a faithful wife for the glory of God; if she feels her natural affections welling up too strongly, she is to repress them; it will not do to act from natural affection—she must think of the glory of God. A man is to guide his affairs with energy and discretion, not from an honest desire to fulfill his responsibilities as a member of society and a father, but—that "God's praise may be sung." . . . A man is not to be just from a feeling of justice; he is not to help his fellow men out of good-will to his fellow men; he is not to be a tender husband and father out of affection: all these natural muscles and fibres are to be torn away and replaced by a patent steel-spring—anxiety for the "glory of God."

George Eliot entirely agrees with Feuerbach that "man is to be loved for man's sake," that "love should be immediate, undetermined

THE ESSENCE OF CHRISTIANITY

by anything else than its object."[21] "Benevolence and justice," she writes, "are strong only in proportion as they are directly and inevitably called into activity by their proper objects." The doctrine that the glory of God must be the absorbing and influential aim of human thought and action does not contribute to morality; rather it "must tend to neutralise the human sympathies; the stream of feeling will be diverted from its natural current in order to feed an artificial canal." Men have been moral not because of, but despite, this belief. George Eliot rejoices in the fact that "the constitution of human nature forbids the complete prevalence of such a theory. Fatally powerful as religious systems have been, human nature is stronger and wider than religious systems, and though dogmas may hamper, they cannot absolutely repress its growth. . . ."

She concludes her examination of Cumming's teaching by drawing a contrast between the idea of God as it is a valuable moral influence (as with Dinah Morris) and the morally pernicious idea of God held by Dr. Cumming. "The idea of God is really moral in its influence—it really cherishes all that is best and loveliest in man," she explains, "only when God is contemplated as sympathising with the pure elements of human feeling, as possessing infinitely all those attributes which we recognise to be moral in humanity." When God is conceived in this way, the sense of the divine presence intensifies all noble feeling and encourages all noble effort "on the same principle that human sympathy is found a source of strength." "The idea of a God who not only sympathises with all we feel and endure for our fellow men, but who will pour new life into our too languid love, and give firmness to our vacillating purpose is an extension and multiplication of the effects produced by human sympathy; and it has been intensified for the better spirits who have been under the influence of orthodox Christianity, by the contemplation of Jesus as 'God manifest in the flesh.'" Dr. Cumming's God is the opposite of all this:

He is a God who, instead of sharing and aiding our human sympathies, is directly in collision with them; who, instead of strengthening the bond between man and man . . . thrusts himself between them and forbids them to feel for each other except as they have relation to Him. He is a God who, instead of adding His solar force to swell the

111

tide of those impulses that tend to give humanity a common life in which the good of one is the good of all, commands us to check those impulses, lest they should prevent us from thinking of His glory.

Another Christian doctrine which George Eliot and Feuerbach felt to be detrimental to morality is that of an after-life in which are meted out rewards and punishments. George Eliot's chief moral objections to the doctrine of personal immortality were that it tended to turn an individual's attention away from the needs and sufferings of his fellow men and that it made the practice of virtue an act of self-interest rather than an act of love. She feared that a belief in divine reward and retribution deadens men's sympathies by allowing them to place the responsibility for their fellows' happiness or unhappiness upon God, instead of assuming it themselves. On the other hand, a recognition that man's earthly existence is his only one, and that we largely contribute to the fates of our fellow beings, is the ground of a higher morality in that it widens our sympathies and encourages us to assume ourselves the role of mediator, of Christ. God, or Providence, no longer stands between man and man. George Eliot wrote to Charles Bray, in January 1853: "I begin to feel for other people's wants and sorrows a little more than I used to do. Heaven help us! said the old religions—the new one, from its very lack of that faith, will teach us all the more to help one another" (Letters, II, 82). And in her essay on Edward Young she contended that "it is conceivable that in some minds the deep pathos lying in the thought of human mortality—that we are here for a little while and then vanish away, that this earthly life is all that is given to our loved ones and to our many suffering fellow men, lies nearer the fountains of moral emotion than the conception of extended existence" (Essays, p. 54). As her understanding of the varieties of human experience deepened, she came to feel more sympathetic towards those who clung to a belief in immortality; nevertheless, her "most rooted conviction" was "that the immediate object and the proper sphere of all our highest emotions are our struggling fellow men and this earthly existence" (Letters, III, 231).

In 1848 Ludwig Feuerbach terminated his lectures on the Essence of Religion in Heidelberg with the following words: "I hope that my auditors will be converted, that they may henceforth be no longer friends of God but friends of men, no longer believers but thinkers, no longer devotees who pray but workers who work, no longer candidates for the hereafter but students of the here below, no longer Christians who, according to their confession and their own avowal, are half angels and half beasts, but men, entirely men."[22]

EXPERIMENTS IN LIFE

"Whoever would know what the agnostic and evolution philosophy of the time has to teach about man, his social life, his moral responsibilities, his religious aspirations, should go to the pages of George Eliot in preference to those of any other." Thus wrote George Willis Cooke in 1883. George Eliot, according to him, has so made the theories of positive science and evolutionary philosophy a part of her mental processes, "that she has painted life thoroughly in accordance with their spirit." It is impossible, in fact, to understand the full significance of the new philosophy for human life "without a study of her books":

> What Comte and Spencer have taught in the name of philosophy, Tyndall and Haeckel in the name of science, she has applied to life and its problems. . . . She is their interpreter through that wonderful insight, genius and creative power which enabled her to see what they could not themselves discover,—the effect of their teachings on man as an individual and as a social being.

Cooke was a supernaturalist and therefore rejected much of George Eliot's philosophy; he felt her teachings to be extremely important, however, because she applied to life what she held in theory: "she not only speculated, she also felt and lived."

His view of the role of science and philosophy in George Eliot's art is, I think, essentially correct. Her novels are *not* best described as moralized fables, "the last word of a philosophy endeavouring to teach by example."[2] Her novels are not so much direct embodiments of the new philosophy as exploratory applications of it to the human situation. "The new philosophy," writes Cooke, "she applied to life, revealed its relations to duty, love, sorrow, trial and death."[3] George Eliot used the novel not only to teach (in a specifically aesthetic way), but also to discover and to verify. In his essay on "George Eliot as a Religious Teacher," Josiah Royce held that Strauss and Feuerbach "expounded theories that she afterward sought to test by an appeal to living human experience." "She was an appreciative student of many systems," Royce explains, "but she let none of them rule her. She heard what they had to say, and then she went to actual human life to see whether the theory held good" (p. 286). Only in a few instances did she allow ideology to interfere with her clear vision of life:

> On the whole, we must see throughout in George Eliot's works an intense earnestness, and a conscientious effort to comprehend the realities of the human heart. She feels what she tells, and to her the religious consciousness whereof she writes is a fact of her own heart. . . . Thus in her writings the best power of analytic vision is joined with depth of emotion. She is, then, the best possible witness to her own doctrines. She has seen and felt what she describes as the true religious life.[4]

Royce and Cooke have, I believe, a subtler perception of the relation in George Eliot of thought and feeling than does Henry James, who holds that her works are eminently intellectual performances, "not the result of experience, or of moral and sensuous impressions."[5] In any event, she herself believed that her procedure was what Royce and Cooke describe it to be.

George Eliot's moral purpose in her art is most clearly set forth in a letter to Clifford Allbutt in August 1868:

> the inspiring principle which alone gives me courage to write is, that of so presenting our human life as to help my readers in getting a clearer conception and a more active admiration of those vital ele-

ments which bind men together and give a higher worthiness to their existence, and also to help them in gradually dissociating these elements from the more transient forms on which an outworn teaching tends to make them dependent. (*Letters,* IV, 472)

We have seen that in the cosmology, sociology, and psychology of science and in the philosophy of Ludwig Feuerbach, George Eliot found many principles which aided her in fulfilling this purpose. But it was art—not science or philosophy—to which she turned in order to discover the moral bearing of these principles and to test the truth of their moral claims. Her primary artistic materials were "pain and relief, love and sorrow" which, she claimed, "have their peculiar history" and "make an experience and knowledge over and above the swing of atoms" (*Letters,* VI, 99).

For George Eliot the novel was an instrument of knowledge, as her letter of January 1876 to Dr. Joseph Frank Payne very clearly indicates. Payne had written a long letter to her asking for some word which would reconcile him to the loss of his mother. He had admired George Eliot's description, in "The Legend of Jubal," of the way in which the knowledge of death ennobles life by thrilling "love and wedded bliss . . . into finer tenderness" (*The Legend of Jubal and Other Poems,* p. 8) and by leading men to seek immortality through heroic creativity; but he found that it did not "make me less long to see those I love again." "If you can say one word to lighten this dark subject," wrote Payne, "how happy I should be. But let me not put it as an individual wish. It is the longing of all freethinkers now that I am trying to express, and this, as the traditional religion decays (if it does), will be the yearning of all mankind. Death is the great problem which man will have to grapple with again" (*Letters,* VI, 216, note 2). George Eliot could not give Payne the word he sought, for such matters, she felt, could only be dealt with through art. Thus, in her reply, she explained why she could not help him except through the medium of art and described to him the way in which she employed her novels as "experiments in life":

Your letter will have associated you with questions which are the most frequently in my thoughts—questions which are my chief prompters to write anything at all. But my writing is simply a set of experiments in life—an endeavor to see what our thought and emotion may be capable of—what stores of motive, actual or hinted as possible, give promise of a better after which we may strive—what gains from past revelations and discipline we must strive to keep hold of as something more sure than shifting theory. I become more and more timid—with less daring to adopt any formula which does not get itself clothed for me in some human figure and individual experience, and perhaps that is a sign that if I help others to see at all it must be through that medium of art. (*Letters* VI, 216–17)

This is the most revealing statement George Eliot ever made about the role of her art in her quest for values.

Taking the letters to Allbutt and Payne together, we see that George Eliot strove to discover for herself and to present to her fellows enduring truths which would ennoble human existence and which would take the place of the outmoded institutions and beliefs that, she felt, must be eventually abandoned by all because they do not accord with man's growing knowledge of reality. She hoped to discover these truths by exploring the resources and tendencies of human motive, thought, and emotion; and by sifting our social, cultural, and religious inheritance from the past in order to determine the enduringly human elements in it. Because of her distrust of "shifting theory" and her reluctance "to adopt any formula which does not get itself clothed . . . in some human figure and individual experience," art was the only means she could confidently employ for the discovery, verification and expression of these truths.

The empirical epistemology, with its emphasis upon the concrete, the particular, the experienced as the source and test of truth, led George Eliot to distrust abstractions and systems (even the systems of empirical philosophers) and to rely upon art in her search for moral truths. Feuerbach, we recall, claims validity for his method because "both in substance and in speech, it places philosophy in the *negation of philosophy, i.e.,* it declares *that* alone to be the true philosophy which is converted *in succum et sanguinem,* which is incarnate in Man."[6] The novel, which deals pre-eminently with flesh and blood experience, and which is produced by "emotion blending with thought" (*Letters,* VI, 124), is, then, clearly a vehicle of true philosophy. Of course, this applies only to the realistic novel; that is, to the novel which is based upon the author's own experience, which is imaginative in that on the basis of the known it fills in unapparent facts, and which conforms in action and character to the laws of human and physical nature.

George Eliot's novels are usually the result of an evolutionary process. With regard to "Mr. Gilfil's Love Story," she wrote to her publisher, John Blackwood: "I am unable to alter anything in relation to the delineation or development of character, as my stories always grow out of my psychological conception of the dramatis personae. For example the behaviour of Caterina in the gallery is essential to my conception of her nature and to the development of that nature in the plot" (*Letters,* II, 299). She frequently began with a group of characters, thoroughly conceived, and the relations of the characters to each other and to their medium. She then allowed the characters and the plot to develop organically. In her account of the genesis of *Adam Bede* she explained: "When I began to write it, the only elements I had determined on besides the character of Dinah were the character of Adam, his relation to Arthur Donnithorne and their mutual relation to Hetty. . . . Everything else grew out of the characters and their mutual relations" (*Letters,* II, 503). Naturally, she set out to explore specific problems—one does not experiment at random—and her experiments in life were conducted, like all experiments, in accordance with a set of presuppositions concerning how things happen. But the writing of a novel was a process of organic unfolding: the ending was not predetermined; rather, it evolved out of the initial configurations of character and circumstance.

There is evidence that *The Mill on the Floss* and *Middlemarch* were the result of an evolutionary process. During the early stages of the composition of *The Mill on the Floss* George Eliot wrote to John Blackwood: ". . . my stories grow in me like plants, and this is only in the leaf-bud. I have faith that the flower will come. Not enough faith, though, to make me like the idea of beginning to print till the flower is fairly out—till I know the end as well as the beginning" (*Letters,* III, 133). Of "Miss Brooke" she wrote in her journal: "I am experimenting in a story, which I began without any very serious intention of carrying it out lengthily. It is a subject which has been recorded among my possible themes ever since I began to write fiction, but will probably take new shapes in the development" (*Letters*, V, 124). After a careful study of the "Quarry for *Middlemarch*" Jerome Beaty has concluded that the frequent changes of plan in the notebook and the disparities between the final notebook plan and the completed novel indicate that George Eliot's conceptions of character, situation, and plot evolved as she wrote. "The greatest planning stage," Mr. Beaty observes, "was the writing itself"; "writing was to her a process: the act of embodying skeletal notebook plans in the flesh of fiction acted upon her and suggested to her expressions and events she could not have foreseen" (p. 115). Mr. Beaty's study of the revisions that she made in Chapter LXXI re-enforces this conclusion. Her reworking of the crucial scene in which Rosamond is moved to confess that Will really loves Dorothea, for example, indicates that George Eliot was herself "only growing aware of the motivation as she wrote it." In the process of writing, it seems, she both expressed and discovered what she had to say. Mr. Beaty concludes that "writing to George Eliot was not an unpremeditated outpouring; neither was it a mechanical following of detailed blueprint. It was a process of evolution and discovery."[7]

George Eliot's characters, plots, and themes did not always evolve out of the interaction of the human materials. Sometimes the idea came first and she invented characters and a story to embody it. She wrote to Frederic Harrison of having "gone through again and again the severe effort of trying to make certain ideas thoroughly incarnate, as if they had revealed themselves to me first in the flesh and not in the spirit." *The Spanish Gypsy* and, very probably, parts of *Felix Holt*,[8] *Romola*, and *Daniel Deronda* were created in this way. She disclosed to Harrison that she was working on *The Spanish Gypsy*, "a drama, which I put aside at Mr. Lewes' request, after writing four acts, precisely because it was in that stage of Creation or 'Werden,' in which the idea of the characters predominates over the incarnation" (*Letters*, IV, 300, 301). In her "Notes on 'The Spanish Gypsy'" she describes the subject of the poem as she originally conceived it: "A young maiden, believing herself to be on the eve of the chief event of her life—marriage—about to share in the ordinary lot of womanhood . . . has suddenly announced to her that she is chosen to fulfil a great destiny, entailing a terribly different experience from that of ordinary womanhood." This subject was suggested to George Eliot by a painting of the Annunciation, and she "came home with this in . . . mind, meaning to give the motive a clothing in some suitable set of historical and local conditions." She explains that her conception of the initial situation with its tragic theme—the difficulty of the "adjustment of our individual needs to the dire necessities of our lot"—determined the setting, the characters, and the working out of the plot.[9] Her art here does not discover the truth it communicates; it embodies preconceived ideas.

Yet even in such extreme cases of working from the abstract to the concrete (and *The Spanish Gypsy* is the most extreme case), George Eliot's fictions are less moralized fables than experiments in life, experiments designed to verify rather than to discover. Her art here is an instrument for verifying previously held theories. It is a means of reducing questionable hypothesis to unquestionable feeling, of getting hold of "something more sure than shifting theory" by refusing "to adopt any formula which does not get itself clothed . . . in some human figure and individual experience." Lewes, we recall, contended that the a priori method is "eminently philosophic when it merely *goes before* the facts, anticipating what will be the tardy conclusions of experience." But it must be used "as it was by Kepler and Goethe, who looked upon nature from the heights, but having seen or fancied they saw a something in the plains, at once descended to verify the truth of their observation."[10] George Eliot was seeking human truths, and instead of confronting her ideas with the physical order, she sought to verify them by seeing if they could be clothed in human figures and individual experiences. If she occasionally clothed her ideas in a garb that was convincing to few but herself, it was not for want of sincerity. While she was preparing for *Romola,* she wrote to John Blackwood: ". . . don't set your mind on my doing just what I have dreamed. It may turn out that I can't work freely and fully enough in the medium I have chosen, and in that case I must give it up; for I will never write anything to which my whole heart, mind, and conscience don't consent" (*Letters,* III, 417).

George Eliot saw the difficulty of human existence; she had a deep sense of man's need, revealed in his myths, philosophies, and theologies to understand and be reconciled to his lot. Since the traditional beliefs of Western culture had been called in doubt by the new philosophy, she turned to art as the best means of discovering a vision of life which would ennoble human existence, which would give modern man a renewed sense of religious orientation in the cosmos. She conceived the role of the artist to be that of a mediator between man and the harsh, non-moral conditions of his life; she rejoiced when she was assured that there were lives in which her art had "done something to 'strengthen the good and mitigate the evil'" (*Letters,* VI, 258). She felt that the artist functions as mediator not only by illuminating the meaning and dignity of life, but also by intensifying the reader's sympathy towards his fellows. Love and fellow-feeling between men, she felt, are the chief moral forces which "lighten the pressure of hard non-moral outward conditions" (*Letters,* IV, 365).

We can gain a clearer insight into George Eliot's use of the novel as an instrument of moral education, I think, if we consider the following (to some minds crucial) questions raised by Martin Svaglic in his essay, "Religion in the Novels of George Eliot": "Is it possible to say whether George Eliot ever believed in freedom of the will, and if so, to what extent? There is much talk of inexorable laws and resignation to the inevitable in her work. Yet if men are not free, why write books proposing virtue as the way of life?"[11]

George Eliot was a thorough determinist whose moral philosophy was based on the conviction that moral education, like the sciences of sociology and psychology, is possible only because men's actions are *not* the products of an arbitrary free will. She held, with John Stuart Mill, that human actions are the "invariable consequents of our antecedent states of mind" (*Logic,* p. 582), and that "all states of mind are immediately caused either by other states of mind, or by states of body" (*Logic,* p. 590). States of mind and body are the result of an enormous number of co-operant causes, internal and external, none of which are outside the realm of nature. Among these causes, and not the least important, are our own volitions or desires. We can, within certain limits, change ourselves if we wish. It is true that our desire to form ourselves is determined by forces over which we have no control, but once it has been brought into being, it becomes itself an extremely important cause of our behavior. Felix Holt, for example, explains to

Esther Lyon that his determination to sacrifice personal gratification in order to devote himself to the cause of the workingmen is the product not so much of innate unselfishness as of profound experience which has led him to choose a course of action that will frustrate some of his own desires:

> It all depends on what a man gets into his consciousness—what life thrusts into his mind, so that it becomes present to him as remorse is present to the guilty, or a mechanical problem to an inventive genius. There are two things I've got present in that way: one of them is the picture of what I should hate to be. I'm determined never to go about making my face simpering, or solemn, and telling lies for profit; or to get tangled in affairs where I must wink at dishonesty and pocket the proceeds, and justify that knavery as part of a system that I can't alter. . . . The other thing that's got into my mind like a splinter . . . is the life of the miserable—the spawning life of vice and hunger. I'll never be one of the sleek dogs. . . . It is the old word—'necessity is laid upon me.' (Chap. XXVII)

Although George Eliot did not believe that man has free will (in the sense of absolute, uncaused volition), she did believe that the individual has the ability to choose the better over the worse course if his motive and determination (themselves products of antecedent causes) are powerful enough. *Her aim as a teacher of morality was to initiate causes which would supply motives and strengthen determination.* Thus there is no real inconsistency with her determinism in Eliot's exhortation to Mrs. Ponsonby to exert her will:

> . . . every fresh morning is an opportunity that one can look forward to for exerting one's will. I shall not be satisfied with your philosophy till you have conciliated necessitarianism—I hate the ugly word—with the practice of willing strongly, willing to will strongly, and so on, that being what you certainly can do and have done about a great many things in life, whence it is clear that there is nothing in truth to hinder you from it—except you will say the absence of a motive. But that absence I don't believe in, in your case—only in the case of empty barren souls. (*Letters,* VI, 166)

It appears that as a moralist George Eliot felt a rigid belief in determinism to be dangerous if it issues (as it had for Mrs. Ponsonby) in a feeling of enslavement which can poison motive and diminish moral energy. But it is clear that she held it possible to conciliate necessitarianism with the practice of willing strongly and that she had reservations not about the truth of the law of universal causation but about the possible psychological effects of a belief in it.

Closely connected with the issue of free will and determinism is, of course, the question of whether or not men are morally responsible for their actions—what if the individual happens to have an empty barren soul? How, it may be asked, can George Eliot construct and teach a morality if she does not believe in free will and hence cannot hold men morally responsible for their deeds? She has never expressed herself in print on this problem, and it does not seem to have caused her any concern; but it is possible to reconstruct her attitude towards the bestowal of praise and blame upon human behavior. It seems clear that she could not have theoretically held men morally responsible for their actions without contradicting her own philosophy, for when human behavior is viewed objectively or scientifically it is seen to be the product of internal and external conditions which the individual cannot possibly have chosen for himself. The fact that she is sympathetic toward almost all her characters, including many whom she finds morally deficient, suggests that she did feel them to be largely, if not entirely, the victims of circumstance and of their own inborn natures. But she does not preach that to understand all is to forgive all; and she does judge the behavior of her characters. She presents their actions as blameworthy or noble, and she expects the reader to share empathically the characters' sense of guilt or virtue. As a realist she recognized that men are not morally responsible for their actions; but as a moralist who based her practice upon the findings of psychology, she felt that moral judgment of past actions can have a potent influence upon future behavior. Freedom from judgment, on the other hand, breeds lawlessness. She would have agreed completely with the observation of Sidney Hook (a determinist) that "a sense of blame, shame, and responsibility has a sound therapeutic use in the moral education of men."[12] She probably would have held that for the practical purposes of morality an individual should be made to feel responsible for acts which he can be educated to desist from or to repeat in the future. A sense of moral responsibility and of the potency of his own free will is not difficult to inculcate in an individual, for it accords far better with his subjective experience of himself than do the doctrines of determinism and freedom from responsibility, which are highly objective and theoretical interpretations of experience.

George Eliot's endeavor to educate men morally through art was implemented rather than contradicted by her determinism; for her aim was not so much to propose virtue as a way of life or to preach specific ethical doctrines as to develop in her readers habits of mind and feeling which would lead naturally to moral actions. She felt that "the education of mankind through the affections and sentiments" is the true basis of moral development (*Letters, IV*, 13). In an article on Thomas Carlyle, written in 1855 for the *Leader*, she contended that "he is the most effective educator . . . who does not seek to make his pupils moral by enjoining particular courses of action, but by bringing into activity the feelings and sympathies that must issue in noble action."[13] She expressed similar views in 1878, when she wrote to Mrs. Peter Alfred Taylor (a feminist): "My function is that of the *aesthetic*, not the doctrinal teacher—the rousing of the nobler emotions, which make mankind desire the social right, not the prescribing of special measures" (*Letters* VII, 44). Carlyle's power as a moral teacher lay, George Eliot felt, not chiefly in his philosophy but in his concrete, sympathetic presentations of human beings: "No novelist has made his creations live for us more thoroughly than Carlyle has made Mirabeau and the men of the French Revolution, Cromwell and the Puritans. What humour in his pictures! Yet what depth of appreciation, what reverence for the great and godlike under every sort of earthly mummery!"[14] By 1815, then, she had come to regard the vivid representation of human experience as a far more effective means of moral education than theories, sermons, and tracts.

George Eliot's conception of the way in which art arouses moral dispositions is set forth clearly in her essay on Riehl, written in 1856, shortly before she began writing fiction. "Appeals founded on generalizations and statistics," she argued, "require a sympathy ready-made, a moral sentiment already in activity; but a picture of life such as a great artist can give, surprises even the trivial and the selfish into that attention to what is apart from themselves, which may be called the raw material of moral sentiment." Pictures of the life of the lower classes such as we find in the novels of Scott and Kingsley, the poems of Wordsworth, and the pictures of Hornung do more "towards linking the higher classes with the lower, towards obliterating the vulgarity of exclusiveness," she felt, "than hundreds of sermons and philosophical dissertations. Art is the nearest thing to life; it is a mode of amplifying experience and extending our contact with our fellowmen beyond the bounds of our personal lot" (*Essays*, p. 193). To be morally efficacious, art must be realistic. In his essay on "The Lady Novelists," written in 1852, G. H. Lewes had contended that works of art "are the avenues through which we reach the sacred adytum of Humanity, and learn better to understand our fellows and ourselves." Only that literature is effective, he continued, "which has reality for its basis."[15] The great danger of unrealistic art, George Eliot felt, is that "our sympathy with the perennial joys and struggles, the toil, the tragedy, and the humour in the life of our more heavily laden fellowmen" is "perverted, and turned towards a false object instead of the true one" (*Essays*, p. 193).

The connection between realism and the moral function of art which George Eliot established in her essay on Riehl is again set forth in Chapter XVII of *Adam Bede,* where she defends both her realistic technique and her choice of subject matter from common life. Her object was that her readers should come to understand, sympathize with, and feel the human worth of "the real breathing men and women, who can be chilled by your indifference or injured by your prejudice; who can be cheered and helped onward by your fellow-feeling, your forbearance, your outspoken, brave justice." She strove to counteract the prejudice and snobbery which blocks sympathy and leads men, because of the outward differences between themselves and their fellows, consciously or unconsciously to deny that all men have a common nature and are equal in human worth.

This led not only to her realistic and sympathetic treatment of common life in *Scenes of Clerical Life, Adam Bede, The Mill on the Floss, Silas Marner,* and *Felix Holt,* but also to her presentation of Jewish life in *Daniel Deronda.* "Not only towards the Jews," she wrote to Mrs. Harriet Beecher Stowe,

... but towards all oriental peoples with whom we English come in contact, a spirit of arrogance and contemptuous dictatorialness is observable which has become a national disgrace to us. There is nothing I should care more to do, if it were possible, than to rouse the imagination of men and women to a vision of human claims in those races of their fellow-men who most differ from them in customs and beliefs.

"I therefore felt urged," George Eliot explains, "to treat Jews with such sympathy and understanding as my nature and knowledge could attain to" (*Letters,* VI, 301).

George Eliot's novels are designed to amplify the reader's experience, to develop his faculty of vision, and to arouse his sympathy for his fellows.[16] The reading of her novels, she hoped, would be similar to an actual experience of life, an experience which would be a potent force in the reader's moral education. She tried so to construct her novels "that the presentation will lay hold on the emotions as human experience—will . . . 'flash' conviction on the world by means of aroused sympathy" (*Letters,* IV, 301).

"The essence of the moral life," observes Lionel Trilling, "would seem to consist in doing that most difficult thing in the world, making a willing suspension of disbelief in the selfhood of someone else."[17] George Eliot would certainly agree that regarding others as they are in and for themselves, as beings with subjectivities like our own to whom we are objects, is the basis of moral behavior. The moral education of her chief characters consists precisely in their movement from a state in which they regard others as things or as extensions of their own egos to a state in which they regard others as subjective objects, as people with inner lives of their own.

Moral life rests upon the individual's ability to imagine and to feel the inner states of others; and George Eliot strove not only to show this ability developing in her characters but also to instill it in her readers. She did not approach this task by preaching that we should love our neighbors, or practice the golden rule, or exercise our free will to choose virtue; rather she sought to enlarge our vision and sympathy by vividly and sympathetically presenting the interior states of her characters. In life we are isolated from our fellows, with only a very indirect access to their consciousness. In reading novels in which the psychology of the characters is realistically portrayed we have a direct experience of the inner states of others and an immediate intuition of our common humanity; we come to "conceive with that distinctness which is no longer reflection but feeling—an idea wrought back to the directness of sense, like the solidity of objects"—that others have "an equivalent centre of self, whence the lights and shadows must always fall with a certain difference" (*Middlemarch,* Chap. XXI). As a result of this experience, we become far more able to suspend our disbelief in the selfhood of our fellows, and our moral faculties of vision and sympathy are strengthened.

> If Art does not enlarge men's sympathies [George Eliot wrote to Charles Bray], it does nothing morally. I have had heart-cutting experience that opinions are a poor cement between human souls; and the only effect I ardently long to produce by my writings, is that those who read them should be better able to *imagine* and to *feel* the pains and joys of those who differ from themselves in everything but the broad fact of being struggling erring human creatures. (*Letters,* III, 111)

The cosmological, sociological, psychological, and epistemological principles which I have discussed in the preceding chapters were instrumental in shaping George Eliot's vision of life, and a knowledge of them is indispensable to a thorough understanding of her fiction. To assign these principles their proper role and importance, however, we should regard them not as the abstract counterpart of the thematic content of her novels, but as the presuppositions of her experiments in life. "It is because George Eliot was not a mere speculative thinker," wrote Cooke, "that her teachings become so important."[18] Having examined the theoretical basis of her quest for values, I should like now to turn my entire attention to her most authoritative utterances, her novels, her experiments in life, through which she tested the worth of abstract formulas by seeing if they could get themselves clothed for her in human figures and individual experiences.

THE THREE STAGES OF
MORAL DEVELOPMENT

There are three basic ways, in George Eliot's novels, in which self relates to the world. It may relate to the world egoistically (or subjectively), in which case the distinction between the inward and the outward is obscured; self is seen as the center of the world and the world as an extension of self. It may be overwhelmed and threatened with annihilation by the hard reality of the world; it then experiences a state of disillusionment or disenchantment in which the world, even the human order, is seen as a totally alien, non-human existence and self as dehumanized, as completely insignificant or spiritually homeless. Or, retaining its integrity but giving up its egocentricity, it may relate to the world at once meaningfully and objectively, seeing the world as an autonomous existence of which it is a part.

These relations of self to reality are familiar to us, of course, from our examination of the conflict between the empirical and the metaphysical cosmologies and epistemologies. Moral development, for George Eliot, consists in a movement from the subjective to the objective approach to reality. The three stages of moral development take place within the indifferent but orderly cosmos of positive science; a discovery of the true nature of the cosmos is part of the process of maturation. In the course of moral evolution, experience of suffering (the second stage) leads to vision and vision intensifies sympathy. In the third stage of moral development, George Eliot's characters arrive at some version of Feuerbach's religion of humanity. The ideas that we have been examining in the first half of this study give rise, then, to a moral vision that is dramatized again and again in George Eliot's fiction.

I

The way in which egoism sees all things in their relation to self rather than in their relations to each other is well illustrated in the pier-glass simile by which George Eliot describes Rosamond Vincy's habit of mind:

Your pier-glass or extensive surface of polished steel made to be rubbed by a house-maid will be minutely and multitudinously scratched in all directions; but place now against it a lighted candle as a centre of illumination, and lo! The scratches will seem to arrange themselves in a fine series of concentric circles round that little sun. It is demonstrable that the scratches are going everywhere impartially, and it is only your candle which produces the flattering illusion of a concentric arrangement, its light falling with an exclusive optical selection. These things are a parable. The scratches are events, and the candle is the egoism of any person now absent—of Miss Vincy, for example. Rosamond had a Providence of her own . . . . (*Middlemarch*, Chap. XXVII)

The egoist tends to assume that the order of things corresponds to the desires of the mind; and instead of cultivating a true vision of causal sequences, he delights in imaginatively shaping the future into accord with present wishes. Many of George Eliot's egoists—Arthur Donnithorne, Hetty Sorrel, Esther Lyon, Fred and Rosamond Vincy, and Gwendolen Harleth, for example—engage in such vivid daydreaming. Esther Lyon's imagination of her Utopia—"which, like other Utopias, was filled with delightful results, independent of processes"—is typical: "She had seen the very mat in her carriage, had scented the dried rose-leaves in her corridors. . . . She had trodden the marble-firm gravel of her garden-walks and the soft deep turf of her lawn . . . ; and she had had several accomplished cavaliers all at once suing for her hand . . ." (*Felix Holt*, Chap. XXXVIII). The egoist has a vague idea that the ease, luxury, love, and respect that he so earnestly desires must (or should) somehow come to him because he so earnestly desires them and because his own worthiness (beauty, good-taste, ability to enjoy, etc.) makes him so deserving of them. This attitude results not only in frustration for the egoist but also in pain for his fellows.

The egoist is often a gambler: he may engage in actual games of chance, like Fred Vincy, Gwendolen Harleth, and Lapidoth (Mirah's father), with the confident expectation that he will win; or he may be a worshipper of fortune and live in hope that the realization of his desires or escape from punishment for wrong-doing will somehow be granted to him. Take the case of Godfrey Cass. Because of his secret marriage Godfrey is afraid of being disowned by his father and cut off forever from Nancy Lammeter. He lives in dread of the disclosure of his secret which may come through Dunstan or through his wife. Godfrey often thinks of confession, but he continues to get himself more deeply involved in lies and debts. When a crisis appears imminent, Godfrey flees "to his usual refuge, that of hoping for some unforeseen turn of fortune, some favourable chance which would save him from unpleasant consequences—perhaps even justify his insincerity by manifesting its prudence." "In this point of trusting to some throw of fortune's dice," George Eliot comments, "Godfrey can hardly be called old-fashioned. Favourable Chance is the god of all men who follow their own devices instead of obeying a law they believe in. . . . The evil principle deprecated in that religion is the orderly sequence by which the seed brings forth a crop after its kind" (*Silas Marner,* Chap. IX).

Events take their natural course: such characters as Godfrey, Arthur Donnithorne, Mrs. Transome and lawyer Jermyn, Tito Melema, Bulstrode, and Gwendolen Harleth are eventually victims of the nemesis set in motion by their lawless actions. And because of the connectedness of things, many others must share the consequences of the egoist's random, short-sighted, or deliberately selfish behavior. Since his desires are not chastened by submission to law and his actions are not governed by a true vision of the relations of things, the egoist is truly at the mercy of circumstances, and his desires are more often frustrated than satisfied. After Harold was born, there grew in Mrs. Transome a hungry desire that her imbecile first son should die:

> Such desires make life a hideous lottery, where every day may turn up a blank; where men and women who have the softest beds and the most delicate eating . . . yet grow haggard, fevered, and restless, like those who watch in other lotteries. Day after day, year after year, had yielded blanks; new cares had come, bringing other desires for results quite beyond her grasp, which must also be watched for in the lottery . . . . (*Felix Holt,* Chap. I)

The egoist is not always impractical or ignorant of the nature of things. Schemers like Tito, Rosamond, and Grandcourt are very good at getting their own way (though unforeseen evils often follow); and a man like Harold Transome has a good understanding of the relation between means and ends (Chap. VIII). Harold's practicality does not negate the fact that his approach to reality is basically subjective; for his ends are always selfish and he regards others not as fellow beings with a center of self of their own, but as objects to be manipulated for the achievement of his purposes. Harold tells his mother that he never forgets places and people, "how they look and what can be done with them"; and George Eliot observes that he had an "indifference to any impressions in others which did not further or impede his own purposes" (Chap. I). Later we are told that he "had a way of virtually measuring the value of everything by the contribution it made to his own pleasure. His very good-nature was unsympathetic: it never came from any thorough understanding or deep respect for what was in the mind of the person he obliged or indulged" (Chap. XLIII). The egoist's calculations often misfire for his want of real insight into the feelings of other people. Lawyer Jermyn, for example, "was anything but stupid; yet he always blundered when he wanted to be delicate or magnanimous; he constantly sought to soothe others by praising himself. Moral vulgarity cleaved to him like an hereditary odour" (Chap. IX). And Harold Transome, in the role of suitor, altogether misconceives the nature of Esther Lyon.

In the relations between man and man the subjective point of view leads to error and suffering. The individual projects his own interests or (more innocently) his own nature into others. This prevents him from knowing others as they really are and makes communication and mutually satisfying relationships impossible. The painful but not basically ignoble mistakes that Adam, Romola, and Dorothea make about Hetty, Tito, and Casaubon are instances, in part, of a higher nature projecting its own qualities into a lower nature. What is taken to be the nature of another is often only a reflection of self. The egoist frequently has a love of power, a craving for mastery over other people as well as over the course of events. Sometimes he has the illusion that others must want to do what he wants them to do; and sometimes he very deliberately contrives to have them act as he wishes. The feelings of others are given no importance. As we have seen, the egoist does not regard his fellows as beings objective to himself who are at the same time subjects in their own right, but (if he is not completely indifferent to them) he regards them either as extensions of himself or as objects to be manipulated in the same way that things are manipulated. This often brings great suffering to those who are so regarded; for not only do they find their purposes frustrated, but also their sense of their own selfhood is challenged, and they feel dehumanized or depersonalized.

The subjective relation of the self to the world, then, is morally unsatisfactory in terms both of ethics and of personal satisfaction. The comfortable illusions with which the egoist surrounds himself may at any moment be shattered; and, since his egoism has cut him off from genuine contact with the world and his fellows, he will, if disillusioned, have no relief from his loneliness and despair. There are no ideal loyalties or intense interests in things outside of self to give life value in the absence of personal gratification. Mrs. Transome "moved to and fro amongst the rose-coloured satin of chairs and curtains—the great story of this world reduced for her to the little tale of her own existence—full obscurity everywhere, except where the keen light fell on the narrow track of her own lot, wide only for a woman's anguish" (Chap. XXXIV). The claims which the egoist makes for self can never be satisfied, and he may, like the somewhat Byronic Gwendolen Harleth, find the world to be a dull, drab place:

"To be middling with me [says Gwendolen] is another phrase for being dull. And the worst fault I have to find with the world is, that it is dull. Do you know, I am going to justify gambling in spite of you. It is a refuge from dullness."

"I don't admit the justification," said Deronda. "I think what we call the dullness of things is a disease in ourselves. Else how could any one find an intense interest in life? And many do." (Chap. XXXV)

II

Man is innately egoistic; it is natural for the mind initially to view all things as extensions of or as related to self. It is equally natural, however, for experience to make clear to the individual the disparity between self and non-self. The discovery of the otherness in things and people comes in many ways, all of which are painful, though in varying degrees. Hetty, Romola, and Mirah are driven to the verge of suicide by their experience of alienation from the world, and Silas Marner becomes a dehumanized hermit and miser. The egoist is wakened from his self-indulgent dreams to the harsh reality of life.[1] He is taken out of his private world and enters the world of his fellow men, who are also fellow sufferers. Harold Transome feels the irresistible pressure of that outward under which all men suffer when he learns that Jermyn is his father: "for the first time the iron had entered into his soul, and he felt the hard pressure of our common lot, the yoke of that mighty resistless destiny laid upon us by the acts of other men as well as our own" (Chap. XLIV). There are many responses to the experience of disenchantment. Some characters are destroyed; some are ennobled by their suffering; some are affected only momentarily; and some fly back to subjectivity, seeking an opiate by which they can escape and retain their sense of selfhood.[2]

One of the first lessons man learns through extensive experience is that nature is indifferent to human beings, that its appearance of being friendly or hostile is the product of a limited, subjective point of view. George Eliot writes in *Adam Bede:*

For if it be true that Nature at certain moments seems charged with a presentiment of one individual lot, must it not also be true that she seems unmindful, unconscious of another? For there is no hour that has not its births of gladness and despair, no morning brightness that does not bring new sickness to desolation as well as new forces to genius and love. There are so many of us, and our lots are so different:

133

what wonder that Nature's mood is often in harsh contrast with the great crisis of our lives? We are children of a large family, and must learn, as such children do, not to expect that our hurts will be made much of—to be content with little nurture and caressing, and help each other the more. (Chap. XXVII)

The order of nature is non-moral, unresponsive to man; to find a religious orientation in the cosmos and a home for his soul in the world the individual must turn to the moral order as it exists in other individuals and in society. In her poem "Erinna," George Eliot presents the plight of the Greek poetess who, according to tradition, died in early youth when chained by her mother to the spinning wheel.[3] Erinna is condemned

> To spin the byssus drearily
> In insect labour, while the throng
> Of gods & men wrought deeds that poets wrought in song.

She pours out her pain in song. She first bewails Cybele's indifference to her plight:

> But thou art deaf to human care:
> Thy breasts impartial cherish with their food
> Strength alike of ill & good.

Cybele, the great earth mother, represents nature, which is non-moral, careless of human needs and desires, indifferent to good and evil. Erinna is comforted by the thought of Athena, and she hymns her praise:

> But Pallas, thou dost choose & bless
> The nobler cause, thy maiden height
> And terrible beauty marshalling the fight
> Inspire weak limbs with stedfastness.
>
> . . . .
>
> Counsel is thine, to sway the doubtful doom
> Of cities with a leaguer at their gate;
> Thine the device that snares the hulk elate
> Of purblind force & saves the hero or the State.

134

Athena represents the love and intelligence which establish the human, moral order; she succors man by interposing herself between him and the blind forces within and without which threaten to destroy him. We recall George Eliot's assertion to John Morley that "in the moral evolution we have 'an art which does mend nature.' It is the function of love in the largest sense, to mitigate the harshness of all fatalities." The object of the moral order is "to lighten the pressure of hard non-moral outward conditions" (*Letters*, IV, 364-365).

George Eliot is fully aware of the strength of man's psychological need for a response to his consciousness, for a humanized world. The world of things is humanized by the individual's identification of himself with objects and places and by association and long familiarity. Mr. Tulliver, for example, decides to work under his bitter enemy Wakem because he cannot bear the thought of leaving Dorlcote Mill:

> . . . the strongest influence of all [in his decision] was the love of the old premises where he had run about when he was a boy. . . . The Tullivers had lived on this spot for generations. . . . It was when he got able to walk about and look at all the old objects, that he felt the strain of this clinging affection for the old home as part of his life, part of himself. He couldn't bear to think of himself living on any other spot than this, where he knew the sound of every gate and door, and felt that the shape and colour of every roof and weather-stain and broken hillock was good, because his growing senses had been fed on them. Our instructed vagrancy . . . can hardly get a dim notion of what an old-fashioned man like Tulliver felt for his spot, where all his memories centred, and where life seemed like a familiar smooth-handled tool that the fingers clutch with loving ease.

"I should go off my head in a new place," Mr. Tulliver tells Luke: "I should be like as if I'd lost my way (Book III, Chap. IX). The great calamity of Mrs. Tulliver's life takes place when she loses her precious china and linen:

> The objects among which her mind had moved complacently were all gone—all the hopes, and schemes, and speculations, all the pleasant little cares about her treasures which had made the world quite com-

prehensible to her for a quarter of a century, since she had made her first purchase of the sugar-tongs, had been suddenly snatched away from her, and she remained bewildered in this empty life. (Book IV, Chap. II)

The chief agencies which humanize the world for us are social institutions and other individuals; for in them and in our fellows we find objects which are endowed with consciousness (or are the product of consciousness) and which mediate between our consciousness and the completely alien, unconscious world of physical nature. Feuerbach contends that consciousness of the world is consciousness of the limitations of our own ego, and that man cannot pass directly from his initial egoistic state to an awareness of the world without introducing, preluding, and moderating

> this contradiction by the consciousness of a being who is indeed another, and in so far gives me the perception of my limitation, but in such a way as at the same time to affirm my own nature, make my nature objective to me. The consciousness of the world is a humiliating consciousness . . . ; but the first stone against which the pride of egoism stumbles is the *thou,* the *alter ego.* The *ego* first steels its glance in the eye of a *thou* before it endures the contemplation of a being which does not reflect its own image. . . . I reconcile myself with the world only through my fellow man. Without other men, the world would be for me not only dead and empty, but meaningless.[4]

It is dangerous for man to create a self-reflexive picture of the world, for this cuts him off from reality; but it is essential that man find in the external world a response to his consciousness. Nature provides no response; Cybele is "deaf to human care." Love, science, art, tradition, society, and one's fellow men, however, make a home in the world for the consciousness. They create a human world which is objectively real and at the same time responsive.

Sometimes, however, in a diseased state of affairs, the human world is indifferent or turns hostile, becomes unhuman or inhuman. The indifference of the human world is the theme of George Eliot's poem "In a London Drawingroom":

The sky is cloudy, yellowed by the smoke.
For view there are the houses opposite
Cutting the sky with one long line of wall
Like solid fog: far as the eye can stretch
Monotony of surface & of form
Without a break to hang a guess upon.
No bird can make a shadow as it flies,
For all is shadow, as in ways o'erhung
By thickest canvass, where the golden rays
Are clothed in hemp. No figure lingering
Pauses to feed the hunger of the eye
Or rest a little on the lap of life.
All hurry on & look upon the ground,
Or glance unmarking at the passers by.
The wheels are hurrying too, cabs, carriages
All closed, in multiplied identity.
The world seems one huge prison-house & court
Where men are punished at the slightest cost,
With lowest rate of colour, warmth & joy.

From a center of human society, a drawing room, in a center of human civilization, London, the consciousness seeks in vain for a resting place. Just as "no bird can make a shadow as it flies," so the consciousness can find no echo, no image of itself; it and the world are wholly disparate. The world of the poem is urban, commercial London. Its motifs are sameness and hurry. Its dwellings are not human, individual; instead of providing interest, room for speculation, allowing the consciousness to expand and take hold of something outside itself, they wall it in. There is no variety of color, light and shade, for the factory smoke has obscured the sun:

far as the eye can stretch
Monotony of surface & of form
Without a break to hang a guess upon.

Each human being is alone, self-enclosed, hurrying on, unconscious of the things and people around him, preoccupied with his own private business or mission. Those who look at their fellow pedestrians "glance unmarking"; there is no human look of recognition or response. Some go by in cabs and carriages, "all closed"; their identities are swallowed up by the vehicles they ride in; they are dehumanized. The last three lines of the poem render a judgment on this world. It seems to be "one huge prison-house" because it imprisons the consciousness within itself, walling it in. But in likening the world to a prison-house and court the consciousness is, in a way, solving its problem. Unable to accept an indifferent world, the mind arbitrarily, out of its need, gives the world volition. It projects a part of its own nature into the world and conceives of it as a hostile agency, bent upon punishing man by its indifference—the world is *consciously* indifferent. Thus the self saves its sense of identity. The alternative to this artificial (though psychologically quite natural) solution is annihilation. This is made clear in the following passage from George Eliot's letter of June 4, 1848, to Sara Hennell:

> Alas for the fate of poor mortals which condemns them to wake up some fine morning and find all the poetry in which their world was bathed only the evening before utterly gone—the hard angular world of chairs and tables and looking-glasses staring at them in all its naked prose. . . .
>
> I feel a sort of madness growing upon me—just the opposite of the delirium which makes people fancy that their bodies are filling the room. It seems to me as if I were shrinking into that mathematical abstraction, a point—so entirely am I destitute of contact that I am unconscious of length or breadth, and by the time you see me again, I shall have lost all possibility of giving you any demonstration of a spiritual existence—like a poor sprite metamorphosed into a pomegranate seed or some such thing. (*Letters*, I, 264)

It is interesting to note that George Eliot was in strange surroundings (on vacation at St. Leonard's) when she wrote this letter.

Perhaps George Eliot's most poignant treatment of the theme of alienation is in the story of Silas Marner, which, according to John Blackwood's report, "sprang from her childish recollection of a man with a stoop and expression of face that led her to think that he was an alien from his fellows" (*Letters*, III, 427). In Chapter I Silas has everything that makes his life human and meaningful stripped away from him. His trouble springs initially from the too great trust which he placed in his friend, William Dane: "whatever blemishes others might discern in William, to his friend's mind he was faultless." When he is accused of theft, Silas realizes that William has deceived him. He tells his inquisitors: "I am sore stricken; I can say nothing. God will clear me." But the lots declare him guilty, and Silas, whose trust in man has been sorely bruised, now loses his faith in divine justice: he declares that "there is no just God that governs the earth righteously, but a God of lies, that bears witness against the innocent." "Poor Marner went out with that despair in his soul —that shaken trust in God and man, which is little short of madness to a loving nature." The final blow falls upon Silas when Sarah, his betrothed, casts him off and marries William. Silas leaves his native town and emigrates to Raveloe.

In Raveloe Silas lives in almost complete estrangement from society, his only contact with his neighbors being in matters of business. In his new surroundings he is one of "those scattered linen-weavers" who "were to the last regarded as aliens by their rustic neighbours, and usually contracted the eccentric habits which belong to a state of loneliness." In addition to being a stranger, a linen-weaver (whose skill is suspicious), and an odd looking sort of man, he is also an epileptic; and his fits, which made him an object of special respect in Lantern Yard, make him an object of fear and distrust to his new neighbors. His appearance "would have had nothing strange for people of average culture and experience"; he suffers from the narrowness of the superstitious and provincial inhabitants of Raveloe.

But not only is Silas alien to his fellows; his new neighbors and surroundings are entirely alien and unintelligible to him. He lives now in a "strange world" which is a "hopeless riddle" to him. Raveloe is different from Lantern Yard in every way—in appearance, economy, customs, religion; and his experience is like that of the primitive man who has left the territory ruled by the tribal divinities and entered a land of strange gods. Even his own past, disconnected as it is from the present, becomes remote and unreal for him. George Eliot remarks that

even people whose lives have been made various by learning, sometimes find it hard to keep a fast hold on their habitual views of life, on their faith in the Invisible, nay, on the sense that their past joys and sorrows are a real experience, when they are suddenly transported to a new land, where the beings around them know nothing of their history, and share none of their ideas—where their mother earth shows another lap, and human life has other forms than those on which their souls have been nourished.

Silas' life comes to center around his loom and his money. He becomes dehumanized in his mechanical activity and his hoarding; his life is narrowed and hardened "more and more into a mere pulsation of desire and satisfaction that had no relation to any other being. . . . Strangely Marner's face and figure shrank and bent themselves into a constant mechanical relation to the objects of his life, so that he produced the same sort of impression as a handle or a crooked tube, which has no meaning standing apart" (Chap. II). At the same time, Silas endows his loom and his money with consciousness and they become his companions, responding to his feelings.

Silas Marner is the story not only of Silas' despair and alienation from the human world; it is the story also of his slow rehabilitation and integration into the life of Raveloe. George Eliot reflects, after Silas' money is stolen, that although his life may have appeared withered and shrunken, "in reality it had been an eager life, filled with immediate purpose which fenced him in from the wide, cheerless unknown. . . . But now the fence was broken down—the support was snatched away" (Chap. X). The theft of his money, which brings Silas to the lowest point of desolation, is the turning point in his relations with his fellows:

> Left groping in the darkness, with his prop utterly gone, Silas had inevitably a sense, though a dull and half-despairing one, that if any help came to him it must come from without; and there was a slight stirring of expectation at the sight of his fellow-men, a faint consciousness of dependence on their goodwill. (Chap. X)

Through Dolly Winthrop and especially through Eppie, whom the loss of his gold has prepared him to welcome and love, Silas comes to partake in the customs and forms of Raveloe life; he becomes once more a part of the world around him. He even comes to have faith in the goodness of the world. Referring to the incident at Lantern Yard, Dolly Winthrop says: "And if you could but ha' gone on trustening, Master Marner, you wouldn't ha' run away from your fellow-creatures and been so lone." "Ah," Silas replies, "but that 'ud ha' been hard . . . ; it 'ud ha' been hard to trusten then." But now Silas can share Dolly's faith in the divine love: "There's good i' this world—I've a feeling o' that now; and it makes a man feel as there's a good more nor he can see, i' spite o' the trouble and the wickedness" (Chap. XVI). Silas' feelings about the invisible are, we see, the direct product of his experiences with his fellow men.

III

The despair of moral isolation and alienation from the world is often produced by the absence or loss of ties with a communal group (family, city, nation, sect, etc.) or with a tradition. This is the experience of Hetty Sorrel when her pregnancy forces her to leave Hayslope, of Don Silva when he has renounced his Spanish duties and heritage, of Romola when her disillusionment with Savonarola impels her to leave Florence, and of Mirah Lapidoth when she is completely alone and on the verge of suicide in London. Conversely, connection and identification with a cause, a group, or a tradition give the individual a sense of being a meaningful part of the world; they give him a sense of religious orientation in the cosmos. When the individual is in this way identified with something external and superior to self, seeing self as a part of the world rather than the world as part of self, he transcends not only the limitations and distortions of the egoistic point of view, but also much of the frustration which attends the individual lot.

Mordecai's aspirations for the Jews and Felix Holt's identification with the cause of the working men enable these men to accept their personal reverses with strength and dignity. When Felix is in prison, Esther is discouraged for him and says, "See how you may fail!" Felix replies:

But I'm proof against that word failure. I've seen behind it. The only failure a man ought to fear is failure in cleaving to the purpose he sees to be best. As to just the amount of result he may see from

141

his particular work—that's a tremendous uncertainty: the universe has not been arranged for the gratification of his feelings. As long as a man sees and believes in some great good, he'll prefer working towards that in the way he's best fit for, come what may. (Chap. XLV)

When Gwendolen complains to Deronda about the pain and dullness of life, he tells her: ". . . try to care about something in the vast world besides the gratification of small selfish desires. Try to care for what is best in thought and action—something that is good apart from the accidents of your own lot." "The refuge you are needing from personal trouble," he tells her a bit later, "is the higher, the religious life, which holds an enthusiasm for something more than our own appetites and vanities" (Chap. XXXVI).

In different ways, Caleb Garth and Philip Wakem both achieve the higher, the religious life. Caleb has much in common with Felix Holt and with Adam Bede; his religion centers around the faithful performance of his work and his identification with the world of labor. Caleb has "no keenness of imagination for monetary results in the shape of profit and loss"; but he does have a clear vision of the way in which the world's work is carried on and a desire to partake in the life of society by honest, enduring labor:

> Caleb Garth often shook his head in meditation of the value, the indispensable might of that myriad-headed, myriad-handed labour by which the social body is fed, clothed, and housed. It had laid hold of his imagination in boyhood. The echoes of the great hammer where roof or keel were a-making, the signal-shouts of the workmen, the roar of the furnace, the thunder and plash of the engine, were a sublime music to him . . . —all these sights of his youth had acted on him as poetry without the aid of the poets, had made a philosophy for him without the aid of philosophers, a religion without the aid of theology. His early ambition had been to have as effective a share as possible in this sublime labour. (Chap. XXIV)

Caleb's imagination extends into the future; he identifies himself with his work and rejoices in the good which it will bring to future generations. When he gets the commission to put Mr. Brooke's estate into good order, he is excited by the opportunity to do some work "that those who are living and those who come after will be better for." " 'It's a great gift of God, Susan,' " he exclaims. " 'That it is, Caleb,' said his wife, with answering fervour. 'And it will be a blessing to your children to have had a father who did such work: a father whose good work remains though his name may be forgotten' " (Chap. XL). As we see from her reply, Mrs. Garth, like her husband, approaches life objectively and with vision: "She had that rare sense which discerns what is unalterable, and submits to it without murmuring" (Chap. XXIV). Mary Garth, too, exemplifies the objective approach to reality: ". . . honesty, truth-telling fairness, was Mary's reigning virtue: she neither tried to create illusions, nor indulged in them for her own behoof" (Chap. XII). Though her lot has never been easy, Mary experiences no great frustration; "for, having early had strong reason to believe that things were not likely to be arranged for her peculiar satisfaction, she wasted no time in astonishment and annoyance at that fact." Mary had "a well of affectionate gratitude within her, which was all the fuller because she had learned to make no unreasonable claims" (Chap. XXXIII).

In Philip Wakem we see the power of unselfish love for another person to give life a meaning apart from the pains and pleasures of our individual lot. The combination of his deformity and his sensitivity makes his life a torment to Philip, who cannot resign himself to his stunted existence. "But I can't give up wishing," he replies when Maggie expounds her philosophy of passivity and renunciation:

> It seems to me we can never give up longing and wishing while we are thoroughly alive. There are certain things we feel to be beautiful and good, and we *must* hunger after them. . . . there are many . . . things I long for . . . —things that other men have, and that will always be denied to me. My life will have nothing great or beautiful in it; I would rather not have lived. (Book V, Chap. I)

Philip's love for Maggie has a large element of egoism in it; he feels that if he can win her love (and eventually her hand) his life will have a redeeming beauty and happiness.

Philip is ultimately saved, however, not by Maggie's love for him but by his love for her, which is purified of egoism when Maggie's love for Stephen makes her unavailable to him. When Maggie returns to St. Ogg's in disgrace, Philip writes her to let her know that, despite all, his love for her has made life a good to him:

> ... no anguish I have had to bear on your account has been too heavy a price to pay for the new life into which I have entered in loving you. . . . The new life I have found in caring for your joy and sorrow more than for what is directly my own, has transformed the spirit of rebellious murmuring into the willing endurance which is the birth of strong sympathy. I think nothing but such complete and intense love could have initiated me into that enlarged life which grows and grows by appropriating the life of others; for before, I was always dragged back from it by ever-present painful self-consciousness. I even think sometimes that this gift of transferred life which has come to me by loving you, may be a new power to me.
>
> Then—dear one—in spite of all, you have been the blessing of my life. . . . And remember that I am unchangeably yours: yours—not with selfish wishes, but with a devotion that excludes such wishes. (Book VII, Chap. III)

Through his love, Philip is approaching a state of disinterested objectivity similar to that which Theophrastus Such, another misfit, has reached when he tells us that "the habit of getting interested in the experience of others has been continually gathering strength, and I am really at the point of finding that this world would be worth living in without any lot of one's own."[5]

The way in which Philip finally regards Maggie is typical (except, of course, for the passion) of the objective relation of self to other people. When we regard others objectively we see things, including ourselves, from their point of view; we put aside, for the time, the claims of our own ego and imaginatively project ourselves into the interior life of the other person, feeling for him as he feels for himself (or as we feel for ourselves). In January 1875 George Eliot wrote to Mrs. Elma Stuart: "I am very fond of that old Greek saying that the best state is that in which every man feels a wrong done to another as if it were done to himself" (*Letters,* VI, 112).

The objective approach to reality involves the recognition of moral law which is independent of self and to which the individual must submit himself. An important function of religion, for George Eliot, is to make the individual conscious of a rule of right which is superior to impulse. The very nature of religious assemblies, she wrote, is that they involve "the recognition of a binding belief or spiritual law which is to lift us into willing obedience and save us from the slavery of unregulated passion or impulse" (*Letters,* V, 448). The objective relation of self to reality involves also an awareness of the autonomy of the world and of other people, a vision of the true relations of things, and an acceptance of the inevitable and a striving for the possible. In "A College Breakfast-Party," George Eliot presents the moral development of the species as in large part the process whereby

> human consciousness awaking owned
> An Outward, whose unconquerable sway
> Resisted first and then subdued desire
> By pressure of the dire Impossible
> Urging to possible ends the active soul
> And shaping so its terror and its love.

Through experience, by having the true nature of things painfully impressed upon his consciousness, the egoist frequently comes to adopt the objective point of view. After they have been married and childless for many years, Godfrey, moved by the discovery of Dunstan's body and Silas' money, tells Nancy that Eppie, whom he has been wanting to adopt, is really his own child. Nancy consents to adopt her and Godfrey is confident that his wish will finally be realized: "It seemed an eminently appropriate thing to Godfrey, for reasons that were known only to himself; and by a common fallacy, he imagined the measure would be easy because he had private motives for desiring it" (Chap. XVII). Godfrey, however, encounters determined resistance from Marner and especially from Eppie, and he is made aware of the existence of powerful feelings in others and of the irrevocability of his actions. Nancy remarks that they "can't alter her bringing up and what's come of it." Godfrey replies: "No . . . there's debts we can't pay like money debts, by paying extra for the years that have slipped by. While I've been putting off and putting off, the trees have been growing—it's too late now." Godfrey recognizes now that "I'd no right to expect anything but evil could come of that marriage [his first]—and when I shirked doing a father's part too." Godfrey recognizes now how little right he had to be a cross to Nancy because of their childlessness:

"And I got *you*, Nancy, in spite of all; and yet I've been grumbling and uneasy because I hadn't something else—as if I deserved it."
"You've never been wanting to me, Godfrey," said Nancy with quiet sincerity. "My only trouble would be gone if you resigned yourself to the lot that's been given us."
"Well, perhaps it isn't too late to mend a bit there. Though it *is* too late to mend some things, say what they will." (Chap. XX)

Arthur Donnithorne undergoes a change of attitude similar to Godfrey's. He learns that the evil consequences of past wrongdoing can be only partially mitigated—and Arthur is ready to undergo any self-sacrifice to lessen the evil. Arthur does much to mitigate the evil for the Poysers and the Bedes, but he can do nothing to make it up to Hetty. At the very end of the novel he says to Adam: "I could never do anything for her, Adam . . . and I'd thought so of the time when I might do something for her. But you told me the truth when you said to me once, 'There's a sort of wrong that can never be made up for' " (Epilogue).

Often the three stages of relation between self and the world which I have been describing are, in the order presented, also stages of intellectual and moral development through which George Eliot's characters go in the process of maturation. "We are all of us," she writes, "born in moral stupidity, taking the world as an udder to feed our supreme selves" (*Middlemarch*, Chap. XXI). Almost all of her major characters experience the second stage in which harsh reality breaks in upon and destroys the illusions (some of them innocent enough) about self and the world which are concomitant with inexperience and with immature or selfish subjectivity. Her characters cannot reach the third and ultimate stage of moral development without going through the trial and sorrow which results from their experience of the world's harshness or indifference. This experience makes clear to them the real relations of things and makes them sharers in the common lot. If it does not drive them back into illusion or into an embittered, defensive egoism, it nurtures in them the vision and sympathy necessary for the highest human fellowship. In 1871 George Eliot wrote to Alexander Main:

> You speak of having had trouble, but—
> "He who hath never warr'd with misery,
> Nor ever tugg'd with danger and distress,
> Hath had n' occasion nor no field to try
> The strength and forces of his worthiness."
> That quatrain of old Daniel brings up—does it not—Goethe's famous
> "Wer nie sein Brod mit Thränen ass"—
> and these sayings will remain true while this earth is a world of suffering. For who could be prepared for true fellowship without having had his share of sorrow as well as joy? (*Letters*, V, 213)

In the third stage of moral development, the individual's painful sense of the world's independent, alien existence is moderated by his vision of his connection, through the web of relations, with the rest of existence and by his awareness of other human beings as subjective objects. He is moved, often, by an identification with and enthusiasm for groups and ends which transcend his individual existence; and his life-purpose becomes not the pursuit of personal gratification but the achievement of genuine significance through living for others. This, for George Eliot, is the true religious life. The individual's feeling of solidarity with his fellows gives him a sense of religious orientation in the cosmos.

The movement from subjectivity to objectivity, from living in and for self to living in and for others, with its concomitant growth in vision and sympathy through experience and suffering, is the basic configuration of moral and psychological experience in the world of George Eliot's novels. Clearly, the pattern emerged from her personal experience and from her acceptance of the cosmological, psychological, and epistemological theories which I have described. But, as Barbara Hardy remarks, "classification is too rough a process. . . . The pattern remains, the people change."[7]

It should be added that George Eliot's novels are not, after all, the last word in a philosophy endeavoring to teach by example, but experiments in life; experiments whose ability to yield "something more sure than shifting theory" lies in their emphasis upon the felt, the evolved, and the particular. To complete the critical process, therefore, I shall turn from theories and categories to a close study of the development of individual characters.

That there are close connections between the positivistic tradition and George Eliot's thought, and between her thought and the imaginative world of her novels, I have already to some degree demonstrated; as I discuss her novels these connections should become quite clear. My primary aim in the following chapters, however, is not to demonstrate that her novels reveal the influence of positivism, but to use a knowledge of her intellectual milieu to get a clearer idea of what the novels are about, of what the story really is. Whatever its independent value as intellectual biography and as history of ideas may be, the real value for literary criticism of whatever extra-literary information I have presented so far is that it enriches our experience of the work of art; it helps us to see it better. The best way to use this information as we read George Eliot is to allow it to become assimilated into our experience of the fiction.

THE THREE STAGES:
ADAM BEDE AND MAGGIE TULLIVER

I

It is not difficult to see why Gerald Bullett feels that Adam Bede has his author's "unqualified moral approval."[1] Like Caleb Garth, Adam has an excellent knowledge of "business" and a strong sense of his relation to the life around him. He has the realist's awareness of the connectedness of things. "I've seen pretty clear," he tells Arthur, "ever since I could cast up a sum, as you can never do what's wrong without breeding sin and trouble more than you can ever see" (Chap. XVI). Adam's conception of man's function in life is expressed in his praise of Arthur Donnithorne at the birthday feast:

> I believe he's one o' those gentlemen as wishes to do the right thing, and to leave the world a bit better than he found it, which it's my belief every man may do, whether he's gentle or simple, whether he sets a good bit o' work going and finds the money, or whether he does the work with his own hands. (Chap. XXIV)

Adam has not only a vision of the right, but also the strength of will to act according to his convictions, even when this involves privation for himself. His resolution is fed by his strong sense of responsibility towards those dependent upon him and by his modest conception of the importance of his own pleasures in the scheme of things. As he works through the night on the coffin that his father, away on a drunken escapade, had failed to make on time, Adam thinks to himself: " 'They that are strong ought to bear the infirmities of those that are weak, and not to please themselves.' There's a text wants no candle to show't; it shines by its own light. It's plain enough you get into the wrong road i' this life if you run after this and that only for the sake o' making things easy and pleasant to yourself" (Chap. IV). Clearly, Adam Bede is not one of George Eliot's blind, self-seeking egoists.

But most recent critics have seen that Adam is not a flawless, static figure; the novel is, in fact, the story of his education.[2] Adam in the beginning of his story has serious deficiencies, deficiencies which are often the counterparts of his virtues. He is often subjective in his atti-tudes towards other people. He attributes to others—notably Arthur and Hetty—virtues which they don't have; his praise of Arthur at the birthday feast turns out to be excruciatingly ironic. His illusions about Arthur and Hetty leave him open to the shock of disillusion-ment, a shock in his case equivalent in force and effect to that pro-duced by the loss of religious faith.[3]

Adam's chief moral fault is his hardness. His strong resolution sometimes leads him into pride and stubbornness. He tells Arthur, who is his opposite: "It isn't my way to be see-saw about anything: I think my fault lies th' other way. When I've said a thing, if it's only to myself, it's hard for me to go back" (Chap. XVI). Being strong himself, Adam is unsympathetic towards weakness in others. He has very little sympathy for his alcoholic father. After his father's death Adam experiences a remorseful awareness of his fault: "Adam's mind rushed back over the past in a flood of relenting and pity" (Chap. IV). At Thias' funeral Adam reflects to himself:

> Ah! I was always too hard. . . . It's a sore fault in me as I'm so hot and out o' patience with people when they do wrong, and my heart gets shut up against 'em, so as I can't bring myself to forgive 'em. I see clear enough there's more pride nor love in my soul. . . . Mayhap the best thing I ever did in my life was only doing what was easiest for myself . . . the real tough job for me 'ud be to master my own will and temper, and go right against my own pride. (Chap. XVIII)

Adam's awareness of his hardness as a fault, however, is not enough to produce a marked change in his behavior. Understanding and sympathy spring from a similarity between our own experience and that of others, and Adam has had no experience of weakness, irresolution, or overmastering passion in himself to make him tender towards those who have these failings. Herbert Spencer, we recall, points out that "strong persons, though they may be essentially sympathetic in their natures, cannot adequately enter into the feelings of the weak."[4] If Adam is to change, the change must be the result of an organic process which involves a widening of his experience and a corresponding development of new sensibilities. In some respects, his hardness is closely allied to his realism, to his clear perception of the order of things and his inflexibility in abiding by his vision of consequences. Before his discovery of Hetty's relation with Arthur, Adam allows his imagination to dwell upon their possible life together after marriage:

But Adam had no sooner caught his imagination leaping forward in this way—making arrangements for an uncertain future—than he checked himself. "A pretty building I'm making, without either bricks or timber. I'm up i' the garret a'ready, and haven't so much as dug the foundation." Whenever Adam was strongly convinced of any proposition, it took the form of a principle in his mind: it was knowledge to be acted on, as much as the knowledge that damp will cause rust. Perhaps here lay the secret of the hardness he had accused himself of: he had too little fellow-feeling with the weakness that errs in spite of foreseen consequences. Without this fellow-feeling, how are we to get enough patience and charity towards our stumbling, falling companions in the long and changeful journey? And there is but one way in which a strong determined soul can learn it—by getting his heart-strings bound round the weak and erring, so that he must share not only the outward consequence of their error, but their inward suffering. That is a long and hard lesson, and Adam had at present only learned the alphabet of it in his father's sudden death, which, by annihilating in an instant all that had stimulated his indignation, had sent a sudden rush of thought and memory over what had claimed his pity and tenderness. (Chap. XIX)

This passage describes the way in which Adam is to be educated—through the suffering caused him by Hetty's fate.

The most dramatic manifestation of Adam's rash severity is in his behavior towards Arthur, first when he fights him in the wood and then when he wants to see Arthur punished for what he has done to Hetty. Mr. Irwine, who is afraid that Adam's vengeful hatred will lead to further violence, tries to convince Adam that Arthur is already suffering greatly and that his desire for revenge is an unjust, dangerous passion that will only cause more trouble. Mr. Irwine's admonitions prevent Adam from acting rashly, but it is Adam's suffering on Hetty's account that prepares the way for his ultimate reconciliation with Arthur. Adam's suffering, which reaches a climax on the morning of the trial, enlarges his sympathy and tenderness by giving him an insight into experiences hitherto unknown to him:

> Deep, unspeakable suffering may well be called a baptism, a regeneration, the initiation into a new state . . . all the intense emotions which had filled the days and nights of the past week, and were compressing themselves again like an eager crowd into the hours of this single morning, made Adam look back on all the previous years as if they had been a dim sleepy existence, and he had only now awakened to full consciousness. It seemed to him as if he had always before thought it a light thing that men should suffer; as if all that he had himself endured and called sorrow before, was only a moment's stroke that had never left a bruise. Doubtless a great anguish may do the work of years, and we may come out from that baptism of fire with a soul full of new awe and new pity.
>
> "O God," Adam groaned . . . , "and men have suffered like this before . . . and poor helpless young things have suffered like her."

Adam's own experience of suffering, then, enables him to envision the suffering of others, and this combination of experience and vision makes him sympathetic towards his fellows. Adam had not intended to be present at the trial, but when he hears that the Poysers will have nothing to do with Hetty, he decides to go. He tells Bartle Massey: "I'll stand by her—I'll own her—for all she's been deceitful. They oughtn't to cast her off—her own flesh and blood. We hand folks over to God's mercy, and show none ourselves. I used to be hard sometimes: I'll never be hard again. I'll go, Mr. Massey—I'll go with you" (Chap. XLII). The triumph of love over justice in Adam repeats the essential pattern of Christianity, in which, according to Feuerbach, the forgiving, redeeming love of the human Christ is ultimately a more potent force than God the lawgiver who is the objectification of the impersonal reason. Adam had never relied much on providence, but now it seems to him a divine thing not only to be responsible, to help oneself, but also to love and forgive others.

When Adam encounters Arthur again in the wood, at the same place where they had fought eight months earlier, he is moved to compassion by Arthur's care-worn appearance: ". . . the figure before him touched him with the signs of suffering. Adam knew what suffering was—he could not lay a cruel finger on a bruised man." Arthur tells Adam that he is going away with the army so that the Bedes and the Poysers will not have to leave the neighborhood; he hopes in this way to mitigate the evil consequences of his sin. Adam is uncooperative for he thinks he sees in Arthur's words "that notion of compensation for irretrievable wrong, that self-soothing attempt to make evil bear the same fruits as good," which most of all "rouses his indignation." When Arthur insists that he is only trying "to do the best" and claims that his suffering is greatest because the fault is his, Adam forgives him in words which show the influence of his earlier experiences upon his present relenting:

> I was too hard with my father, for doing wrong. I've been a bit hard t' everybody but *her*. I felt as if nobody pitied her enough— her suffering cut into me so; and when I thought the folks at the Farm were too hard with her, I said I'd never be hard to anybody myself again. But feeling overmuch about her has perhaps made me unfair to you. I've known what it is in my life to repent and feel it's too late: I felt I'd been too harsh to my father when he was gone from me—I feel it now, when I think of him. I've no right to be hard towards them as have done wrong and repent. (Chap. XLVIII)

One of the chief themes in *Adam Bede* is the nemesis that lies in wrong-doing and the irrevocability of the past. In her review of William Rathbone Greg's *The Creed of Christendom* George Eliot gave much attention to Greg's criticism of the Christian "conception of pardon of sin, or repentance and conversion." Not only does this conception relieve man of permanent responsibility for his own acts and place more emphasis upon contrition than upon sinlessness; but it also blinds man to a great impetus to right action, the fact "that everything done is done irrevocably, that even the omnipotence of God cannot *uncommit* a deed, cannot make that undone which has been done; that every act of his *must* bear its allotted fruit according to the everlasting laws." The ineluctable working out of nemesis, in a purely natural way, constitutes a significant part of the action in many of George Eliot's novels. Greg's subsequent remarks further illuminate her thematic intent in the Arthur-Hetty story. He does not deny the value of repentance, but he interprets it naturalistically:

> Repentance, contrition of soul, bears, like every other act, its own fruit—the fruit of purifying the heart, of amending the future: not as man has hitherto conceived—of effacing the past. The commission of sin is an irrevocable act, but it does not incapacitate the soul for virtue. Its consequences cannot be expunged, but the course need not be pursued. Sin, though it is ineffaceable, calls for no despair, but for efforts more energetic than before. Repentance is still as valid as ever; but it is valid to secure the future, not to obliterate the past.[5]

Arthur Donnithorne's repentance is of that genuine, efficacious kind which seeks to amend the future, but his efforts would be of no avail without Adam Bede's forgiveness and cooperation.

The modification in Adam's character which leads him to forgive Arthur is produced largely by the suffering caused him by Arthur's sin with Hetty. The Arthur-Hetty story has its causes within itself; the growth in Adam of a higher moral nature is the result of his relation to Arthur and Hetty. The somber theme of the Arthur-Hetty story is complemented by the theme of Adam's story which stresses the moral growth that results from suffering. Like Adam, however, George Eliot abhors the facile doctrine of compensation and is careful to point out that the good which has come of Adam's pain does not make its evil cause the less evil in its effects on others:

> That is a base and selfish, even a blasphemous, spirit, which rejoices and is thankful over the past evil that has blighted or crushed another,

because it has been made a source of unforeseen good to ourselves: Adam could never cease to mourn over that mystery of human sorrow which had been brought so close to him: he could never thank God for another's misery. . . . But it is not ignoble to feel that the fuller life which a sad experience has brought us is worth our own personal share of pain: surely it is not possible to feel otherwise, any more than it would be possible for a man with cataract to regret the painful process by which his dim blurred sight of men as trees walking had been exchanged for clear outline and effulgent day. (Chap. LIV)

We should note that George Eliot's analogy connects Adam's moral development with a clarification of vision. The analogy refers to the story of Jesus curing the blind man and suggests (as did her earlier description of Adam's initiation through suffering as "a baptism, a regeneration") the religious nature (in a Feuerbachian sense, of course) of Adam's experience.

Adam's moral growth is manifested not only in his forgiveness of Arthur and Hetty, but also in his increased tenderness towards and need of others. His greater indulgence towards Seth "was part of that growing tenderness which came from the sorrow at work within him." He was aware

that common affection and friendship were more precious to him than they used to be,—that he clung more to his mother and Seth, and had an unspeakable satisfaction in the sight or imagination of any small addition to their happiness. The Poysers, too—hardly three or four days passed but he felt the need of seeing them, and interchanging words and looks of friendliness with them. . . . (Chap. L)

Adam's sorrow lived in him "as an indestructible force, only changing its form, as forces do, and passing from pain into sympathy—the one poor word which includes all our best insight and our best love." It is in such periods of learning to live with grief as Adam was experiencing, George Eliot notes, "that the sense of our lives having visible and invisible relations beyond any of which either our present or prospective self is the centre, grows like a muscle that we are obliged to lean on and exert." At the end of the novel Adam is much more fully a member of the human community than he had been at the beginning.

It is the growth of new and higher sensibilities in Adam that leads to his love for Dinah; while he was feeling that he could never love again "the power of loving was all the while gaining new force within him; . . . the new sensibilities bought by a deep experience were so many new fibres by which it was possible, nay, necessary to him, that his nature should intertwine with another" (Chap. L). Adam was far more fitted to stand alone, had far less need of another, before his sorrow. Adam himself sees that his feeling for Dinah is the outgrowth of all his past experience: "I should never ha' come to know that her love 'ud be the greatest o' blessings to me, if what I counted a blessing hadn't been wrenched and torn away from me, and left me with a greater need, so as I could crave and hunger for a greater and a better comfort" (Chap. LIII). Adam's love for Hetty had been connected with his religious feelings; his love for Dinah is the product, too, of religious feeling, but feeling of a higher nature. The marriage of Dinah and Adam is by no means contrived or superfluous to the design of the novel; it is the natural culmination of the major action and theme of the novel:

> His feeling towards Dinah, the hope of passing his life with her, had been the distant unseen point toward which that hard journey from Snowfield eighteen months ago had been leading him. Tender and deep as his love for Hetty had been—so deep that the roots of it would never be torn away—his love for Dinah was better and more precious to him; for it was the outgrowth of that fuller life which had come to him from his acquaintance with deep sorrow. (Chap. LIV)[6]

II

From the beginning of her life to the end Maggie Tulliver finds herself in a world in which the satisfaction of her needs of heart and mind is impossible.[7] Maggie's frustration must not be confused with that of Dorothea Brooke, whose desire for a widely beneficent function for her life is thwarted by the meanness of opportunity; or with that of self-satisfied egoists like Gwendolen Harleth whose claims upon life are excessive and who have therefore a Byronic sense of the world's worthlessness. F. R. Leavis argues that Maggie is essentially identical with the young Marian Evans:

She has the intellectual potentiality for which the environment into which she is born doesn't provide much encouragement; she has the desperate need for affection and intimate personal relations; and above all she has the need for an emotional exaltation, a religious enthusiasm, that shall transfigure the ordinariness of daily life and sweep her up in an inspired devotion of self to some ideal purpose.[8]

The first two points are well made, but the third is misleading. The early Maggie desires not so much a religious enthusiasm as recognition and self-fulfillment. She has much to give others, but she wants much in return: "Poor Maggie was by no means made up of unalloyed devotedness, but put forth large claims for herself where she loved strongly" (Book III, Chap. II). Maggie's wants are not coarse—she has a sensitive nature—and in her pursuit of gratification she is not heedless of others; but this does not make Maggie another Saint Theresa whose "passionate, ideal nature demanded an epic life" (*Middlemarch,* Prelude).

What Mr. Leavis does not make clear is that Maggie's spiritual hunger is not (as with Dorothea) the source, but the product of her frustration; and that her hunger is not initially "for ideal exaltations,"[9] but for an approach to life which will reconcile her to the hardness of her lot. At the time of her father's downfall Maggie is described as "a creature full of eager, passionate longings for all that was beautiful and glad; thirsty for all knowledge; with an ear straining after dreamy music that died away and would not come near to her; with a blind unconscious yearning for something that would link together the wonderful impressions of this mysterious life, and give her soul a sense of home in it." This is not the same as Dorothea's ardent, theoretic yearning "after some lofty conception of the world which might frankly include the parish of Tipton and her own rule of conduct there" (*Middlemarch,* Chap. I). Maggie longs for beauty, gladness, knowledge, and the sensuous delight of music; if she had these things, along with love and understanding, Maggie would be content. As it is, all the satisfactions that her nature craves are denied to her: "No wonder," George Eliot comments, "when there is this contrast between the outward and the inward, that painful collisions come of it" (Book III, Chap. V). The painful disparity which she experiences between inner desire and outer fact leads Maggie to crave an understanding of life that will give her soul a sense of home in it; and out of her suffering and her search arises the moral sensibility which leads us to regard Maggie as noble despite her weakness and error.

The first great crisis in Maggie's life comes with her father's bankruptcy and illness. As Tom and Maggie begin their sorrowful homeward journey from Mr. Stelling's, George Eliot likens their experience to the expulsion from Eden: "They had gone forth together into their new life of sorrow, and they would never more see the sunshine undimmed by remembered cares. They had entered the thorny wilderness, and the golden gates of their childhood had for ever closed behind them." Tom and Maggie must now adjust themselves to a life far different from the comfortable one to which they had been accustomed. The shock of disillusionment is greater perhaps for Tom than it is for Maggie. Tom had always felt quite secure about his family's wealth and respectability; and, aided by his gentleman's education, his imagination had pictured a future filled with horses, fine dogs, and much esteem from his fellows: "He was awakened now with a violent shock" (Book II, Chap. VII). Tom painfully but rather quickly brings his conceptions into accord with the nature of things and is able to work off his frustrations by a concentrated effort to re-establish the family honor and fortune. The family misfortune, unhappily, does not shake him out of his narrow self-righteousness, but only confirms it.

Tom's preoccupation and his increased severity of judgment are part of the new hardness that life has for Maggie. Maggie had never been at ease with her lot. "What was it," wondered sympathetic and perceptive Philip Wakem, "that made Maggie's dark eyes remind him of the stories about princesses being turned into animals?" "I think," George Eliot answers, "it was that her eyes were full of unsatisfied intelligence, and unsatisfied, beseeching affection" (Book II, Chap. V). The only genuine response that Maggie found in her medium was in her father's love and protection and in her brief encounters with Philip Wakem. Otherwise, her need for love and approval was either an unfulfilled longing or a painfully bruised sensibility. Maggie escaped from her frustrations by pounding nails into the head of her fetish doll, by running away to the gypsies ("it seemed to her the only way of escaping opprobrium, and being entirely in harmony with circumstances"—Book I, Chap. XI), or by fancying "it was all different, refashioning her little world into just what she should like it to be." "Maggie's was a troublous life," George Eliot explains, "and this was the form in which she took her opium" (Book I, Chap. VI). After her father's failure life becomes so hard for Maggie, and the pressure of reality so inescapable, that the need of a real solution, a true and enduring source of moral strength becomes imperative.

At first Maggie's sorrow for herself is entirely subsumed in her love and pity for her father. As long as her father is in a childishly dependent state, Maggie feels "the strong tide of pitying love" within her "almost as an inspiration, a new power, that would make the most difficult life easy for his sake." But when he becomes fully conscious of his misfortune Mr. Tulliver is continually wrapped in "sullen incommunicative depression," and Maggie now gets "no answer to her little caresses, either from her father or from Tom— the two idols of her life" (Book IV, Chap. II).

Maggie's surroundings provide no home for her spirit; for not only is there no human response, but even her familiar possessions and occupations have been taken from her. Added to her previous experience "of conflict between the inward impulse and outward fact, which is the lot of every imaginative and passionate nature" is a complete deprivation of every device, response, or object of passionate devotion which could give even an illusory comfort. It is at this point, "when sorrow has become stale, and has no longer an emotive intensity that counteracts its pain," that despair threatens; "it is then that the peremptory hunger of the soul is felt, and eye and ear are strained after some unlearned secret of our existence, which shall give to endurance the nature of satisfaction" (Book IV, Chap. II). Sometimes Maggie feels that if she could become absorbed in fancies, could have all Scott's novels and all Byron's poems she might find

happiness enough to dull her sensibility to her actual daily life. And yet . . . they were hardly what she wanted . . . no dream-world would satisfy her now. She wanted some explanation of this hard, real life . . . the privation of all pleasant things that had come to *her* more than to others: she wanted some key that would enable her to understand, and, in understanding, endure, the heavy weight that had fallen on her young heart. (Book IV, Chap. III)

Maggie's despair, which is truly pitiable but hardly the result of her "higher nature" in George Eliot's sense of that term, develops in her a sensitivity to human suffering and a craving for spiritual comfort that initiate her into a new stage of moral culture. Out of the deprivation of all personal satisfactions springs the need for a religious enthusiasm; for "something that will present motives in an entire absence of high prizes, something that will give patience and feed human love when the limbs ache with weariness, and human looks are hard upon us—something, clearly, that lies outside personal desires, that includes resignation for ourselves and active love for what is not ourselves" (Book IV, Chap. III).

Bob Jakin sees Maggie mourning over the loss of her favorite books, and, out of compassion for her heart's need, he brings her more books, among which is a used copy of Thomas à Kempis' *The Imitation of Christ*. Hitherto Maggie has been entirely alone in her trouble, "with no other part of her inherited share in the hard-won treasures of thought, which generations of painful toil have laid up for the race of men, than shreds and patches of feeble literature and false history." Now there comes to her a voice from the past speaking out of a full experience of sorrow and consolation, and Maggie has a "sudden vision" of a new approach to life. She feels as if she has been "wakened in the night by a strain of solemn music [far different from the "dreamy music" of sensuous indulgence], telling of beings whose souls had been astir while hers was in stupor." From Thomas à Kempis Maggie learns that the pursuit of personal satisfaction is the source of all discontent, that only by forsaking love of self can inner tranquillity be achieved. Maggie is won to the objective point of view in which self is seen not as the center of the world, but as part of the world, as no more important than all the other selves which are sharers in the common lot:

It flashed through her like the suddenly apprehended solution of a problem, that all the miseries of her young life had come from fixing her heart on her own pleasure, as if that were the central necessity of the universe; and for the first time she saw the possibility of shifting the position from which she looked at the gratification of her own desires—of taking her stand out of herself, and looking at her own life as an insignificant part of a divinely-guided whole.

There is a good deal of egoism and exaggeration in Maggie's renunciation. She longs alternately for the eternal peace that à Kempis' theology promises and for the enjoyment of "an everlasting crown" which is to be won by self-sacrifice. In her conscious abandonment of egoism Maggie seeks "the path of martyrdom and endurance, where the palm-branches grow, rather than the steep highway of tolerance, just allowance, and self-blame, where there are no leafy honours to be gathered and worn." The fault is not that of à Kempis, but Maggie's, for she sees in renunciation a means to the satisfaction she had been craving in vain: "She had not perceived—how could she until she had lived longer?—the inmost truth of the old monk's outpourings, that renunciation remains sorrow, though a sorrow borne willingly" (Book IV, Chap. III). In time, through more experience of failure and suffering, Maggie learns this.

Though Maggie's is not a completely genuine or realistic renunciation (hence it does not last), the moral discipline which her reading of *The Imitation of Christ* leads her to impose upon herself has a permanent effect and does much to account for her refusal to marry Stephen Guest at the end of the novel. For Maggie comes to feel that in the fulfillment of duty and in the submission of personal desires to a rule of conduct which transcends self lies the sacredness of life; and her desire born of despair for such a sanctification of her existence makes it impossible for her ever to be content with mere self-gratification.

Maggie's allowing herself to become involved in relationships with Philip Wakem and Stephen Guest is quite understandable. In Philip she finds the only genuine response to her intelligence that she ever knows. Perhaps even more important is the fact that Philip has a great need of her; Philip arouses her pity and tenderness and she has, when she declares her love for him, "a moment of belief that, if there were sacrifice in this love, it was all the richer and more satisfying" (Book I, Chap. IV). Maggie is always uneasy, however, about the duplicity and disloyalty that are involved (because of her father's narrow vindictiveness) in her relation with Philip, and she is somewhat relieved when Tom forces her to terminate the relationship. With Philip "the appeal was more strongly to her pity and womanly devotedness than to her vanity or other egoistic excitability of her nature" (Book VI, Chap. VII); but Maggie's attraction to Stephen Guest springs from her egoistic delight in his masculine homage and from the day-dream visions of wealth, luxury, ease, and refinement that are prompted by Stephen's presence.

Maggie has a powerful moral urge to resist a relationship which will violate her ties of trust, duty, and affection to Philip and Lucy, but, after much conflict, it is overcome by the enchantment into which she is thrown by Stephen's presence. During her two barren years of teaching at a boarding-school "she had slipped back into desire and longing: she found joyless days of distasteful occupation harder and harder—she found the image of the intense and varied life she yearned for, and despaired of, becoming more and more importunate." Maggie's earlier discipline is still an active force, for she tells Lucy, with significant self-judgment, "I think I get worse as I get older— more selfish. That seems very dreadful" (Book VI, Chap. II). But her long privation has intensified her susceptibility to pleasure. When Stephen's singing and his furtive attentions put Maggie in a state of great excitement, George Eliot explains:

> In poor Maggie's highly-strung, hungry nature—just come away from a third-rate schoolroom, with all its jarring sounds and petty round of tasks—these apparently trivial causes had the effect of rousing and exalting her imagination in a way that was mysterious to herself. It was not that she thought distinctly of Mr. Stephen Guest . . . ; it was rather that she felt the half-remote presence of a world of love and beauty and delight, made up of vague, mingled images from all the poetry and romance she had ever read, or had ever woven in her dreamy reveries. . . . The music was vibrating in her still . . . and she could not stay in the recollection of that bare, lonely past. She was in her brighter aerial world again. (Book VI, Chap. III)

When she is in such states of dreamy enchantment, Maggie's moral sensibility, her "higher nature," is inert; memory and vision give way to self-indulgent fantasies about the future or to absorption in the experience of the present moment. She has no consciousness of ties rooted in the past or of future consequences for herself and for others.

When the spell is for some reason broken, however, Maggie's vision and sympathy, the products of her early suffering, and her religious desire for a self-transcendent sanctification of her life, the result of her despair and her reading of Thomas à Kempis, are awakened into activity. When Stephen comes to her Aunt Moss's to beg her to marry him, Maggie resists his argument that all ties other than that made by their love are unnatural and hence not binding: "Love is natural," she replies, "but surely pity and faithfulness and memory are natural too. And they would live in me still, and punish me if I did not obey them" (Book VI, Chap. XI). When Maggie returns to St. Ogg's the argument is renewed, this time internally:

... it seemed to her as if all the worst evil in her had lain in ambush till now, and had suddenly started up full-armed, with hideous, over-powering strength! There were moments in which a cruel selfishness seemed to be getting possession of her: why should not Lucy—why should not Philip suffer? *She* had had to suffer through many years of her life; and who had renounced anything for her? And when something like that fulness of existence—love, wealth, ease, refinement, all that her nature craved—was brought within her reach, why was she to forego it, that another might have it—another who perhaps needed it less? But amidst all this new passionate tumult there were the old voices making themselves heard with rising power, till, from time to time, the tumult seemed quelled. *Was* that existence which tempted her the full existence she dreamed? Where, then, would be all the memories of early striving—all the deep pity for another's pain, which had been nurtured in her through years of affection and hard-ship—all the divine presentiment of something higher than mere personal enjoyment, which had made the sacredness of life? She might as well hope to enjoy walking by maiming her feet, as hope to enjoy an existence in which she set out by maiming the faith and sym-pathy that were the best organs of her soul. And then, if pain were so hard to *her,* what was it to others?—"Ah, God! preserve me from inflicting—give me strength to bear it." (Book VI, Chap. XIII)

Maggie never deliberately chooses to indulge her passion for Stephen; when she glides down the Floss with him she is in a state of intoxicated passivity. In Maggie, George Eliot wrote to John Blackwood, she has presented "a character essentially noble but liable to great error—error that is anguish to its own nobleness" (*Letters*, III, 318).

Both Joan Bennett and Gerald Bullett feel that "Maggie was hurried by her author to a premature death" because George Eliot had created in Maggie's conflict between her love for Stephen and her loyalty to Philip and Lucy a moral dilemma which she was unable satisfactorily to resolve. Mrs. Bennett's argument is "that the problem facing Maggie and Stephen at the crisis is not a satisfactory vehicle for the conception the author intended to symbolize by it." Maggie's decision, according to Mrs. Bennett, "was to depend on the rational conception of virtue—the weighing of foreseeable consequences," her motive being "to cause as little unhappiness as the circumstances would allow." But by this criterion Maggie's decision not to marry Stephen is hardly justifiable; Stephen's position is really more acceptable, for Maggie's refusal can hardly benefit Lucy and Philip, while it is a cause of great pain to Stephen and to Maggie herself. "In fact," writes Mrs. Bennett, "Maggie falls back on the assumption that 'all self-sacrifice is good.'" Mr. Bullett argues that "the problem is stated in terms of human kindness, and it proves insoluble."[10] The objections raised by these critics have much logical force; they are vitiated, however, by the fact that the major premise simply is not true. Neither Mrs. Bennett nor Mr. Bullett fully understands George Eliot's theory of morality and the problem she is raising in *The Mill on the Floss*.[11] Dr. Kenn, as Mrs. Bennett points out, sees that in many respects an ultimate marriage between Maggie and Stephen would be "the least evil"; but he sees even more clearly that Maggie's "conscience must not be tampered with: the principle on which she had acted was a safer guide than any balancing of consequences" (Book VII, Chap. II).

Maggie refuses to marry Stephen for a combination of reasons, each of which is the natural result of her previous moral experience. On the Dutch boat going to Mudport, Maggie awakens with horror to the reality of her situation. By her breach of faith and her selfishness she had rent the ties that had given meaning to duty, and had made herself an outlawed soul, with no guide but the wayward choice of her own passion. . . . Her life with Stephen could have no *sacredness:* she must forever sink and wander vaguely, driven by uncertain impulse; for she had let go the clue of life—that clue which once in the far-off years her young need had clutched so strongly. (My italics; this and subsequent passages are from Book VI, Chap. XIV.)

Maggie's choice is not between kindness or unkindness, or between degrees of pleasure and pain for those involved; it is between a life which is motivated and sanctified by the recognition of a moral law which is independent of personal desire and a meaningless life guided by nothing but random impulse. When Stephen argues that her refusal to marry him will serve no one's happiness, but will cause him unbearable anguish, Maggie replies:

We can't choose happiness either for ourselves or for another: we can't tell where that will lie. We can only choose whether we will indulge ourselves in the present moment, or whether we will renounce that, *for the sake of obeying the divine voice within us—for the sake of being true to all the motives that sanctify our lives.* I know this belief is hard: it has slipped away from me again and again; but I have felt that if I let it go for ever, I should have no light through the darkness of this life. (My italics)

The sanctification of her life lies, for Maggie, in obedience to that which she feels to be her duty, in faithfulness to the ties of love, trust, and dependence which have grown out of her past life. Feuerbach's conception of the religious nature of human relationships is clearly operative here. Stephen contends that the natural law which has manifested itself in the overwhelming force of their love is superior to every other claim; but Maggie argues that "if we judged in that way, there would be a warrant for all treachery and cruelty—we should justify breaking the most sacred ties that can ever be formed on earth. If the past is not to bind us, where can duty lie? We should have no law but the inclination of the moment."

Faithfulness to past ties is not merely an abstract principle of conduct for Maggie; the rule draws its force from powerful feelings,

feelings which are deeply rooted in her past experience and which are re-enforced by the moral faculties of vision and sympathy which that experience has nurtured:

> There was at least this fruit from all her years of striving after the highest and the best—that her soul, though betrayed, beguiled, ensnared, could never deliberately consent to a choice of the lower. And a choice of what? O God—not a choice of joy, but of conscious cruelty and hardness; for could she ever cease to see before her Lucy and Philip, with their murdered trust and hope?

Maggie's "memories, and affections, and longings after perfect goodness" are the very stuff of her conscience; "they would never quit me for long" she tells Stephen, "they would come back and be pain to me—repentance." It is because she has suffered so herself from the world's hardness that Maggie cannot bring herself deliberately to inflict pain upon others: "I can't argue any longer—I don't know what is wise; but my heart will not let me do it. I see—I feel their trouble now: it is as if it were branded on my mind. *I* have suffered, and had no one to pity me; and now I have made others suffer. . . . I cannot marry you: I cannot take a good for myself that has been wrung out of their misery." It was too late, Maggie knew, "too late already not to have caused misery: too late for everything, perhaps, but to rush away from the last act of baseness—the tasting of joys that were wrung from crushed hearts." Maggie's moral sensibility, of course, would never permit her to experience joy in a life with Stephen; just as it will not allow her to choose a course that would rend her from all that her past life "has made dear and holy" to her.

Life for Maggie on her return to St. Ogg's is very hard indeed, and her strength and resolution are sorely tried. Tom, whom she feared but could never cease to love, refuses to shelter or even to hear her. Her mother, Aunt Glegg, Bob Jakin, and Dr. Kenn stand by her, but the pressure of community opprobrium threatens to drive her out of St. Ogg's; and in strange surroundings, Maggie tells Dr. Kenn, "I should have no stay. I should feel like a lonely wanderer—cut off from the past" (Book VII, Chap. II). At times Maggie is roused from her self-pity, sense of desolation, and yearning for "that far, far off rest, from which there would be no more waking for her into this struggling earthly life" by the thought that her own suffering is a source of moral power that will enable her to succor her struggling fellow-men: "Ought she to shrink in this way from the long penance of life, which was all the possibility she had of lightening the load to some other sufferers, and so changing that passionate error into a new force of unselfish human love" (Book VII, Chap. V). But circumstances and society offer no channels into which Maggie's desire to live for others can flow, and she is uncertain of her strength to bear future trials.

Maggie's final temptation comes when Stephen renews by letter his plea for her to join him. The force of the temptation lies not so much in her desire for the alleviation of her own lot as in her pity for Stephen's misery; but the habit of obedience to that highest nature which is bound up with her past leads her after a brief struggle to seek a renewal of inspiration and high resolve:

> She sat quite still, far into the night: . . . only waiting for the light that would surely come again. It came with the memories that no passion could long quench: the long past came back to her, and with it the fountains of self-renouncing pity and affection, of faithfulness and resolve. The words that were marked by the quiet hand in the little old book that she had long ago learned by heart, rushed even to her lips, and found a vent for themselves in a low murmur . . .: "I have received the Cross, I have received it from Thy hand; I will bear it, and bear it till death, as Thou hast laid it upon me." . . . Her soul went out to the Unseen Pity that would be with her to the end. Surely there was something being taught her by this experience of great need; and she must be learning a secret of human tenderness and long-suffering, that the less erring could hardly know? "Oh God, if my life is to be long, let me live to bless and comfort—" (Book VII, Chap. V)

Maggie is aware of her own moral education: her own experience of great need has prepared her, she feels, to understand and to sympathize with the needs of others. Her epiphany is presented in Christian terms, but it is clear that George Eliot is here rendering her own version of the essence of Christianity. Maggie has arrived by a completely natural process at the Religion of Humanity; she draws upon the species for strength and she participates through love and sorrow in the life of mankind. Her sense of God (mankind) as a sustaining and directing force enables her to transcend the moral provincialism of St. Ogg's and gives her a sense of religious orientation in the cosmos. She not only feels God as a mediator between herself and the oppressive external order; she also feels a Christ-like, self-sacrificing love which impels her to act as a mediator for others.

At this point the flood comes, and Maggie, entirely unconscious of self, heroically braves the perils of the storm to rescue Tom at the mill. Tom, who had cruelly and self-righteously condemned Maggie because "his own eyes . . . gave no warning of their imperfection" (Book VII, Chap. III), now becomes reconciled to Maggie by a new vision of profound moral realities. Maggie's forgiving, selfless love suddenly adds a religious dimension to life for Tom. As they faced each other in the boat on the wide waters

> the full meaning of what had happened rushed upon his mind. It came with so overpowering a force—it was such a new revelation to his spirit, of the depths in life, that had lain beyond his vision which he had fancied so keen and clear—that he was unable to ask a question. They sat mutely gazing at each other: Maggie with eyes of intense life looking from a weary, beaten face—Tom with a certain awe and humiliation. . . . But at last a mist gathered over the blue-grey eyes, and the lips found a word they could utter: the old childish— 'Magsie!' (Book VII, Chap. V)

There is no dilemma for Maggie's death to resolve; she dies at her moment of greatest moral clarity and hope.

THE THREE STAGES: *MIDDLEMARCH*

One of the principal unifying elements in *Middlemarch* is the fact that most of the major characters (as well as many minor ones) clearly exemplify varieties of the subjective and objective approaches to reality.[1] Dorothea and Lydgate are both predominantly objective in their approach to reality, but they have blind spots which lead them into error and tend to frustrate their noble ambitions. In addition to Lydgate (as physician and scientist) and Dorothea (especially at the end), Farebrother and the Garths are objective in their relation to the world and to their fellows. At the same time, of course, *Middlemarch* abounds in egoists: Casaubon, Fred Vincy, Rosamond, Featherstone, and Bulstrode are, each in his individual way, classic studies of the subjective approach to reality. Clearly, one of George Eliot's chief interests in *Middlemarch* is the presentation on a large scale of the roles which the subjective and objective habits of mind play in shaping human destiny.

Fred Vincy is the only extreme egoist to be successfully nurtured to objectivity. His natural disposition to regard himself as the worthy object of cosmic dispensations was heightened by his university education and by the great expectations that he had with regard to his uncle Featherstone's fortune. As a result he was given to visions of ease, pleasure, and position rather than to visions of consequences and plans for a career. His world crumbled when he did not receive Featherstone's money; harsh reality broke in upon his dreams of easy wealth. Now he had to face the real business of life and to earn through his own merit not only a place in the world, but also the hand of Mary Garth. And when he learned of Farebrother's feelings for Mary, he became far less sure of his own accomplishments and attractions.

The final step in Fred's development came when Farebrother, his rival, warned him about the dangers of his renewed gambling. Farebrother, who deserved Mary far more than did Fred, was tempted to be quiet and let Fred ruin himself; but he knew that Mary loved Fred: "I want you," he told Fred, "to make the happiness of her life and your own." Fred was deeply moved by the vicar's loving act:

Some one highly susceptible to the contemplation of a fine act has said that it produces a sort of regenerating shudder through the frame and makes one feel ready to begin a new life. A good deal of that effect was just then present in Fred Vincy.

"I will try to be worthy," he said, breaking off before he could say "of you as well as of her." (Chap. LXVI)

Farebrother was here the true agent of God; through him the divine quality of human love was made manifest to Fred. Fred's values were no longer self-created; through Farebrother, and through the Garths, too, Fred came to recognize something higher than himself and began to participate in the life of the species. But he could not have come to find God in his fellow men rather than in himself without the experience of disillusionment and humiliation which began with the reading of the will.

Featherstone and Bulstrode, unlike Fred, did not reach the third stage of moral development. Featherstone was an extraordinarily manipulative man; his greatest pleasures in life lay in cunningly getting his own way and in having power over others. His determination to do as he liked at the last was thwarted by Mary Garth's refusal to obey his commands. His final and most significant gesture of manipulation was met by a resistance that he was powerless to overcome, and he died in an agony of frustration. The irony was compounded when his land fell into the hands of Bulstrode. Like Casaubon, Featherstone failed in his effort to control the lives of others from the grave.

The mainspring of Bulstrode's behavior, too, was a strong desire for personal pre-eminence and dominion over others. Perfectly exemplifying Feuerbach's description of the religious habit of mind, Bulstrode saw his own desires as directives from without. He justified his actions to himself by regarding himself as an instrument of God and seeing the fulfillment of his own ambitions as identical with God's glory. Morality had nothing to do with his relations to his fellows: sin, for Bulstrode, "seemed to be a question of doctrine and inward penitence, humiliation an exercise of the closet, the bearing of his deeds a matter of private vision adjusted solely by spiritual relations and conceptions of the divine purpose " (Chap. LIII). His relation to God enabled him to bypass humanity; his moral life was divorced from reality.

Bulstrode's peace of mind was dependent upon his transgressions being kept a private matter between himself and God. His system of illusions and rationalizations was destroyed, however, when Raffles appeared in Middlemarch. Bulstrode's past, which had become very dim in his mind, descended upon him as a tangible nemesis. To stay the divine vengeance in its new, solid form, Bulstrode undertook "a kind of propitiation which was not simply a doctrinal transaction"; he tried to correct the injustice which had been done to Will Ladislaw. But Bulstrode had now entered the real world which he could not completely control, even by behaving morally. When he offered Will the fortune which should have been his mother's, Ladislaw scornfully refused the money because of its tainted source: "It was the first time he [Bulstrode] had encountered an open expression of scorn from any man higher than Raffles; and with that scorn hurrying like venom through his system, there was no sensibility left to consolations" (Chap. LXI). The failure of his strategies for controlling reality (through religion and through economic power) was brought home to Bulstrode even more devastatingly when he was denounced at a meeting of the town's leading citizens. He saw with horror "that his life was after all a failure, that he was a dishonoured man, and must quail before the glance of those towards whom he had habitually assumed the attitude of a reprover—that God had disowned him before men and left him unscreened to the triumphant scorn of those who were glad to have their hatred justified" (Chap. LXXI). He left Middlemarch "to end his stricken life in that sad refuge, the indifference of new faces" (Chap. LXXXV). The universe, which was once in the hands of an omnipotent God who was especially friendly to Nicholas Bulstrode, had now only hostility or indifference to offer. Bulstrode was saved from a sense of total alienation by his wife's faithfulness; but he was cut off from her too by his dread that she would call him a murderer if he told her the whole truth.

We have seen that in his scientific pursuits Lydgate rigorously employed the empirical methodology. Furthermore, his relation to his work was sound; the pursuit of knowledge was with him an intellectual passion rather than, as with Casaubon, a means of exalting his own ego. Lydgate's goals were social as well as intellectual; he hoped to contribute to medical progress by making "a link in the chain of discovery." The medical profession provided him with what Dorothea Brooke was looking for, an opportunity "to do good small work for Middlemarch and great work for the world." Lydgate had the qualities which make for greatness and the opportunity to employ his abilities; but he also had grave weaknesses which prevented him from realizing his potentialities.

"Lydgate's spots of commonness," George Eliot observed, "lay in the complexion of his prejudices, which, in spite of noble intentions and sympathy, were half of them such as are found in ordinary men of the world" (Chap. XV). Though an experimentalist and an innovator in the field of medicine, in his social attitudes Lydgate had not risen above his class. In the affairs of practical life "he walked by hereditary habit; half from . . . personal pride and unreflecting egoism . . . , and half from that *naiveté* which belonged to preoccupation with favourite ideas" (Chap. XXXVI). Much of Lydgate's trouble stemmed from his lack of realism in money matters; he was unconsciously extravagant, having naturally expensive tastes and an inbred assumption that he should have the best as a matter of course. His conceit—which was "massive in its claims and benevolently contemptuous" (Chap. XV)—led him to have "a fearless expectation of success, a confidence in his own powers and integrity" and a "contempt for petty obstacles or seductions of which he had had no experience" (Chap. XIII). He was not a believer in providence, like Fred Vincy; his egoism, his conceit, was of a different sort. He believed in the power of his will to conquer all obstacles; like Conrad's youths, he felt indestructible and was ready to do battle with the cosmos. Because the more experienced Farebrother had a "low estimate of possibilities," Lydgate "thought that there was a pitiable infirmity of will" in him (Chap. XVIII).

Lydgate's attitude towards women was quite blindly traditional. He did not like Dorothea's style of woman; he gave adornment the first place among wifely functions and wanted, in marriage, to recline "in a paradise with sweet laughs for bird-notes and blue eyes for heaven" (Chap. XI). Dorothea had too active and independent an intelligence for his taste: "He held it one of the prettiest attitudes of the feminine mind to adore a man's pre-eminence without too precise a knowledge of what it consisted in" (Chap. XXVII). His vulnerability to women, his susceptibility to being misled by his own preconceptions, was made manifest in his experience with Laure. Instead of being warned by this experience, however, he became even more insulated from reality. He *thought* that he had been educated, that he would now be scientific in his dealings with women, and he therefore became falsely and dangerously self-confident: "henceforth," he told himself, "he would take a strictly scientific view of woman, entertaining no expectations but such as were justified beforehand" (Chap. XV). Rosamond had little trouble ensnaring him; for Lydgate, we are told, fell to spinning the gossamer web of young love's illusions "from his inward self with wonderful rapidity, in spite of experience supposed to be finished off with the drama of Laure—in spite too of medicine and biology" (Chap. XXXVI).

"Poor Lydgate!" exclaims George Eliot, "or shall I say, Poor Rosamond! Each lived in a world of which the other knew nothing." Lydgate, viewing Rosamond in the light of his preconceptions and desires, had no idea of what Rosamond was really like or of how she regarded him. And Rosamond "was entirely occupied not exactly with Tertius Lydgate as he was in himself, but with his relation to her" (Chap. XVI). Lydgate, we are told, was "virtually unknown" to Middlemarchers; he was "known merely as a cluster of signs for his neighbours's false suppositions" (Chap. XV). He appealed to Rosamond because of his foreignness, his distinction in manner and appearance, and, especially, his good family connections: "In Rosamond's romance it was not necessary to imagine much about the inward life of the hero, or of his serious business in the world . . ." (Chap. XVI). To Rosamond Lydgate meant primarily an elevation in social status. After their first meeting she vividly imagined the aristocratic life they would have together: "There was nothing financial, still less sordid, in her previsions: she cared about what were considered refinements, and not about the money that was to pay for them" (Chap. XII).

Their marriage brought disillusionment to both Rosamond and Lydgate. Lydgate soon discovered that Rosamond was interested in his talent only as a means to prestige; he came "to look through less and less of interfering illusion at the blank unreflecting surface her mind presented to his ardour for the more impersonal ends of his profession and his scientific study, an ardour which he had fancied that the ideal wife must somehow worship as sublime, though not in the least knowing why." When during her pregnancy Rosamond went horseback riding against his orders, he learned that she had a "terrible tenacity," and he got "an amazed sense of his powerlessness" over her (Chap. LVIII). Their financial and social difficulties intensified their alienation from each other: ". . . it was as if they were both adrift on one piece of wreck and looked away from each other" (Chap. LXXV). To Lydgate it seemed that Rosamond no more identified herself with him in his troubles "than if they had been creatures of different species and opposing interests" (Chap. LVIII).

Lydgate and Rosamond were driven even farther apart by the bitterness and ill temper which accompanied Lydgate's consciousness of having fallen from the contemplation of wide and noble ends into a preoccupation with the petty, sordid cares brought on by his money problems:

Some gentlemen have made an amazing figure in literature by general discontent with the universe as a trap of dulness into which their great souls have fallen by mistake; but the sense of a stupendous self and an insignificant world may have its consolations. Lydgate's discontent was much harder to bear: it was the sense that there was a grand existence in thought and effective action lying around him, while his self was being narrowed into the miserable isolation of egoistic fears, and vulgar anxieties for events that might allay such fears. (Chap. LXIV)

Lydgate had never been tempted by drink, opium, or gambling, but he began now to gamble and win at billiards; he "was acting, watching, speaking with that excited narrow consciousness which reminds one of an animal with fierce eyes and retractile claws" (Chap. LXVI). Fortunately, he lost and gave up the idea of continuing his gambling on a larger scale.

Lydgate's worst trial came when he was involved in the scandal surrounding Raffles' death; even Farebrother did not stand by him, and to Rosamond, he recognized, "he was always . . . a being apart, doing what she objected to" (Chap. LXXV). At this point he was rescued from despair by Dorothea's ardent faith in him; he "felt that he was recovering his old self in the consciousness that he was with one who believed in it." Dorothea wanted to use her money to help him follow, after all, in the footsteps of his heroes Louis and Laennec; but he was a much changed man. His belief in will shattered by his experience of failure, he did not have sufficient confidence in himself to accept her money: "I have not given guarantees enough. I must not at least sink into the degradation of being pensioned for work that I never achieved." There was also his sense of responsibility for Rosamond's happiness. He had resigned himself, he told Dorothea, to the fact that he "must do as other men do, and think what will please the world and bring in money" (Chap. LXXVI).

From a naive believer in activity, Lydgate had been transformed into an exponent of resignation. He recognized the irreversibility of his acts and he accepted responsibility for them: "Lydgate had accepted his narrowed lot with sad resignation. He had chosen this fragile creature and had taken the burthen of her life upon his arms. He must walk as he could, carrying that burthen pitifully" (Chap. LXXXI). One wonders, however, whether he did not resign himself too readily and to too much.

Rosamond, meanwhile, was bitterly disappointed in her life with

Lydgate, and became "in her secret soul . . . utterly aloof from him. The poor thing saw only that the world was not ordered to her liking, and Lydgate was part of that world" (Chap. LXIV). Her attention came to center on Will Ladislaw, around whom "she constructed a little romance which was to vary the flatness of her life: Will Ladislaw was always to be a bachelor and live near her, always to be at her command." She felt that Will would have made a much more suitable husband for her. "No notion," George Eliot hastened to comment, "could have been falser than this, for Rosamond's discontent in her marriage was due to the conditions of marriage itself, to its demand for self-suppression and tolerance and not to the nature of her husband" (Chap. LXXV).

Rosamond's world began to collapse when Will turned on her after Dorothea found them together. Rosamond knew that Will had received a harsh blow, but she was confident of her power to soothe and subdue him, for "she had been little used to imagining other people's states of mind except as a material cut into shape by her own wishes." Will, however, vented the fury of his frustration on Rosamond:

> Rosamond, while these poisoned weapons were being hurled at her, was almost losing the sense of her identity, and seemed to be waking into some new terrible existence. She had no sense of chill resolute repulsion, of reticent self-justification such as she had known under Lydgate's most stormy displeasure: all her sensibility was turned into a bewildering novelty of pain; she felt a new terrified recoil under a lash never experienced before. What another nature felt in opposition to her own was being burnt and bitten into her consciousness.

When Will at last lapsed into mute rage Rosamond had "no force to fling out any passion in return; the terrible collapse of the illusion toward which all her hope had been strained was a stroke which had too thoroughly shaken her: her little world was in ruins, and she felt herself tottering in the midst as a lonely bewildered consciousness" (Chap. LXXVIII). Her subjective picture of the world was further broken down by her experience with Dorothea, whose kindness belied all her expectations. Dorothea's "strange unexpected manifestation of feeling made Rosamond's soul to totter all the more with a sense that she had been walking in an unknown world which had just broken in upon her."

Rosamond's harsh awakening had two important effects. Her confession that when Dorothea discovered them together Will was telling her how he loved Dorothea made possible the reconciliation between Will and Dorothea. Her experience of the world's otherness also led Rosamond back to Lydgate: "Poor Rosamond's vagrant fancy had come back terribly scourged—meek enough to nestle under the old despised shelter" (Chap. LXXXI). No great permanent alteration took place in Rosamond, however, and Lydgate in later years, though he gained an excellent practice, considered himself a failure and was not without bitterness towards his wife: "He once called her his basil plant; and when she asked for an explanation, said that basil was a plant which had flourished wonderfully on a murdered man's brains" (Finale).

Dorothea Brooke, like Lydgate, had an ardent desire to be a power for good in the world, but her social sympathy and her "passionate, ideal nature" which "demanded an epic life" (Prelude) were frustrated by the meanness of opportunity. She had no home ties which bound her to immediate and satisfying duties. She had lost her parents when she was twelve and, being then educated in Switzerland, she did not find herself identified with the history or interests of any particular community. Her social position cut her off from any vital class feelings or activities: She was oppressed by the "gentlewoman's world, where everything was done for her and none asked for her aid—where the sense of connection with a manifold pregnant existence had to be kept up painfully as an inward vision, instead of coming from without in claims that would have sharpened her energies" (Chap. XXVIII). Her energies and affections were undirected; she was left free to dwell on "vague ambitions" and to soar "after some illimitable satisfaction" (Prelude). The social life in which she was expected to find her satisfactions "seemed nothing but a labyrinth of petty courses, a walled-in maze of small paths that led no whither" (Chap. III). The failure of society to provide a path for her energies and her consequent feeling that "all existence seemed to beat with a lower pulse than her own" (Chap. XXVII) were instrumental in producing the state of mind that resulted in her "life of mistakes, the offspring of a certain spiritual grandeur ill-matched with the meanness of opportunity" (Prelude).

With her Christian consciousness and her spiritual passion, Dorothea was an anomaly among her neighbors, and her social medium oppressed her not only by its barrenness of opportunity but also by its lack of understanding. She "knew of no one who thought as she did about life and its best objects" (Chap. V). Even her sister Celia failed to understand her. When Dorothea discovered Sir James Chettam's romantic interest in her, she became angry and announced to Celia that she would have nothing further to do with his cottages:

"Poor Dodo," Celia went on, in an amiable staccato. "It is very hard: it is your favourite *fad* to draw plans!"

"*Fad* to draw plans! Do you think I only care about my fellow-creatures' houses in that childish way? I may well make mistakes. How can one ever do anything nobly Christian, living among people with such petty thoughts?" . . . The *fad* of drawing plans! What was life worth—what great faith was possible when the whole effect of one's actions could be withered up into such parched rubbish as that? When she got out of the carriage, her cheeks were pale and her eyelids red.

Dorothea's reaction here was extreme; but since building cottages was the only socially significant activity she had found, she took it with desperate seriousness. Dorothea's "passionate desire to know and to think" had, "in the unfriendly mediums of Tipton and Freshitt . . . issued in crying and red eyelids" (Chap. IV).

Lydgate's failure was, as he himself knew, more the result of his own deficiencies than of circumstances: "It always remains true," George Eliot commented, "that if we had been greater, circumstances would have been less strong against us" (Chap. LVIII). Dorothea made mistakes similar to Lydgate's, but her errors and the frustration of her noble aims resulted chiefly from the defects of her social medium—"for there is no creature whose inward being is so strong that it is not greatly determined by what lies outside it" (Finale). The demands of St. Theresa's nature for an epic life were satisfied because her inner urges found a response in outward conditions; "She found her epos in the reform of a religious order." Later Theresas were less fortunate: "With dim lights and tangled circumstances they tried to shape their thought and deed in noble agreement; but after all, to common eyes their struggles seemed mere inconsistency and formlessness; for these later-born Theresas were helped by no coherent social faith and order which could perform the function of knowledge for the ardently willing soul" (Prelude).

Dorothea's failure of knowledge in marrying Mr. Casaubon was a product of both dim lights and tangled circumstances. The social machinery for courtship was partly to blame. Their premarital relationship was of short duration and was conventionally formal, so that Dorothea experienced no check to her unreal image of Casaubon. Her experience of men was slight, and she had naive views about the marriage relationship. There was nothing in her experience or in her cast of mind for Mr. Casaubon's pettiness to register upon, especially since he presented none of the signs that she had come to associate with pettiness and many signs which suggested greatness of mind and soul. Signs were all that she had to go by, and signs are deceptive. Her case was not singular; she suffered from the common liability of the human lot, the difficulty of truly knowing another person. Her tendency was to see others in the most favorable light. She erred, and suffered for her error, with Casaubon; but she was right about Ladislaw and Lydgate, and her action towards them issued in noble results. She could easily have been mistaken; even Farebrother was hesitant about Lydgate.

Dorothea failed to see that Casaubon's pedantic assertions about love and religion were merely parades of the conventional signs of feelings which he had never experienced. Casaubon's most passionate love-making took the form of "frigid rhetoric" which was "as sincere as the bark of a dog, or the cawing of an amorous rook"; "Dorothea's faith supplied all that Mr. Casaubon's words seemed to leave unsaid" (Chap. V):

> . . . she looked as reverently at Mr. Casaubon's religious elevation above herself as she did at his intellect and learning. He assented to her expressions of devout feling, and usually with an appropriate quotation; he allowed himself to say that he had gone through some spiritual conflicts in his youth; in short, Dorothea saw that here she might reckon on understanding, sympathy, and guidance. (Chap. III)

179

The signs were meaningful to Dorothea because she had experienced that which they point to, but she could not discriminate between herself and Casaubon, between the life within and the life without. She did not relate to Casaubon as he was in and for himself but to a reflection of herself. Her mental process corresponded to the way in which, according to Feuerbach, man creates his image of God out of the qualities and yearnings of his own nature. The few deficiencies she sensed in Casaubon were, she felt, really the result of the inability of her lower nature to comprehend the ways of perfection: "She filled up all blanks with unmanifested perfections, interpreting him as she interpreted the works of Providence, and accounting for seeming discords by her own deafness to the higher harmonies" (Chap. IX).

In her relation with Casaubon, Dorothea fell into the mental habits of the egoist. She failed to see him as a subject to whom she was an object. She did not regard him as an autonomous individual with needs and desires of his own, but rather as a means to her own ends. Her subjective approach to Casaubon was not the result of a basically egoistic nature; it was the product rather of her frustration. As we have seen, she found in her environment no one who thought and felt as she did, no path for her energies, no response to her needs. She found only indifference and misunderstanding. She felt the world to be alien and unyielding, but she could not accept this, for she had a passionate need to relate significantly to the life around her. She was ardent and affectionate and craved a generous response from the world, a pair of eyes looking into her own with welcome and admiration, a voice speaking her own language. The intensity of her need led her to rebel against her frustration and to create a response where there was none. She saw her own eyes in a mirror and heard the echo of her own voice and readily believed that they were the eyes and voice of another. But she thought that it was she who was a mirror, imperfectly reflecting the greatness of the other: " 'He thinks with me,' said Dorothea to herself, 'or rather, he thinks a whole world of which my thought is but a poor two-penny mirror'" (Chap. III).

Despite her early education in the difference between self and non-self, Dorothea's yearnings became a set of fixed ideas, making her perception quixotic—as George Eliot suggested by the epigraph to Chapter II. Celia was her Sancho. Dorothea's illusory picture of

Casaubon and of the life she would have with him was the effort of her imagination, seizing upon the first hint of suitable material that came its way, to fulfill the wishes that reality denied. Casaubon's knowledge, she felt, would liberate her from society's "walled-in maze of small paths that led no whither," and would reveal to her a course of actions which would be both grand and immediately satisfying:

> I should learn everything then. . . . There would be nothing trivial about our lives. . . . I should learn to see the truth by the same light as great men have seen it by. And then I should know what to do, when I got older: I should see how it was possible to lead a grand life here—now—in England. I don't feel sure about doing good in any way now: everything seems like going on a mission to people whose language I don't know. (Chap. III)

Dorothea was immensely gratified by Casaubon's desire to marry her, but her mind never dwelt upon *his* motives and expectations, only upon the release from anxiety and the personal fulfillment that *she* would experience. Casaubon's appearance on the scene was a manifestation of the divine good will which was to be gratefully and unquestioningly accepted. The universe, so long indifferent, was at last responding to her needs.

Mr. Casaubon, of course, was seeking in his relationship with Dorothea the gratification of *his* needs and desires. Casaubon was doomed to disappointment, for he would discover not only that Dorothea was not what he had imagined, but also that some of his own desires were illusory. He was deficient in self-knowledge because he confused his ideas with his feelings. Dorothea had naive ideas about marriage because her ideas were a product of her feelings and were unchecked by social knowledge. Casaubon's ideas about marriage, on the other hand, had no relation to the emotions he actually experienced; they were imbibed from traditional lore. He had read the classics and the literature of courtly love, and he assumed that his feelings would correspond to those described. He found, even in the early days of courtship, that for him the "stream of feeling" was "an exceedingly shallow rill," and "he concluded that the poets had much exaggerated the force of masculine passion" (Chap. VII).

Casaubon had no spontaneous feelings to give direction and intrinsic significance to his actions, and consequently his behavior was directed by and gauged to accommodate the expectations of society. He found himself leading a life of sterile formality: in religion, in authorship, and finally in marriage, "the sense of acquitting himself and acting with propriety [came to] predominate over any other satisfaction." One of his reasons for seeking a wife was that this was a thing which everyone did: ". . . it had occurred to him that he must not any longer defer his intention of matrimony. . . . he had always intended to acquit himself by marriage" (Chap. XXIX).

Casaubon's scholarly labors were divorced from life both in subject matter and in method. His learning stood like a screen between himself and the world; it served him in the stead of direct experience. He lived in a world of words, papers, and arguments which had little connection with any kind of reality. He was not concerned with truth, but with acquitting himself worthily. As we have seen, his overall method in his "Key to all Mythologies" was metaphysical and a priori. He treated his initial assumption "that all the mythical systems or erratic mythical fragments in the world were corruptions of a tradition originally revealed" (Chap. III) as a truth to which all evidence must conform. He sought logical consistency; there were no unyielding facts outside his own mind to which he must submit himself. Dorothea soon recognized that she could not find in him the theoretical guide and justification of life that she was seeking.

Casaubon was a lonely and unhappy man, and he looked to Dorothea to protect him from the pressures of the world. His nature did not have enough sensuous force "to thrill out of self-consciousness into passionate delight," but he was sharply aware of his own feelings and of the world's resistance to them. His preoccupation with self made his claims excessive. But while he made great claims for himself and expected the world to honor them, his actual progress was small, and his uncertainties about the outcome were great: "the difficulty of making his Key to all Mythologies unimpeachable weighed like lead upon his mind" (Chap. XXIX). His attitude became defensive and suspicious; he erected barriers between himself and the world out of fear that he would be seen and judged in his shivering nakedness. His uneasy feeling that he was not, in fact, what he was expected to be and what he wished to be flooded his consciousness with images of a scornful, unbelieving world which his pride could not bear. To confound his enemies, real and imaginary, by writing an immortal book became the sole purpose of his life. Everything was seen as related to it, either favorably or adversely, and the rest of the world was seen but dimly. He was given "to think that others were providentially made for him, and especially to consider them in the light of their fitness for the author of a 'Key to all Mythologies' " (Chap. X).

Casaubon sought a wife not only because he was bent upon fulfilling society's expectations that he would marry, but also because he hoped for relief from his loneliness and insecurity. Holding the traditional views about the submissiveness and intellectual inconsequence of women, he felt that a wife would be a buffer between himself and the unappreciative world. In talking to Dorothea "he presented all his performance and intention with the reflected confidence of the pedagogue, and rid himself for the time of that chilling ideal audience which crowded his laborious uncreative hours with the vaporous pressure of Tartarean shades" (Chap. X). Dorothea, he thought, exactly suited his needs: "Providence, in its kindness, had supplied him with the wife he needed. . . . Whether Providence had taken equal care of Miss Brooke in presenting her with Mr. Casaubon was an idea which could hardly occur to him" (Chap. XXIX). His vision blurred by traditional conceptions and by the pressure of his own needs, he failed to read aright the signs which Dorothea presented to him. He turned to her, much as she turned to him, for satisfactions which the resisting and threatening otherness of the world had failed to provide. He did not form an image of her from his own qualities, but from his preconceptions and desires. His egoism and insecurity craved a responsive, applauding world, and Dorothea was to supply it. She was to see him as he wished to be seen and as he wished to see himself; she was to clothe his unsightly nakedness with a warm, soft covering of faith, hiding himself from himself. Her admiring glance was to replace the searching, damning, or unresponsive looks of Carp, the archdeacon, and "the leading minds of Brasenose."

After his marriage, however, Casaubon discovered that Dorothea was not what he had imagined; she was full of wifely devotedness, but she made demands for herself, and her devotedness "was accompanied with a power of comparison by which himself and his doings were seen too luminously as a part of things in general" (Chap. XLII). Instead of regarding him with unmingled awe and admiration, she judged him. Instead of drowning out the self-distrustful voice of his secret consciousness with ardent faith and reassurance, she made it sound all the louder to his inward ear. Instead of "getting a soft fence against the cold, shadowy, unapplausive audience of his life," he had "only given it a more substantial presence." She "was not only his wife: she was a personification of that shallow world which surrounds the ill-appreciated author" (Chap. XX).

As a consequence, Casaubon shrank from Dorothea and closed his mind to her. Even when she had ceased to manifest disappointment in him and offered him love and compassion, he repulsed her; for her compassion was a form of judgment and implied that she knew him to be a failure. He could not conceive that she would not therefore reject and condemn him; "he distrusted her affection; and what loneliness is more lonely than distrust" (Chap. XLIV). To allow her near him was to open himself to the possibility of being further injured. Even the threat of imminent death did not break down his isolating pride; it only increased his fears and suspicions, and he responded to her compassionate presence with a chill glance.

Casaubon attempted to use his power as a husband in order to make Dorothea serve his purposes; he felt that her intellectual and moral qualities "were a peculiar possession for himself, and he wanted to engross them" (Chap. XLVIII). His jealousy of Will Ladislaw was not sexual. He knew that Will held him and his work in low esteem, and he was afraid of a future marriage between Dorothea and Will —or even of a close acquaintanceship—because it might interfere with his plan for having Dorothea complete his book. He could not bear the thought of his book being unfinished: "Even his religious faith wavered with his wavering trust in his own authorship, and the consolations of the Christian hope in immortality seemed to lean on the immortality of the still unwritten Key to all Mythologies" (Chap. XXIX).

In order to keep Will and Dorothea apart, Casaubon provided in his will that Dorothea should forfeit his entire estate if she married Ladislaw. Like Bulstrode and Featherstone, he attempted to manipulate others through the power of money. Like Featherstone, he too was defeated in the end. He was within a half-hour of gaining Dorothea's promise to complete his book when his plans were frustrated by death. When the terms of his will were made known, all he had striven for was undone. His faults might have been sanctified by compassion in Dorothea's memory, "but now her judgment, instead of being controlled by duteous devotion, was made active by the imbittering discovery that in her past union there had lurked the hidden alienation of secrecy and suspicion." Society, whose judgments pride had made his law, was revolted by the meanness of his action. His "exorbitant claims for himself had even blinded his scrupulous care for his own character and made him defeat his own pride by shocking men of ordinary honour" (Chap. L).

Dorothea, too, after her marriage, experienced severe disillusionment. Her self-reflexive image of Casaubon and her dream of a life of grand action and devotion were shattered. His work eventually revealed itself to her as "questionable riddle-guessing . . . instead of the fellowship in high knowledge which was to make life worthier" (Chap. XLVIII). She had a need for an immediacy of affection as well as a "yearning to know what was afar off and to be widely benignant"; but he regarded her manifestations of devotion "as rather crude and startling" (Chap. XX). Her affection was met by a frigidly correct formality which left her no room to imagine a response where there was none. Instead of finding a response from the world, Dorothea had enslaved herself to an alien being. Instead of finding an escape from the constrictions of her lot, she had committed herself to a lot which was narrower and more suffocating. All paths of escape were closed, even imaginary ones. Before her marriage the future had been rich with vague and glorious possibilities; now she was committed to binding ties. The hopes of the past were dead and the future could only be a continuation of the unhappy present.

The strangeness and incomprehensibility of Rome to Dorothea intensified her feelings of desolation. The reality into which she awakened was so alien to her experience and expectation that it seemed dream-like (while her self-reflecting dream world had seemed quite real); and the "stupendous fragmentariness" of Rome heightened this "dream-like strangeness of her bridal life." The alienness of her surroundings produced a sense of self-alienation; in her bewilderment "the oppressive masquerade of ages" made her own life seem "to become a masque with enigmatical costumes" (Chap. XX). When Dorothea returned to Lowick Manor from her honeymoon journey she found that the changes which had taken place within her since she was last in these surroundings made this once familiar world now seem alien. In her spiritual desolation, she saw the world in its naked prose, and it appeared dead, disenchanted; her experience of it was "a nightmare in which every object was withering and shrinking away from her." The blue-green boudoir, especially, seemed phantasmal in its disenchanted state:

> Her blooming full-pulsed youth stood there in a moral imprisonment which made itself one with the chill, colourless, narrowed landscape, with the shrunken furniture, the never-read books, and the ghostly stags in a pale fantastic world that seemed to be vanishing from the daylight. . . . The ideas and hopes which were living in her mind when she saw this room nearly three months before were present now only as memories. . . . Each remembered thing in the room was disenchanted, was deadened as an unlit transparency . . . (Chap. XXVIII).

Dorothea's experience of the world as dehumanized, a place where self can find neither echo nor room for expansion, is similar to the experiences which George Eliot recounts in her letter of June 4, 1848, to Sara Hennell and expresses in her poem "In a London Drawing-room."

The sense of unreality and self-annihilation which accompanied Dorothea's confrontation of the world's stark otherness was mitigated by the presence in the blue-green boudoir of a miniature of Casaubon's Aunt Julia (Will Ladislaw's grandmother). Dorothea's experience with Casaubon led her to enter empathically into the possible marital troubles of Aunt Julia, and she then imagined Aunt Julia as a being who would understand and sympathize with her. She came to feel that the miniature "had an ear for her and could see how she was looking at it." Her need for responsiveness and companionship led her to endow the miniature with life: "the colours deepened, the lips and chin seemed to get larger, the hair and eyes seemed to be sending out light, the face was masculine and beamed on her with that full gaze which tells her on whom it falls that she is too interesting for the slightest movement of her eyelid to pass unnoticed and uninterpreted" (Chap. XXVIII).

In a way, Dorothea was here repeating the pattern of her early relation to Casaubon; out of her need, she created a response where there was none. An important difference, however, is that in her relation with Aunt Julia Dorothea gave compassion as well as received it. Her own unhappy marriage had already extended the range of her vision and sympathy. The illusory relationship that she had with Aunt Julia was a prefiguration of her later relation with Will Ladislaw in which there was a real responsiveness on both sides, a genuine reciprocity. Just as Dorothea was drawn to Aunt Julia because she imagined her to be unhappy, so the misfortunes in Will's lot, some of which were related to Aunt Julia's troubles, "only gave something more of enthusiasm to her clinging thought" (Chap. LXXVII). Like Aunt Julia's, Will's hair and eyes seemed to send out light; and in his case, as in hers, Dorothea's great craving for sympathy led her somewhat to idealize the giver of it. The light was not all in Will.

Dorothea's disillusionment about Casaubon gradually led her to an understanding of him as he was for himself and of her relation to him as he conceived it. Through the intimate experience of marriage she began "to conceive with that distinctness which is no longer reflection but feeling—an idea wrought back to the directness of sense, like the solidity of objects—that he had an equivalent centre of self, whence the lights and shadows must always fall with a certain difference." When she began to sense his inner state there were stirrings in her "of a pitying tenderness fed by the realities of his lot and not by her own dreams" (Chap. XXI). Instead of rejecting her disappointing husband, as did Rosamond, Dorothea, moved to sympathy by her vision of his subjective state, strove to comfort him and to resign her claims for herself. He, however, would not trust her devotion. When she sensed that he had received bad news about his health, she went to share his sorrow with him, but he made no response to her sympathy. Her pity was overthrown in a fit of rebellious anger, but her vivid imagination of what must be his state of mind restored her resolution to help him as much as she could: "It cost her a litany of pictured sorrows and of silent cries that she might be the mercy for those sorrows—but the resolved submission did come. . . . She would never again expect anything else" (Chap. XLII). Her discontent, however, was not easily quelled; and it reached a climax on the day that Will Ladislaw came to Lowick Church and was ignored by Casaubon.

In order to be properly understood, Dorothea's relation with Will Ladislaw must be seen in the context of her moral and intellectual isolation and frustration. Will Ladislaw was the only person in all her experience with whom she could have communication. Their intimacy had its beginning in their conversations in Rome; Dorothea "felt an immense need of some one to speak to, and she had never before seen any one who seemed so quick and pliable, so likely to understand everything" (Chap. XXI). When Will appeared in the neighborhood of Lowick after her return, she welcomed his presence eagerly:

> Poor Dorothea before her marriage had never found much room in other minds for what she cared most to say; and she had not . . . enjoyed her husband's superior instruction so much as she had expected. . . . But Will Ladislaw always seemed to see more in what she said than she herself saw. . . . Hence the mere chance of seeing Will occasionally was like a lunette opened in the wall of her prison, giving her a glimpse of the sunny air. (Chap. XXXVII)

Will, she felt, "was a creature who entered into every one's feelings, and could take the pressure of their thought instead of urging his own with iron resistance" (Chap. L).

It is very important to recognize that her suffering in marriage altered the nature of Dorothea's needs. Before marriage she had longed chiefly for an epic life, while now she required most of all an affectionate and understanding response from another to mitigate the isolation and positive hardness of her lot. In Will alone she found a look which recognized and reflected her own humanity:

> . . . her soul thirsted to see him. How could it be otherwise? If a princess in the days of enchantment had seen a four-footed creature from among those which live in herds come to her once and again with a human gaze which rested upon her with choice and beseech-

ing, what would she think of in her journeying, what would she look for when the herds passed her? Surely for the gaze which had found her, and which she would know again. (Chap. LIV)

Again and again, in depicting the isolation of Lydgate and Dorothea, George Eliot showed them feeling the people around them to be creatures of another species, incapable of understanding and responding to their needs and aspirations. The relations between Lydgate and Dorothea and Dorothea and Ladislaw were so intense because they were oases of fellowship in an otherwise arid and alien world. In her loneliness and self-repression "it seemed fresh water at her thirsty lips to speak without fear to the one person whom she had found receptive" (Chap. XXVII). After Casaubon's death the knowledge of Will's love for her did much to comfort her, even though she did not see any probability that they could unite their lives: ". . . the first sense of loving and being loved excluded sorrow. It was as if some hard icy pressure had melted, and her consciousness had room to expand" (Chap. LXII).

Dorothea's greatest crisis and the climax of her moral development came when she was cast into despair by her loss of faith in Will when she found him apparently making love to Rosamond. She discovered the full force of her love for Will "in the unshrinking utterance of despair"; but Will was now "a detected illusion." Her personal disappointment did not, however, result in feelings of isolation and alienation, for she had been educated through her marital experience to an awareness of the interior lives of others. The feelings of her fellows continued to exist and to matter for her, whatever her own state might be. After her night of anguish, she found that "she had waked to a new condition." She resigned herself to her fate, she accepted her grief as "a lasting companion," and found that, thus liberated, her mind was flooded with thoughts of others. She had gone to see Rosamond as a result of her intimate conversation with Lydgate; she had hoped to help their marriage and had "set out with a longing to carry some clearness and comfort" into Rosamond's "beclouded youth." When she remembered this, she realized that the event of the preceding day did not involve her alone:

All the active thought with which she had before been representing to herself the trials of Lydgate's lot, and this young marriage union which, like her own, seemed to have its hidden as well as evident troubles—all this vivid sympathetic experience returned to her now as a power: it asserted itself as acquired knowledge asserts itself and will not let us see as we saw in the day of our ignorance. She said to her own irremediable grief that it should make her more helpful, instead of driving her back from effort. (Chap. LXXX)

Dorothea, like Maggie Tulliver, was motivated at her moment of great moral crisis by her past experience and by the vision and sympathy which that experience had nurtured in her. "What should I do," Dorothea asked herself, "how should I act now, this very day if I could clutch my own pain, and compel it to silence, and think of those three?" At this point she experienced a vivid sense of her solidarity with her fellow men; she transcended the limits of self and of her individual lot by identifying self with the world:

She opened her curtains and looked out toward the bit of road that lay in view, with fields beyond outside the entrance-gates. On the road there was a man with a bundle on his back and a woman carrying her baby; in the field she could see figures moving—perhaps the shepherd with his dog. Far off in the bending sky was the pearly light; and she felt the largeness of the world and the manifold wakings of men to labour and endurance. She was a part of that involuntary, palpitating life and could neither look out on it from her luxurious shelter as a mere spectator, nor hide her eyes in selfish complaining. (Chap. LXXX)

This is the thematic climax of *Middlemarch*. Dorothea had become aware of her participation in the life of the species; she had arrived at the Religion of Humanity. Her feelings of alienation were replaced by feelings of connection and commitment at the moment when her personal happiness seemed irrevocably lost. She felt her common nature with her fellows (no longer the herd) despite the absence of a special response to her individuality. She was joined to others by her sense of community in suffering, by her awareness of the common lot as one of labor and endurance. One of the major themes in *Middlemarch* is the power of outer conditions to shape the individual lot.

The climax of Dorothea's story emphasizes the importance of the individual's inner orientation to reality. Her sense of religious orientation in the cosmos rested, at this point, on a firm foundation; for it came from loving, not from being loved.

By going to Rosamond, Dorothea achieved an effective rescue of four lives—Rosamond's, Lydgate's, Will's, and her own (for she discovered that it was she whom Will loved). Her marriage to Will, which she made possible by her own unselfish action, gave Dorothea the satisfaction of love; but this (as the action is arranged) could come to her only after she had truly learned how to live for others.

Many critics have objected to Dorothea's relationship with Will. Henry James complained that Ladislaw "has not the concentrated fervor essential in the man chosen by so nobly strenuous a heroine"; and Leslie Stephen observed that Dorothea "hardly seems to grow wiser at the end; for . . . she takes up with a young gentleman who appears to have some good feeling, but is conspicuously unworthy of the affections of a Saint Theresa." Gerald Bullett feels that the reader must be "deeply dissatisfied with . . . her marriage . . . to a young man who though pleasant enough is palpably not worthy of her."[2] These critics fail to observe that Dorothea's nature and needs have changed as a result of her painful experience of alienation from the world and that she now finds in Ladislaw the love which mitigates the harshness of outward fatalities and makes a home in the world for the human spirit.

Ladislaw is accused by George Eliot's critics of being a dilettante and therefore unfit for the ardent Dorothea; but he is less of a dilettante than a rootless cosmopolitan—similar in many ways to Daniel Deronda. He is by no means devoid of talent and high aspirations, but, somewhat like Dorothea, he has found no channel for his energies; not because none exists, but because his social and family background has left him without a definite place in the world, without a set of positive commitments. *Middlemarch* deals repeatedly with the problem of the young person seeking to place himself in the world; this is one of the ways in which the stories of Dorothea, Ladislaw, Lydgate, Fred Vincy, and Farebrother are artistically interrelated. It is through each other that Dorothea and Will Ladislaw find a definite relation to the life around them.

Through her marriage to Will, Dorothea finds a worthy and satisfying life though certainly not the grand destiny of a St. Theresa. As Joan Bennett remarks, George Eliot's "theme is the adjustment of the aspiring individual to the inhibiting conditions of the actual social world. Marriage with Ladislaw is not meant to be the fulfillment of Dorothea's youthful dreams."[3] Moreover, Dorothea has changed—in George Eliot's opinion, for the better. Was not her vague ambition for some illimitable satisfaction somewhat immature, after all—the product of her youth and of the absence of a definite social commitment? To imagine her as being terribly unfulfilled in her marriage to Ladislaw is to see her as a static character who is the same at the end as she was in the beginning. Her second marriage may disappoint our hopes; but it should in no way violate our expectations if we have understood Dorothea's psychological development and the unalterable limitations imposed upon her by her social medium.

SELF AND SOCIETY

I

Man's moral life is largely determined, for George Eliot, by his relation to society. In society she saw a moral order which tends to mediate between the individual and the alien cosmos and to counteract the egoism which is man's inheritance (a kind of original sin) from his brute ancestors. The social experience of the race is impressed upon the individual by the force of impersonal tradition and by his inheritance of the acquired social characteristics of his progenitors. In his relations to society, hereditary and assumed, are defined the individual's duties and his identity. Those who cut themselves off from their society find, like Don Silva in *The Spanish Gypsy,* that

> on solitary souls, the universe
> Looks down inhospitable; the human heart
> Finds nowhere shelter but in human kind. (p. 312)

The moral lives of George Eliot's characters are deeply influenced by the extent to which they feel themselves to be part of a corporate existence which is greater than themselves. "Our dignity and rectitude," George Eliot wrote, "are proportioned to our sense of relationship with something great, admirable, pregnant with high possibilities, worthy of sacrifice, a continual inspiration to self-repression and discipline by the presentation of aims larger and more attractive than the securing of personal ease or prosperity."[1] The attitude of the individual—his readiness to identify himself with something larger than self—is extremely important; but much also depends upon the nobility of the people or group to which he belongs. As she has dramatized again and again in her fiction, not all communities provide moral sustenance; many are stultifying. Dorothea Brooke's life, for example, is marred by the absence of a medium for the ardent deeds which her Christian heritage has inspired her to perform. Dorothea's inspiration from the past can find no response in the incoherent and prosaic society of the present.

The moral grandeur of a people, or of a community of any kind, is dependent, for George Eliot, upon its conscious possession of an inspiring history and a body of living tradition:

> The eminence, the nobleness of a people, depends on its capability of being stirred by memories, and of striving for what we call spiritual ends—ends which consist not in immediate material possessions, but in the satisfaction of a great feeling that animates the collective body as with one soul. A people having the seed of worthiness in it must feel an answering thrill when it is adjured by the deaths of its heroes who died to preserve its national existence; when it is reminded of its small beginnings and gradual growth through past labours and struggles, such as are still demanded of it in order that the freedom and wellbeing thus inherited may be transmitted unimpaired to children and children's children; when an appeal against the permission of injustice is made to great precedents in its history and to the better genius breathing in its institutions. It is this living force of sentiment in common which makes a national consciousness.

Even if he is not dependent on it for his basic virtues, the individual cannot achieve the highest moral life without an identification with such a corporate body.

> An individual man, [George Eliot continued] to be harmoniously great, must belong to a nation of this order, if not in actual existence yet existing in the past, in memory, as a departed, invisible, beloved ideal, once a reality, and perhaps to be restored. A common humanity is not yet enough to feed the rich blood of various activity which

makes a complete man. The time is not come for cosmopolitanism to be highly virtuous, any more than for communism to suffice for social energy.

George Eliot's sympathy with the spirit of nationalism and with movements of religious enthusiasm stemmed from her conviction that they serve to inspire and to channel exalted moral sentiments. In "The Modern Hep! Hep! Hep!" she made her advocacy of nationalism explicit:

The tendency of things is towards the quicker or slower fusion of races. It is impossible to arrest this tendency: all we can do is to moderate its course so as to hinder it from degrading the moral status of societies by a too rapid effacement of those national traditions and customs which are the language of the national genius—the deep suckers of healthy sentiment. . . . And it is in this sense that the modern insistence on the idea of Nationalities has value.

Early in the essay she approved of the pride of Englishmen in their history, literature, language, and institutions, pointing to "the connection between the patriotic affection and every other affection which lifts us above emigrating rats and free-loving baboons." She hailed the unification of Italy and the liberation of Greece. Both of these movements were inspired, in large part by the people's awareness of their nation's past glory. The restored dignity of Italy was the result chiefly of "the divine gift of a memory which inspires the moments with a past, a present, and a future, and gives the sense of corporate existence that raises man above the otherwise more respectable and innocent brute." Englishmen are determined that, at whatever cost, their country shall never be subject to foreign domination "because there is a national life in our veins. . . . Because we too have our share . . . in that spirit of separateness which has not yet done its work in the education of mankind, which has created the varying genius of nations, and, like the Muses, is the offspring of memory."

George Eliot's object in "The Modern Hep! Hep! Hep!" is to defend the worth of Jewish separateness, to oppose the arguments of Jewish and non-Jewish assimilationists, and to advocate the establishment of a Jewish national homeland in Palestine. Here she utters in her own voice the sentiments and ideas she had given to Mordecai in *Daniel Deronda*. Mordecai, like Daniel's grandfather, advocates separateness with comunication not only for the sake of the Jews, but also for the sake of the world: "Each nation has its own work, and is a member of the world, enriched by the work of each" (*Daniel Deronda*, Chap. XLII). Mordecai's chief aim is to effect a regeneration in the moral life of world Jewry by reviving their consciousness of their glorious heritage and their sense of special destiny. He feels, as George Eliot states it in her essay, that "the organized memory of a national consciousness actually exists in the world-wide Jewish communities"; and he holds that this memory can become a living inspiration to the masses (as it has already become to him) only when the Jews are recognized by the world as a nationality, only when, in Palestine, the race has "an organic centre, a heart and brain to watch and guide and execute":

> The heritage of Israel is beating in the pulses of millions; it lives in their veins as a power without understanding, like the morning exultation of herds; it is the inborn half of memory, moving as in a dream among writings on the walls, which it sees dimly but cannot divide into speech. Let the torch of visible community be lit! Let the reason of Israel disclose itself in a great outward deed, and let there be another great migration, another choosing of Israel to be a nationality. (Chap. XLII)

According to George Eliot's theory, the formation of a Jewish state would provide the appropriate external stimulus to rouse into consciousness the innate unconscious tendencies which exist in all Jews as a result of their organic racial heritage. The national consciousness of the Jewish people, instead of being only a potentiality, "a power without understanding," would become actualized and articulated; and individual Jews would be morally elevated by their strong sense of connection with the life of their people.

In "The Modern Hep! Hep! Hep!" she asserted that the future of the Jewish race depends largely upon the guidance of men of heroic stature, "upon the hope that among its finer specimens there may arise some men of instruction and ardent public spirit, some new Ezras, some modern Maccabees." Clearly Mordecai, whose first name is

Ezra, is her version of such a man, a man who believes like Zarca in *The Spanish Gypsy* that

> Royal deeds
> May make long destinies for multitudes. (p. 156)

Zarca's aspirations and his philosophy of nationalism are similar to Mordecai's; but his task is far more difficult, for his race, the despised and outcast Zincali, have neither a homeland nor an inspiring and unifying heritage. They are

> wanderers whom no God took knowledge of
> To give them laws, to fight for them, or blight
> Another race to make them ampler room;
> Who have no Whence or Whither in their souls
> No dimmest lore of glorious ancestors
> To make a common hearth for piety. (p. 142)

As a reward for his aid in fighting the Spaniards, the Moors have promised Zarca a land in Africa for his people; and it is his ambition to rescue the Zincali from the

> dark and marshy wilderness
> Where life is nought but blind tenacity
> Of that which is. (pp. 160–61)

He envisions himself as another Moses, Christ, or Mohammed. In addition to establishing his people as a nation in the eyes of the world, he will, by his actions and his wisdom, create for them a heritage of heroism, loyalty, ceremony and law. The success of this venture which involves the entire future of the race depends, Zarca recognizes, upon two forces: upon his own possession of "the steadfast mind" and "the undivided will to seek the good" which

> compels the elements and wrings
> A human music from the indifferent air (p. 162);

and upon the strength of his people's racial feeling,

the mystic stirring of a common life
Which makes the many one. (p. 145)

Like Mordecai, Zarca is gifted with a nature in which passionate zeal
and a realistic vision of present conditions and future possibilities are
combined, and like Mordecai he believes firmly in the power of individual effort to shape the course of history when it works in harmony
with powerful natural forces. His purpose is thwarted by circumstance, for with his premature death at the hands of Don Silva his
cause is doomed to failure. Even so, his life has grand significance. He
tells Fedalma:

> The greatest gift the hero leaves his race
> Is to have been a hero. Say we fail!—
> We feed the high tradition of the world,
> And leave our spirit in our children's breasts. (pp. 162–63)

The group, cause, or tradition which is a source of inspiration and
an object of identification need not be national or racial in nature; it
may include such things as an evangelical movement in religion or a
revival of classical culture. Felix Holt identifies himself with the cause
of the workingmen; Lydgate is inspired by the heroes of medical research; Mr. Tryan, Dinah Morris, Rufus Lyon, Savonarola, and
Dorothea Brooke are religious enthusiasts. The moral vigor of these
characters and their lofty ideals are the result of their identification
with "something great, admirable, pregnant with high possibilities,
worthy of sacrifice." It is because movements of political, religious,
cultural, or social enthusiasm awaken the minds of men to a consciousness of wider relations and higher ideals than they had known before
that George Eliot was in sympathy with such movements. She depicted a number of such movements in her fiction.

In "Janet's Repentance" and in *Adam Bede* she dramatized the impact of the Evangelical movement upon individuals and communities.
She concluded, in "Janet's Repentance," that

> Evangelicism had brought into palpable existence and operation in
> Milby society that idea of duty, that recognition of something to be
> lived for beyond the mere satisfaction of self, which is to the moral

life what the addition of a great central ganglion is to animal life. No man can begin to mould himself on a faith or an idea without rising to a higher order of experience: a principle of subordination, of self-mastery, has been introduced into his nature; he is no longer a mere bundle of impressions, desires, and impulses. Whatever might be the weaknesses of the ladies who pruned the luxuries of their lace and ribbons, cut out garments for the poor, distributed tracts, quoted Scripture, and defined the true Gospel, they had learned this—that there was a divine work to be done in life, a rule of goodness higher than the opinion of their neighbors; and if the notion of a heaven in reserve for themselves was a little too prominent, yet the theory of fitness for that heaven consisted in purity of heart, in Christ-like compassion, in the subduing of selfish desires. . . . The first condition of human goodness is something to love; the second, something to reverence. And this latter precious gift was brought to Milby by Mr. Tryan and Evangelicism. (Chap. X)

Evangelicism is instrumental in the spiritual rescue of Janet Dempster, and it provides a noble and definite program of action for Mr. Tryan and Dinah Morris.

In *Felix Holt,* Rufus Lyon's social energies find their channel in Dissent. The sluggish life of Treby Magna was stirred not only by Dissent, which grew in force as the town became more industrialized, but also by the "political agitation" which "swept in a great current through the country" as a consequence of the Catholic Emancipation Bill and the Reform Bill: ". . . thus Treby Magna, which had lived quietly through the great earthquakes of the French Revolution and the Napoleonic wars, . . . began at last to know the higher pains of a dim political consciousness" (Chap. III). Felix Holt lives the higher life by devoting himself to the improvement, through education, of the lot of the workingmen. Despite his superior intelligence and training, he feels bound by heredity to the working class. His father, Felix contends, would have been better off if he had remained in his own class: "I mean to stick to the class I belong to." Felix will use his abilities not to advance himself, but to advance his fellows: "That's how the working men are left to foolish devices and keep worsening themselves: the best heads among them forsake their born comrades, and go in for a house with a high door-step and a brass knocker"

(Chap. V). Felix suffers severely from the entanglements of circumstance in the election day riot; but, on the whole, he is fortunate in that he lives in stirring times and his hereditary ties identify him with a cause that is "pregnant with high possibilities."

Moral life can be thwarted or stifled as well as inspired by society. In *The Mill on the Floss* George Eliot depicts the stultifying effects upon Tom and Maggie of the petty provincialism and commercialism of the society of St. Ogg's. George Eliot attributes the sordid, prosaic, wordly lives of the people of St. Ogg's to their unconsciousness of the rich legendary and historical traditions of their town, and to the absorption in their own small interests and customs which makes them oblivious of the great movements in thought, feeling, and action which are stirring the contemporary world. The oppressive feeling one gets while watching the vulgar lives of the Dodsons and Tullivers and their neighbors is comparable to that produced by a journey down the Rhone, observing "those ruined villages which stud the banks in certain parts of its course, telling how the swift river once rose, like an angry, destroying god, sweeping down the feeble generations whose breath is in their nostrils and making their dwellings a desolation." What a different feeling is aroused by the medieval ruins along the banks of the Rhine!

> That was a time of colour, when the sunlight fell on glancing steel and floating banners; a time of adventure and fierce struggle—nay, of living religious art and religious enthusiasm; for were not cathedrals built in those days, and did not great emperors leave their Western palaces to die before the infidel strongholds in the sacred East? Therefore it is that these Rhine castles thrill me with a sense of poetry: they belong to the grand historic life of humanity, and raise up for me the vision of an epoch. But these dead-tinted, hollow-eyed, angular skeletons of villages on the Rhone oppress me with the feeling that human life—very much of it—is a narrow, ugly, grovelling existence, which even calamity does not elevate, but rather tends to exhibit in all its bare vulgarity of conception; and I have a cruel conviction that the lives these ruins are the traces of, were part of a gross sum of obscure vitality, that will be swept into the same oblivion with the generation of ants and beavers. (Book IV, Chap. I)

The inhabitants of St. Ogg's, "whose breath is in their nostrils," will, like the Rhone villagers, be swallowed up by the river of time and change, leaving behind them no ruins to inspire future ages with a sense of the greatness and fierceness and mystery of life. Like that of ants and beavers, their existence will end when their breathing stops.

The town of St. Ogg's has a long and noble history. Its patron saint, Ogg the son of Beorl, was a poor boatman who ferried passengers across the river Floss. One stormy night a young woman carrying a child asked to be taken across the river. The boatmen, obvious progenitors of the town's present inhabitants, refused to ferry her, advising her to wait till morning; "so shalt thou be wise and not foolish. Still she went on to mourn and crave. But Ogg the son of Beorl came up and said, 'I will ferry thee across: it is enough that thy heart needs it.'" After Ogg had ferried her across the river, the woman became transfigured. She was the Virgin, and she blessed Ogg because he did "not question and wrangle with the heart's need, but was smitten with pity, and didst straightway relieve the same." Ogg's boat was to be safe in all storms; "and when the floods came, many were saved by reason of that blessing on the boat." When Ogg died "the boat loosed itself from its moorings, and was floated with the ebbing tide in great swiftness to the ocean, and was seen no more." But, as the legend goes, whenever there was a flood in aftertimes, Ogg and his boat appeared at eventide, "and the Blessed Virgin sat in the prow, shedding a light around as of the moon in its brightness, so that the rowers in the gathering darkness took heart and pulled anew" (Book I, Chap. XII).

The legend of St. Ogg exemplifies, of course, the divine power of living for others, of being guided by the heart's need of a fellow being rather than by our selfish interests and fears. Deeds such as Ogg's, and Romola's in the plague-stricken village, when they become a part of tradition, are a source of guidance, inspiration, and salvation to men of subsequent generations. Like the appearance of St. Ogg's boat, they encourage rowers on life's stormy seas to take heart and pull anew. But the modern inhabitants of St. Ogg's keep no festival in honor of their patron saint. Unlike the citizens of Romola's Florence, they have no sense of community in a shared heritage; their minds are not tinged with awe and devotion by the contemplation of an image of ideal goodness.

The town of St. Ogg's had been the scene of great passions and grand events in its day. Roman legions had camped near it, and "the long-haired sea-kings came up the river and looked with fierce eager eyes at the fatness of the land." Saxon hero-kings, Danes, and Norman conquerors had left their marks upon the town's history and architecture. It had known "the troubles of the civil wars, when it was a continual fighting place, where first Puritans thanked God for the blood of the Loyalists, and then Loyalists thanked God for the blood of the Puritans. Many honest citizens lost all their possessions for conscience' sake in those times, and went forth beggared from their native town." But the present inhabitants of the town are oblivious of their past:

> The mind of St. Ogg's did not look extensively before or after. It inherited a long past without thinking of it, and had no eyes for the spirits that walk the streets. Since the centuries when St. Ogg with his boat and the Virgin Mother at the prow had been seen on the wide water, so many memories had been left behind, and had gradually vanished like the receding hill-tops! And the present time was like the level plain where men lose their belief in volcanoes and earthquakes, thinking to-morrow will be as yesterday, and the giant forces that used to shake the earth are for ever laid to sleep. The days were gone when people could be greatly wrought upon by their faith, still less change it. . . . Protestantism sat at ease, unmindful of schisms, careless of proselytism: Dissent was an inheritance along with a superior pew and a business connection. . . . Public spirit was not held in high esteem at St. Ogg's, and men who busied themselves with political questions were regarded with some suspicion, as dangerous characters: they were usually persons who had little or no business of their own to manage, or, if they had, were likely enough to become insolvent. (Book I, Chap. XII)

The men and women of St. Ogg's appear to be "a kind of population out of keeping with the earth on which they live—with this rich plain where the great river flows for ever onward, and links the small pulse of the old English town with the beatings of the world's mighty heart" (Book IV, Chap. I).

Whatever moral life the townspeople of St. Ogg's do have may be attributed to the fact that their religion "consisted in revering whatever was customary and respectable." Still, there is little trace of religion in St. Ogg's; the moral notions of the townspeople, "though held with strong tenacity, seem to have no standard beyond hereditary custom." Their conceptions of duty and propriety are narrow in range and shallow in spirit. George Eliot felt that any tradition, any order, is better than none; but she recognized that tradition often sanctifies the most unenlightened practices, and that a narrow, clannish tradition like that of the Dodsons and Tullivers often encourages hardness and vindictiveness rather than love and compassion.

George Eliot is concerned with depicting the "oppressive narrowness" of the life of the "emmet-like" Dodsons and Tullivers chiefly that we may understand how it affected Tom and, especially, Maggie. Maggie suffers so from the drabness and harshness of her society because even though she is superior to them in intellect and culture, she is tied to her family and to St. Ogg's by the strongest fibers of her heart (Book IV, Chap. I). She is made to suffer in many ways. The misery brought into her life by her father's failure and illness goes unrelieved by the prosperous Dodson aunts because of their inbred notion of the impropriety of relieving misfortune that is caused by mistaken business practices. Aunt Glegg is appalled by the suggestion that "my money's to go and be squandered on them as have had the same chance as me, only they've been wicked and wasteful." The children must be humbled and made to "feel as they've got to suffer for their father's faults" (Book III, Chap. III). Maggie's relation with Philip Wakem, which could be so innocent and so beneficial to both of them, is forced to take the form of duplicity and then is broken off because of Mr. Tulliver's vengeful hatred of Lawyer Wakem. When Mr. Tulliver has Tom write a promise in the family Bible that he will make Wakem suffer if possible for the injury done to his father, Maggie exclaims: "O father . . . It's wicked to curse and bear malice" (Book III, Chap. IX). George Eliot explains that Mr. Tulliver's traditional beliefs had been subject to no highly modifying religious force from the larger life of society. After her misadventure with Stephen Guest, Maggie is persecuted unmercifully by the women of St. Ogg's who will not heed even Dr. Kenn's plea that Maggie be treated with justice and with Christian love. I have mentioned only a few of the more obvious ways in which Maggie's lot is shaped by the moral poverty of her social medium. Maggie is rescued, as we have seen, by the moral tradition of the past, which comes to her in the form of Thomas à Kempis' *The Imitation of Christ*.

George Eliot's most extensive explorations of the moral implications of the relations between self and society occur in *Daniel Deronda, The Spanish Gypsy,* and *Romola,* and I shall turn now to a close analysis of these works. In discussing them, however, I shall not limit myself exclusively to their treatment of self and society, for that would result in an undesirable distortion of emphasis. Daniel and Romola go through the three stages of moral development, and their interpersonal relations play an important role in their spiritual lives; these things cannot be ignored or slighted. It will be clear, however, that for Deronda, Romola, Fedalma, and Don Silva, the relation of self to society is at the very center of their moral experience.

II

Since Daniel Deronda was innately endowed with high intelligence and a sympathetic nature, his painful experience of the disparity between the inward and the outward quickly molded him into a superior moral being. The first turning point in his mental history occurred when, at the age of thirteen, he was struck by the idea that his "uncle," Sir Hugo Mallinger, might really be his father. Daniel had felt Sir Hugo to be "absolutely perfect." The fact "that Sir Hugo had always been a Whig made Tories and Radicals equally opponents of the truest and best"; Sir Hugo's various writings "were alike in having an unquestionable rightness by which other people's information could be tested." Deronda's new suspicion that Sir Hugo was wicked, that he had wronged him and perhaps his mother, brought a painful sense of disillusionment to the boy and unsettled many of his attitudes. His discovery of the imperfection of the object of his love and identification was, perhaps, "hardly a less revolutionary shock . . . than the threatened downfall of habitual beliefs which makes the world seem to totter for us in maturer life" (Chap. XVI).

Deronda's disillusionment, his anxious uncertainty about his parentage, and his "sense of an entailed disadvantage" (Chap. XVI) produced in him both an ardent sympathy for all fellow sufferers and a paralyzing reluctance to commit himself to a particular cause or to choose a definite path in life. His approach to external reality was objective in the extreme. Just before he saw Mirah preparing to drown herself, he "was forgetting everything else in a half-speculative, half-involuntary identification of himself with the objects he was looking at, thinking how far it might be possible habitually to shift his centre till his own personality would be no less outside him than the landscape" (Chap. XVII). His ability to see himself and the world from points of view other than his own was the source of much of his moral nobility, leading him to act generously in his relations with Hans Myerick, Mirah, Gwendolen, and Mordecai. The trouble was that he lacked a clearly defined point of view of his own; his approach to reality lacked an energizing bias.

Deronda is George Eliot's portrait of the disinherited intellectual. He was speculative and detached; he understood all the implications and complexities of things and often questioned "whether it were worth while to take part in the battle of the world." He recognized that a life of action often involves compromises with one's ideals, a blunting of one's moral sensibilities and passion for truth, and a futile struggle against uncontrollable circumstances. He could summon a "strong array of reasons . . . why he should not draw strongly at any thread in the hopelessly-entangled scheme of things" (Chap. XVII). He was strongly sympathetic, but the moral potency of his sympathy tended to be negated by its universality:

His early-wakened sensibility and reflectiveness had developed into a many-sided sympathy, which threatened to hinder any persistent course of action: as soon as he took up any antagonism, though only in thought, he seemed to himself like the Sabine warriors in the memorable story—with nothing to meet his spear but flesh of his flesh, and objects that he loved. His imagination had so wrought itself into the habit of seeing things as they probably appeared to others, that a strong partisanship, unless it were against an immediate oppression, had become an insincerity for him. His plenteous, flexible sympathy had ended by falling into one current with that reflective analysis which tends to neutralise sympathy. (Chap. XXXII)

Deronda's "sensibility to the half-known facts of his parentage" was one of the main causes of his moral and social paralysis; it "made him an excuse for lingering longer than others in a state of social neutrality. Other men, he inwardly said, had a more definite place and duties." He had been educated as an English gentleman, but he did not have the hereditary functions and loyalties of the gentleman. When he asked Sir Hugo, "What do you intend me to be, sir?" Sir Hugo replied, "Whatever your inclination leads you to, my boy" (Chap. XVI). Like Dorothea Brooke, he had no significant duties imposed upon him from without. His reluctance to pursue a specific goal was also partly a consequence of his insight and sympathy. He had no strong personal ambition; he was not competitive and could not bear the thought of causing others pain in order that he himself should succeed. His life took a more definite shape when his actions were guided by the responsibilties he felt in his relations with Mirah and Gwendolen; but these women became a part of his life quite accidentally, and his relation to them, important and satisfying as it was, did not constitute a vocation for him.

Daniel Deronda, with all his vision and sympathy and desire to live for others, was significantly limited as an active moral being. He was himself aware of his limitation, and he suffered from a deep unrest and sense of unfulfillment. He advised Gwendolen that she could overcome her discontent with her personal lot only by forsaking self and living for others: "The refuge you are needing from personal trouble," he told her, "is the higher, the religious life, which holds an enthusiasm for something more than our own appetites and vanities" (Chap. XXXVI). But he himself was in danger of being debarred from the higher, the religious life; not because he was preoccupied with self, but because he lacked an *enthusiasm* for something in particular. He was aware "that he had fallen into a meditative numbness and was gliding farther and farther from that life of practically energetic sentiment which he would have proclaimed (if he had been inclined to proclaim anything) to be the best life of all and for himself the only life worth living."[2] He longed to be "an organic part of social life, instead of roaming in it like a yearning disembodied spirit, stirred with a vague social passion, but without fixed local habitation to render fellowship real. To make a little difference for the better was what he was not contented to live without; but how make it?" (Chap. XXXII).

What Deronda lacked, of course, was an identification with a special social group, cause, or tradition. And lacking this, he lacked a center of self, a core of prejudices and cherished interests which would define his identity, establish his goals, and channel his thoughts, feelings and actions. His situation was similar to what George Eliot described in "The Modern Hep! Hep! Hep!" as the plight of the Jews who have lost their sense of Jewish identity and separateness and have not yet gained "that inward identification with the nationality immediately around them which might make some amends for their inherited privation." Deronda, like Will Ladislaw, suffered from the rootlessness of the cosmopolitan man. His life entered upon a new epoch when his mother, her rebellious spirit weakened by illness, fulfilled her duty to her father and to her race and told Daniel of his Jewish birth:

It was as if he had found an added soul in finding his ancestry—his judgment no longer wandering in mazes of impartial sympathy, but choosing, with that noble partiality which is man's best strength, the closer fellowship that makes sympathy practical—exchanging that bird's-eye reasonableness which soars to avoid preference and loses all sense of quality, for the generous reasonableness of drawing shoulder to shoulder with men of like inheritance. (Chap. LXIII)

Deronda had been prepared to feel the significance of his Jewishness by his experience with Mordecai. His relation with Mordecai had been shaped by his delicate sympathy and by his inherited racial consciousness. As we have seen, George Eliot believed that the experience of the race modifies organic structure, and that these modifications are transmitted biologically. In this way there have evolved special racial characteristics and a kind of racial unconscious. In each individual there are inherent unconscious tendencies which need only the appropriate external stimuli to bring them to conscious fruition. After Deronda discovered his parentage and learned that his grandfather, like Mordecai, was an ardent advocate of Jewish separateness, he had "a quivering imaginative sense of close relation to the grandfather who had been animated by strong impulses and beloved thoughts, which were now perhaps being roused from their slumber within himself" (Chap. LVI). He was thus organically predisposed to assume for himself the aspirations of Mordecai and of his grandfather to establish a Jewish homeland in Palestine.[3] He told Mordecai:

It is you who have given shape to what, I believe, was an inherited yearning—the effect of brooding, passionate thoughts in many ancestors—thoughts that seem to have been intensely present in my grandfather. Suppose the stolen offspring of some mountain tribe brought up in a city of the plain, or one with an inherited genius for painting, and born blind—the ancestral life would lie within them as a dim longing for unknown objects and sensations, and the spell-bound habit of their inherited frames would be like a cunningly-wrought musical instrument, never played on, but quivering throughout in uneasy mysterious moanings of its intricate structure that, under the right touch, gives music. Something like that, I think, has been my experience. Since I began to read and know, I have always longed for some ideal task, in which I might feel myself the heart and brain of a multitude —some social captainship, which would come to me as a duty, and not be striven for as a personal prize. You have raised the image of such a task for me—to bind our race together in spite of heresy. . . . I mean to try what can be done with that union—I mean to work in your spirit. Failure will not be ignoble, but it would be ignoble for me not to try. (Chap. LXIII)

The power of the racial consciousness and of the racial cause is manifested not only in Deronda's responsiveness to Mordecai when it appeared very unlikely that he was a Jew, but also in the inability of his mother to maintain her rebellion against her father and her race. His mother, the famous singer Alcharisi, had placed Daniel in the charge of Sir Hugo because she did not want to be burdened with the responsibility of caring for him and also because she wanted him to escape the stigma of being a Jew. Her father had hoped she would have a son who could carry out his Jewish ideas, but he died before Daniel was born, and Daniel's mother was then free to do as she wished. But Daniel's grandfather had his will in the end, for her memories of him acted as a law for Daniel's mother in her prolonged final illness. It was no wonder, remarked Deronda, that despite elaborate efforts at concealment the facts of his birth should have come to light:

The effects prepared by generations are likely to triumph over a contrivance which would bend them all to the satisfaction of self. Your will was strong, but my grandfather's trust which you accepted and did not fulfil—what you call his yoke—is the expression of something stronger, with deeper, farther-spreading roots, knit into the foundations of sacredness for all men. You renounced me—you still banish me—as a son. . . . But that stronger Something has determined that I shall be all the more the grandson whom also you willed to annihilate. (Chap. LIII)

Her Jewish heritage, which remained with her even though she had been baptized, was a force for good in Deronda's mother, compelling her to bend her selfish nature to a higher law.

In his relation to society Daniel Deronda is perhaps the most fortunate of George Eliot's characters. Once his initial problem of rootless cosmopolitanism is resolved by the discovery of his Jewish heritage, he has an opportunity to lead an epic life, like St. Theresa's—the kind of life that Dorothea so yearned for but could not find. There is no conflict in his lot between duty and inclination, or between public duty and private duty—though Gwendolen's dependence does cause him some uneasiness. The less fortunate Mordecai could not devote himself totally to his ideal goal because the villainy of his father imposed upon him the sacred duty of caring for his mother. George Eliot has given Deronda what she conceives to be the ideal human lot. For him, love and duty, personal affections and social sentiments, lie along the same path; his discovery of his Jewish identity at once gives him a heroic vocation and imperative duties and makes it possible for him to marry the woman he loves, Mirah. Once he discovers his true social identity all the elements of his life fall into place.

III

The harmony between the personal and the social, the individual and the general, which Daniel Deronda comes to experience is exceptional in George Eliot's world. His high fulfillment is approached by Felix Holt; though with Felix there was initially the threat of a conflict, for Felix was convinced that the pettiness of woman would force him to sacrifice the joys of marriage if he would be true to his social cause. Conflict rather than harmony is the rule in George Eliot's fiction—conflict between love and duty, private duty and public duty, duty and desire, self and society. The individual is often the victim of hereditary forces which are beyond his control. The higher life frequently requires the sacrifice of legitimate personal satisfactions, and family or community ties may frustrate self-fulfillment.

The story of Fedalma, like that of Deronda, turns upon the protagonist's discovery of her true social identity; but the issue in this case is tragic. Fedalma is called imperatively to a destiny perhaps grander than Deronda's. By helping Zarca to establish the Zincali as a nation, she will

> live a goddess, sanctifying oaths
> Enforcing right, and ruling consciences,
> By law deep-graven in exalting deeds,
> Through the long ages of her people's life. (p. 291)

The fulfillment of her great duty to the race and to her father requires, however, the renunciation of her love, Don Silva, and of all her dreams of woman's happiness. It is not only her own frustration which pains her; she is torn by the thought of Don Silva's suffering at her betrayal:

> his imagined sorrow is a fire
> That scorches me. (p. 151)

The hereditary conditions of her lot involve her in a conflict of irreconcilable duties; unlike Deronda, she is compelled to choose between the satisfaction of her affections and the fulfillment of her hereditary duties. Although she takes what George Eliot considers the best course by sacrificing the lower to the higher, her life is irrevocably maimed.

Fedalma is mastered by the larger life of the race which exists outside her in the form of her father, the king, and within her in the inherited racial tendencies which spring into conscious life and instinctive action when the appropriate stimuli are present. Even before Zarca's annunciation she had experienced a strong yearning for a freer, wider life than would be her lot as Don Silva's wife (p. 114).

Zarca claims that even if he had not made her conscious of her heritage, Fedalma would have suffered from a sense of incompleteness, of doubleness, if her "nature framed for noblest things" (p. 272) had been imprisoned by marriage to Don Silva. But she is doomed to imperfect fulfillment and internal conflict no matter what she does, for in embracing the role of the gypsy queen, she is forever thwarted as a woman.

Fedalma sees her duty and submits to it with heroic resignation and painful self-abnegation. Since she does not share Zarca's passionate confidence that his vision will come to pass, she is afraid to base her resolve on hope:

> Hopes have precarious life.
> They are oft blighted, withered, snapped sheer off
> In vigorous growth and turned to rottenness.
> But faithfulness can feed on suffering,
> And knows no disappointment. (p. 271)

As events turn out, Fedalma's sole resource is faithfulness, her sole satisfaction the performance of a duty felt to be sacred. Her fate, then, is the opposite of Daniel Deronda's; the revelation of her hereditary ties brings about her complete personal frustration, and circumstances further conspire to deny her a compensatory social fulfillment. Yet her life has dignity, purpose, and meaning; for she has imperative duties and a strong sentiment of loyalty.

Fedalma's situation, George Eliot wrote in her "Notes on 'The Spanish Gypsy' and Tragedy in General," is "a symbol of the part which is played in the general human lot by hereditary conditions in the largest sense and of the fact that what we call duty is entirely made up of such conditions." Tragedy lies in the "irreparable collision between the individual and the general. . . . It is the individual with whom we sympathize, and the general of which we recognize the irresistible power."[4] The tragic conflict in *The Spanish Gypsy* is between Fedalma's and Don Silva's love for each other and their hereditary ties which make the fulfillment of that love impossible.

The thwarting of their love, however, does not constitute the tragedy. Fedalma must make a great sacrifice, but it is for a noble

211

end. The tragedy is brought about by Don Silva's rebellion against the unalterable conditions of his lot, a rebellion which brings destruction to his people and a shattering remorse to him and which leads to the premature death of Zarca and renders Fedalma's self-sacrifice futile. The function of tragedy, George Eliot contended, is to show that the individual is compelled to give way to the general; "the tragedy consisting in the struggle involved, and often in the entirely calamitous issue in spite of a grand submission. Silva presents the tragedy of entire rebellion; Fedalma of a grand submission, which is rendered vain by the effects of Silva's rebellion. Zarca, the struggle for a great end, rendered vain by the surrounding conditions of life."[5] Don Silva is George Eliot's major study of the rebel against duty and heredity and of the consequences of such rebellion.

Don Silva's initial conflict is with his uncle, the Prior, who opposes his marriage to Fedalma because of Fedalma's unchristian blood. The Prior fears the effects of Don Silva's divided allegiance and warns that moral anarchy will result from a refusal to be guided by authority:

> What honour has a man with double bonds?
> Honour is shifting as the shadows are
> To souls that turn their passions into laws. (p. 81)

When Don Silva threatens defiance, the Prior portrays, quite accurately as it turns out, the moral anguish that awaits him if he rejects his hereditary ties.

Don Silva feels that love and reason are superior to hereditary bonds and prejudices. He rejects "custom, tradition, and old sanctities" (p. 211) as his lawgivers, arguing that his love for Fedalma "makes highest law, must be the voice of God" (p. 212). When Fedalma refuses to betray her people by returning to Bedmar with him and he resolves to become a member of Fedalma's tribe rather than to lose his love, he tells Zarca:

> I will elect my deeds, and be the liege
> Not of my birth, but of that good alone
> I have discerned and chosen. (p. 299)

During his solitary wait at the gypsy camp—while, unknown to him, Zarca is leading a surprise attack on Bedmar—Silva confronts the bare reality of his situation, and his "thwarted needs" make "loud insurgence" (p. 311). To strengthen his resolve and salve his inner torment, Silva falls back upon his rational perception of the absurdity of society and its values; he cultivates contempt for

> customs and bonds and laws
> Wherewith men make a better or a worse
> Like children playing on a barren mound
> Feigning a thing to strive for or avoid. (p. 311)

He calls upon thought

> To change all forms, dissolve all prejudice
> Of man's long heritage, and yield him up
> A crude fused world to fashion as he would. (p. 312)

He finds, however, that his whole being revolts against the dehumanized world conceived by thought alone. Without the inward and outward manifestations of society, without feeling and fellowship, institutions and traditions, duties and loyalties, the world is mysterious, alien, intolerable to the human spirit:

> He could not grasp Night's black blank mystery
> And wear it for a spiritual garb
> Creed-proof: he shuddered at its passionless touch.
> On solitary souls, the universe
> Looks down inhospitable; the human heart
> Finds nowhere shelter but in human kind.
> He yearned towards images that had breath in them,
> That sprang warm palpitant with memories
> From streets and altars, from ancestral homes
> Banners and trophies and the cherishing rays
> Of shame and honour in the eyes of man. (p. 312)

Now that he has renounced his people and his past, Fedalma alone makes his world human and habitable; and Silva defiantly regards her as his heaven, which it is worth any sacrifice to gain.

213

But Silva cannot in fact renounce his people and his past. The massive, cumulative effects of centuries of racial experience and of lifelong habits of thought and feeling triumph over the strongest rebellious resolve:

> All in vain
> He sought the outlaw's strength, and made a right
> Contemning that hereditary right
> Which held dim habitations in his frame,
> Mysterious haunts of echoes old and far,
> The voice divine of human loyalty. (p. 313)

Silva is tormented by visions of the faces, divine and human, which have always sanctified his life and from which, by his betrayal, he is cut off forever. His defiance is shattered when he finds that his desertion of his post has enabled Zarca to overcome Bedmar and has resulted in the deaths of his dearest comrades: "Silva had but rebelled—he was not free" (p. 340). When Zarca refuses to spare the Prior, Don Silva renounces his oath of brotherhood to the Zincali, asserts his identity as a Spanish Catholic knight, and, maddened by the Prior's death, stabs Zarca. This act severs him forever from Fedalma, making vain the treason he had committed for her sake. At their final parting, he tells Fedalma that, having resisted the temptation of suicide, he has determined to go to Rome to seek reinstatement as a knight so that he may serve Spain and rescue his name from infamy:

> I will not be perpetual rottenness
> Upon the Spaniard's air. (p. 371)

IV

Her father's teachings having kept Romola aloof from the political and religious life of Florence, her religion consisted in intense devotion to those to whom she was bound by ties of kinship and affection. When Tito's treachery rendered impossible the fulfillment of her functions as wife and daughter, life seemed to her to be devoid both of pleasure and of a duty which would give direction to effort and make endurance meaningful. She was saved from aimlessness and despair by the intervention of Savonarola, who awakened her dormant social consciousness and gave her a sense of relationship, as a Florentine woman, to "something great, admirable, pregnant with high possibilities, worthy of sacrifice."

Before she met Tito, Romola had known no joy, and she expected none. Her life with her blind, frustrated father was often wearisome and constricting, but she served willingly because of her intense feeling of devotion and sympathy. She displayed toward her father the "loving, pitying devotedness" and the "patient endurance of irksome tasks" from which Tito excused himself in his relation with Baldassare. Her perpetual self-denial, however, made her all the more responsive to the fulfillment which a relationship with Tito seemed to promise. With him she experienced a "sense of comradeship" which she had never known before. His attentions seemed "like a wreath of spring, dropped suddenly in Romola's young but wintry life" (Chap. VI). She thought for the first time that joy was possible for her, and she was eager to taste it. "I am very thirsty," she told him, "for a deep draught of joy—for a life all bright like you" (Chap. XVII).

As soon as she met Tito, Romola began to read the signs which he presented by the light of her heart's desires. She was, like Dorothea, quite naive about the world of men. She was sure that Tito would share her feelings about helping Bardo in his scholarship: "A girl of eighteen imagines the feelings behind the face that has moved her with its sympathetic youth, as easily as primitive people imagined the humours of the gods in fair weather: what is she to believe in, if not in this vision woven from within?" (Chap. VI). Romola attributed the nobleness of her own nature to Tito. She "only read her own thoughts" in the "dark depths" of his eyes, "as we read letters in happy dreams" (Chap. XVII). Impelled by desire and encouraged by all outward signs, she spun a web of illusions about him and dreamt enchanted dreams about the pagan pleasures of their future life together.

After their marriage, there grew between them a sense of alienation; for Tito was really afraid of intimacy with Romola. He was afraid of her intelligence and her judgment. His wearing of armor increased their alienation, and his sale of Bardo's library climaxed it:

"You are a treacherous man!" exclaimed Romola, who was now without illusions. When Romola lost her trust in Tito, she also lost "her belief in the happiness she had once thirsted for: it was a hateful, smiling, soft-handed thing, with a narrow, selfish heart." He had become so morally repulsive to her that she could not think of remaining with him.

The act of removing her betrothal ring, the symbol of her public union with Tito, brought Romola a presentiment "that there was something in human bonds which must prevent them from being broken with the breaking of illusions." Her "vague but arresting sense that she was somehow violently rending her life in two" is attributed by George Eliot to "that force of outward symbols by which our active life is knit together so as to make an inexorable external identity for us, not to be shaken by our wavering consciousness" (Chap. XXXVI). Much has been made of Feuerbach's influence upon George Eliot's conception of the marriage relation. Feuerbach wrote: "But marriage—we mean, of course, marriage as the free bond of love—is sacred in itself, by the very nature of the union which is therein effected. That alone is a religious marriage, which is a true marriage, which corresponds to the essence of marriage—or love." That marriage whose "bond . . . is merely an external restriction, not the voluntary, contented self-restriction of love . . . is not a true marriage, and therefore not a truly moral marriage."[6] Feuerbach's position, it is argued, led George Eliot to condone Lewes' leaving his legal wife and to regard her union with him as a true, thoroughly moral marriage. This may have been the case, but in *Romola* she suggests that marriage is not simply an inherently religious bond between two persons which draws its sanctity solely from the feelings of the partners. It is also a public fact, a social act, which irrevocably shapes the external or social identities of the partners and which is binding upon them because it is a public pledge of faithfulness. Romola came to feel that no matter what Tito did, she could never cease to be his wife. It is clear that George Eliot agreed with Savonarola's argument:

... you chose the bond; and in wilfully breaking it—I speak to you as a pagan, if the holy mystery of matrimony is not sacred to you—

you are breaking a pledge. Of what wrongs will you complain, my daughter, when you yourself are committing one of the greatest wrongs a woman and a citizen can be guilty of—withdrawing in secrecy and disguise from a pledge which you have given in the face of God and your fellow-men? Of what wrongs will you complain, when you yourself are breaking the simplest law that lies at the foundation of the trust which binds man to man—faithfulness to the spoken word? (Chap. XL)

Philosophically at least, George Eliot was no rebel against the basic laws of society. Without law, she felt, human existence would tremble towards chaos—as it does in the underworld of *Romola*. She recognized also, however—and the issue is most carefully posed in *Romola* —that in some cases rebellion, too, has its sacredness.

Romola, as we have seen, had a passionately held code of faithfulness which "made the religion of her life," but she had little awareness of her social identity and duties: she "had never yet bowed to any obligation apart from personal love and reverence; she had no keen sense of any other human relations." She felt that "there could be no law for her but the law of her affections" (Chap. XXXVI). With the death of her father and with Tito's deceitful sale of the library she was left without an object of strong affection; and hence she was without a sense of duty, value, or purpose. As she fled from Florence she felt herself, for the first time, "alone in the presence of the earth and sky, with no human presence interposing and making a law for her" (Chap. XL).

Her flight was stopped, however, by the interposition of Savonarola, who demanded that she return and fulfill her social duties as a wife and as a citizen of Florence. Men and women can choose their place and function in life, he argued, "no more than they can choose their birthplace or their father and mother. My daughter, you are fleeing from the presence of God into the wilderness." In leaving Florence, Savonarola argued, she was leaving "the only men and women in the world to whom" she owed "the debt of a fellow-citizen." Romola protested that she would never have quitted Florence "as long as there was any hope of my fulfilling a duty to my father there." Savonarola replied:

And do you own no tie but that of a child to her father in the flesh? Your life has been spent in blindness, my daughter. . . . doubtless you were taught how there were pagan women who felt what it was to live for the Republic; yet you have never felt that you, a Florentine woman, should live for Florence. If your own people are wearing a yoke, will you slip from under it, instead of struggling with them to lighten it? There is hunger and misery in our streets, yet you say, 'I care not; I have my own sorrows; I will go away.

Like Maggie if she had remained with Stephen, Romola would have no law but her own impulses and her life would be without sacredness. Daniel Deronda, with neither family ties nor certain social heritage, had suffered from too scattered and impartial a sympathy. Romola, highly endowed like him with intelligence and sympathy, suffered from too narrow an identification. "What!" exclaimed Savonarola, "you say your love for your father no longer tells you to stay in Florence? Then, since that tie is snapped, you are without a law, without religion: you are no better than a beast of the field when she is robbed of her young" (Chap. XL).

Savonarola, by the force of his disinterested concern for her as a fellow being and his passionate devotion to the great ends of human life, succeeded in awakening in Romola a consciousness of her duty to her native city and of her fellowship in suffering with all men. "The higher life," Savonarola proclaimed, "begins for us . . . when we renounce our own will to bow before a divine law." The higher life lies in the religion of the Cross. The stoic philosophy of her father had left her "without a share in the Divine life which quenches the sense of suffering Self in the ardours of an ever-growing love." The crucifix, on the other hand, presents "the image of a Supreme Offering, made by Supreme Love, because the need of man was great." Savonarola exhorted Romola to pattern her life after the great Christian symbol of self-sacrifice. Her own suffering, he contended, had endowed her with a new faculty for understanding and relieving the sorrows of others: "if there is a cry of anguish, you, my daughter, because you know the meaning of the cry, should be there to still it. My beloved daughter, sorrow has come to teach you a new worship: the sign of it [the crucifix] hangs before you" (Chap. XL).

Savonarola's influence over Romola was to a large degree personal —the effect of his fervent belief, his noble and beneficent bearing, and his ardent nature. In the years that followed, Romola felt, particularly in moments of weakness or great hardship, that her strength and her faith in the high purpose of life depended upon her belief not so much in Savonarola's teachings as in Savonarola himself. He was the highest that she knew; he was her God. At the end of the novel she honored him on the anniversary of his death by a private religious ceremony. When she temporarily lost her belief in his goodness and nobility of purpose, she experienced a despair far more profound than any she had known. But Savonarola was more than a great and good individual to her; he was the representative of Florence and of humanity. And it is because he awakened her consciousness of herself as a Florentine and as a fellow sufferer with all men that she could eventually have a sense of moral purpose without his direct inspiration.

Savonarola's teachings were clothed in the garb of theological doctrines that George Eliot felt to be as false as his moral conceptions were true. One of her primary aims in her "experiments in life" was, we know, to see "what gains from past revelations and discipline we must strive to keep hold of as something more sure than shifting theory" (*Letters,* VI, 216). Savonarola's teachings are tested by their efficacy for Romola. Romola never lost the antipathy towards dogma and superstition that her father's philosophy and her brother Dino's desertion of his filial duties had instilled in her; her response to Savonarola, therefore, was essentially that of an agnostic. Her experience, then, provides a key to that which is essentially human and hence of enduring value in Savonarola's vision of life. The following passage, describing her state of mind after her return to Florence, clearly establishes the relative significance for Romola of Savonarola's social and theological teachings and defines the importance in her moral experience of both her new social consciousness and her personal worship of Savonarola:

> Her enthusiasm was continually stirred to fresh vigour by the influence of Savonarola. . . . His special care for liberty and purity of government in Florence, with his constant reference of this immediate object to the wider end of a universal regeneration, had created in her

a new consciousness of the great drama of human existence in which her life was a part; and through her daily helpful contact with the less fortunate of her fellow-citizens this new consciousness became something stronger than a vague sentiment; it grew into a more and more definite motive of self-denying practice. She thought little about dogmas, and shrank from reflecting closely on the Frate's prophecies of the immediate scourge and closely-following regeneration. She had submitted her mind to his and had entered into communion with the Church, because in this way she had found an immediate satisfaction for moral needs which all the previous culture and experience of her life had left hungering. Fra Girolamo's voice had waked in her mind a reason for living, apart from personal enjoyment and personal affection; but it was a reason that seemed to need feeding with greater forces than she possessed within herself, and her submissive use of all offices of the Church was simply a watching and waiting if by any means fresh strength might come. . . .

Her trust in Savonarola's nature as greater than her own made a large part of the strength she had found. . . .

No soul is desolate as long as there is a human being for whom it can feel trust and reverence. Romola's trust in Savonarola was something like a rope suspended securely by her path, making her step elastic while she grasped it; if it were suddenly removed, no firmness of the ground she trod could save her from staggering, or perhaps from falling. (Chap. XLIV)

As a result of her participation in the stirring, crisis-ridden life of the community, Romola came to identify the idea of home "less with the house in the Via de' Bardi . . . than with the towered circuit of Florence, where there was hardly a turn of the streets at which she was not greeted with looks of appeal or of friendliness" (Chap. XLIII). She thought hardly at all of personal happiness and found that the ardor which she used to feel in personal relationships "had transformed itself into an enthusiasm of sympathy with the general life" (Chap. XLIV). The weariness attending her sometimes distasteful labors of mercy was transfigured because "the inspiring consciousness breathed into her by Savonarola's influence that her lot was vitally united with the general lot had exalted even the minor details of obligation into religion. She was marching with a great army; she was feeling the stress of a common life" (Chap. LVI).[7]

Romola chafed, nevertheless, under the yoke of her bond to Tito, whose villainy became more and more apparent to her. Her marriage tie took more and more the form of a "stifling predominance over her of a nature that she despised"; and she determined to seek a separation: "The law was sacred. Yes, but rebellion might be sacred too." Savonarola, she recognized, had faced the same problem in his defiance of the Pope—"the problem of where the sacredness of obedience ended and where the sacredness of rebellion began. To her, as to him, there had come one of those moments in life when the soul must dare to act on its own warrant, not only without external law to appeal to, but in the face of a law which is not unarmed with Divine lightnings—lightnings that may yet fall if the warrant has been false" (Chap. LVI). The execution of her godfather, Bernardo del Nero, who was a leader of the Medicians, turned her rebellion, however, in a new direction—against Savonarola.

After Bernardo's execution, Romola again fled from Florence, her perception of the hopeless entanglement of human affairs and her loss of faith in Savonarola having engendered a new rebellion and a new despair:

> The vision of any great purpose, any end of existence which could ennoble endurance and exalt the common deeds of a dusty life with divine ardours, was utterly eclipsed for her now by the sense of a confusion in human things which made all effort a mere dragging at tangled threads; all fellowship, either for resistance or advocacy, mere unfairness and exclusiveness.

She saw no reason to "care about wearing one badge more than another, or about being called her own name"; for "she despaired of finding any consistent duty belonging to that name." She bought a boat and allowed herself to glide out upon the waters, wishing to be freed from the burden of choice when all motive was bruised, to commit herself, sleeping, to destiny, which would either bring death or else new necessities that might rouse a new life in her" (Chap. LXI).

At this point Romola experienced a rebirth; the drifting boat "had been the gently lulling cradle of a new life" (Chap. LXVIII). She was roused from her aimlessness and despair by an urgent call upon her beneficent activity from a plague-stricken village. The appeal here was directly to her sympathy, a sympathy which had become habitual and unreflecting as a result of her years of devotion to her fellow citizens. But this experience was different from her labors of mercy in Florence in that she was now motivated solely by an immediate feeling of fellowship rather than partly by the ideas of duty and communal identity which she had derived from Savonarola: she "simply lived, with so energetic an impulse to share the life around her, to answer the call of need and do the work which cried aloud to be done, that the reasons for living, enduring, labouring, never took the form of argument" (Chap. LXIX).

The point here is not simply that Romola had escaped from intellectual perplexities by working hard and doing the nearest duty. For George Eliot, our sense of the meaning of life depends not upon thought but upon feeling. The meaning of life can be discussed philosophically, and arguments can be advanced for affirming or denying it. But ultimately arguments do not matter. Even the existence of God is meaningful, as Mill pointed out, only if we feel it to be; and many believers do not. The whole purpose of George Eliot's "experiments in life," after all, was to get hold of "something more sure than shifting theory" by seeing if the imagination could picture ideas being experienced.

When Romola returned to Florence and undertook the care of Tessa and Tito's children, her religious life depended no longer solely upon her identification with the social and political life of Florence. She had found the sanctity of life and a sense of religious orientation in the cosmos through the direct experience of living for others, not as members of her family or of her community, but as fellow human beings. By the end of the novel, then, she had come to participate in the life of the species; she had arrived at the Religion of Humanity. But she could not have arrived at what George Eliot considered to be the religion of the future without the moral discipline which was provided by Savanarola's Christianity and by her labors in the common cause of her fellow citizens. Her worship of the family, of the hero, and of the state were stages through which Romola had to go on her way to the religion of man.

MAN AND MAN

I

In George Eliot's fiction the individual's dignity and rectitude, his sense of the worth and purpose of life, and his feeling that the world contains a home for his spirit are derived not only from his relation to society, but also from his personal relationships. We remember Feuerbach's assertion that to the individual another human being "is the representative of the species, even though he is only one, for he supplies to me the want of many others, has for me a universal significance, is the deputy of mankind."[1] To those of George Eliot's people who generalize their experience in the terms of conventional religion, God's nature and his government of the universe often take their character from the behavior of loved ones, friends, and neighbors. A loss of faith in their fellow men leads to despair or, at the least, to scepticism about the divine love and pity.

Many of George Eliot's characters become aware of their connection with the general life of society or of the species through a personal relationship with someone who is stirred by religious or social passion and has a consciousness of the wider relations of things. Such a relation exists between Romola and Savonarola, Janet Dempster and Mr. Tryan, Esther Lyon and Felix Holt, and Gwendolen Harleth and Daniel Deronda. Romola, Janet, Esther, and Gwendolen are initiated into the higher life—or at least into a new and higher level of consciousness—by their veneration for and emulation of their mentors.

Silas Marner illustrates the way in which love for another being—in this case, for a child—can rescue one from loneliness and despair. Silas Marner's alienation from society and loss of faith in God, which had been produced by the perfidy of his best friend, were overcome by his love for the child Eppie and by the kindly ministrations of Dolly Winthrop. Because he wanted Eppie to be at no disadvantage in the society of Raveloe, Silas became interested in the practices, standards, and institutions of Raveloe life, and in time his surroundings and his own past self were no longer alien to him (Chap. XVI). George Eliot likens Eppie to a rescuing angel who has led Silas away from the city of destruction: "We see no white-winged angels now. But yet men are led away from threatening destruction: a hand is put into theirs, which leads them forth gently towards a calm bright land, so that they look no more backward; and the hand may be a little child's" (Chap. XIV). Silas feared that his reawakened sense of the divine goodness would be destroyed if he lost Eppie: "I might come to think I was forsaken again and lose the feeling that God was good to me" (Chap. XIX). When Eppie decided to stay with Silas rather than to live with Godfrey Cass, Silas told Dolly Winthrop, "I think I shall trusten till I die" (Chap. XXI).

When we go through the list of George Eliot's novels, we see that the rescue of man by man is a recurrent motif. Mr. Tryan rescues Janet Dempster. Dinah Morris rescues Hetty Sorrel from total isolation and despair, and she succors Lisbeth Bede and the Poysers. Bob Jakin rescues Maggie Tulliver, for Bob's act of kindness in giving her books puts Maggie into contact with the regenerating power of *The Imitation of Christ*. Bob Jakin is a modern counterpart of St. Ogg, who was rewarded for listening to the heart's need by being given a special power to rescue his fellows during times of storm and flood. Maggie's final act of heroism—which brings about her reconciliation with Tom—is her effort to rescue Tom and her mother from the flood waters. Mrs. Transome is succored by Esther Lyon, and Esther is saved from a life of pettiness and dissatisfaction by Felix Holt. Romola is rescued from a despairing lawlessness by Savonarola; and she, in turn, acts as an angel of mercy to her suffering fellow citizens, to the plague-stricken villagers, to Tessa, and to Tito's children.

Middlemarch is the scene of many rescues. Farebrother keeps Fred Vincy from falling prey once more to the vice of gambling and in doing so assures Fred's success with Mary Garth. Dorothea rescues Farebrother, Lydgate, Rosamond, and Will Ladislaw. Dorothea is distressed because Farebrother must play whist for money, and after Casaubon's death she gives him a living chiefly because of her "strong desire to rescue him from his chance-gotten money" (Chap. L). When Lydgate gets into serious trouble after the death of Raffles, Dorothea has an immediate desire to stand by him. "What do we live for," she asks Farebrother, "if it is not to make life less difficult to each other?" When Farebrother suggests that Lydgate's character may have become diseased, Dorothea replies that "it may be rescued and healed." Dorothea protests that "people glorify all sorts of bravery except the bravery they might show on behalf of their nearest neighbors" (Chap. LXXII). Her greatest act of rescue comes, of course, when, despite her pain and injured pride, she once again tries to effect a better understanding between Rosamond and Lydgate. George Eliot comments: "It is given to us sometimes even in our everyday life to witness the saving influence of a noble nature, the divine efficacy of rescue that may lie in a self-subduing act of fellowship" (Chap. LXXXII). In *Daniel Deronda* Daniel comes to the rescue, in varying ways, of Gwendolen, Hans Myerick, Mirah, and Mordecai.

George Eliot regarded society as a mediator between man and the hard, non-moral outward conditions of his existence; but the love whose function it is to mitigate the harsh fatalities of the human lot manifests itself most powerfully in the personal relations between men. Like Feuerbach, she felt that the highest, truest teaching of Christianity is that the love of man for man is divine, and that to love, pity, and suffer for one's fellows is to be a God to men.

The moral standards and the behavior of a George Eliot character are often shaped by the values of those whom he loves and esteems. My fellow man, wrote Feuerbach, is "my objective conscience; . . . he is my personified feeling of shame."[2] Fred Vincy's moral growth was to a large degree the product of his love for Mary Garth whose stand-

225

ards for conduct were far higher than his own. George Eliot felt that this kind of moral influence of one person upon another is not unusual: "Even much stronger mortals than Fred Vincy hold half their rectitude in the mind of the being they love best. 'The theatre of all my actions is fallen,' said an antique personage when his chief friend was dead; and they are fortunate who get a theatre where the audience demands their best" (Chap. XXIV).

Although many desire it, few can achieve the epic life of a St. Theresa, a Zarca, or, perhaps, a Daniel Deronda. The individual can, however, derive a sense of the worth and purpose of his life from his relations with those near to him. Each individual constitutes a major part of the environment of those who love and depend upon him, and to a large degree it is he who makes their world a heaven or a hell. George Eliot wrote to Emily Cross on the occasion of Emily's engagement:

> The future must always be in one sense dark, but with a deep love which enables us to be the light and bliss of another, we can never be without reason for saying 'I am glad that I have lived.' That is really the highest good of a wife—to be quite sure in the midst of the dimness and doubt which this difficult world surrounds us with, that there is one close to her whose life is every day the better for her. (*Letters,* VI, 116–17)

George Eliot regarded wedded love as one of the greatest blessings of human life. "What greater thing is there for two human souls," she wrote after Dinah agreed to marry Adam, "than to feel that they are joined for life—to strengthen each other in all labour, to rest on each other in all sorrow, to minister to each other in all pain, to be one with each other in the silent unspeakable memories at the moment of the last parting" (Chap. LIV)

George Eliot tried to awaken men to the great movements and multitudinous connections of social life, but to those whose impulse to grand action was thwarted by the absence of opportunity and the entanglements of circumstance she stressed the unquestionable significance of bringing good to those close around them. To Oscar Browning, for example, she wrote:

One must care for small immediate results as well as for great distant ones—and in my own mind nothing takes greater emphasis than the possibility of being certain that our own character and deeds make a few lives near to us better than they would have been without our presence in the world. Scepticism has less chance of creeping in here than in relation to larger results. (*Letters,* V, 76)

To Mrs. Charles Bray, she insisted that we must not try to ascertain the value of our life by asking whether the universe would have missed us; rather we must ask whether we have been a force for good in the lives of those whose fortunes and affections are bound up with our own.

I cannot quite agree [she wrote] that it is hard to see what has been the good of *your* life. It seems to me very clear that you have been a good of a kind that would have been sorely missed by those who have been nearest to you and also by some who are more distant. And it is this kind of good which must reconcile us to life—not any answer to the question, 'What would the universe have been without me?' The point one has to care for is, 'Are A B and C the better for me?' And there are several letters of the alphabet that could not have easily spared you in the past and that can still less spare you in the present. (*Letters,* VI, 319)

It is from the perspective suggested here that we must view Dorothea's fate. By the time she married Will, Dorothea knew that she would never find the grand life of which she had dreamed when she was courted by Mr. Casaubon; but she had learned also that life can be given a religious meaning and sanctification if we can respond to those opportunities for beneficence and rescue that come our way. In marrying Will, Dorothea at once satisfied the needs of her affections and entered upon "a life filled . . . with a beneficent activity which she had not the doubtful pains of discovering and marking out for herself" (*Middlemarch,* Finale). She gave Will wifely help in his political career and was, undoubtedly, an affectionate mother. George Eliot is not without a strong sense of the waste in Dorothea's lot, but it is clear that she regards Dorothea's as a worthy life—one whose influence upon the sum of human good is hidden but not unimportant.

A religiously significant life can be achieved by all, then, through their relations—"incalculably diffusive" in effect—with those immediately around them. This, of course, is what Romola discovered in the plague-stricken village after she had become disillusioned with the social and political causes of Savonarola: "If everything else is doubtful, this suffering that I can help is certain" (*Romola,* Chap. LXIX). Our life has unquestionable value and purpose, George Eliot felt, as long as our existence is a good to others.

Interpersonal relations play an important role in the moral lives of almost all of George Eliot's characters, and it would be profitable to analyze each of her novels as a structure of meaningful interactions between man and man. We cannot do this here, but we can get a quite good idea of the ethical and religious significance which she found in interpersonal relationships by examining closely two fairly typical examples—the Felix Holt–Esther Lyon and the Daniel Deronda–Gwendolen Harleth relationships. Critics have found these relationships to be equally unconvincing; but it will be apparent, I think, from the following discussion, how much more artistically subtle and psychologically sophisticated George Eliot had become by the time of *Daniel Deronda* in her handling of a very difficult subject. No critic has paid enough attention to the relationship of Daniel and Gwendolen to understand it; and this, I think, is one reason why the unity of the novel has not been properly appreciated.

Though my emphasis will be chiefly on the religious character of the two relationships, it will be apparent that Esther and Gwendolen move through the three stages of moral development, that they arrive at sympathy through experience and vision, and that they find through another individual a meaningful relation to society and to the species. We shall see that George Eliot's conception of interpersonal relations and of the Religion of Humanity is just as Feuerbachian in her last novel, *Daniel Deronda,* as it was in *Adam Bede.*

II

Esther Lyon was nurtured to vision and sympathy (rather too quickly to be artistically convincing) by her contact with the higher nature of Felix Holt. In her unregenerate state Esther was vain, petty, and self-satified. By nature she was like her mother, Annette Ledru, who told Rufus Lyon that she had never cared much about religious matters: *"J'aimais les fleurs, les bals, la musique, et mon mari qui était beau."* Her "native tendencies towards luxury, fastidiousness, and scorn of mock gentility" were strengthened by her experience as a governess in an aristocratic family. The early Esther was the direct forerunner of Rosamond Vincy and Gwendolen Harleth. When she came home to live with her father, Esther "seemed to herself to be surrounded with ignoble, uninteresting conditions, from which there was no issue." She measured the value of the life around her according to her own quite limited tastes and standards: "she had a little code of her own about scents and colours, textures and behaviour, by which she secretly condemned or sanctioned all things and persons. And she was well satisfied with herself for her fastidious taste, never doubting that hers was the highest standard" (Chap. VI). Her mind dwelt upon visions of a sudden change in fortune which would give her a life of luxury and gentility. She was oblivious of the needs and the natures of those around her, ruling the minister's house in Malthouse Yard with the strength that comes from a lack of vision and feeling.

At their first meeting Esther and Felix found themselves immediately in opposition. "A real fine-lady," she remarked to Felix, "does not wear clothes that flare in people's eyes, or use importunate scents, or make a noise as she moves: she is something refined and graceful, and charming, and never obstructive." "A fine lady," he replied, "is a squirrel-headed thing, with small airs, and small notions, about as applicable to the business of life as a pair of tweezers to the clearing of a forest." Esther thought that he was "very coarse and rude"; and he, wiser than Lydgate, recognized her to be the kind of woman who would ruin a man with a lofty purpose (Chap. V). As Felix became friendly with her father, it became clear to Esther that "instead of feeling any disadvantage on his own side, he held himself to be immeasurably her superior: and, what was worse, Esther had a secret consciousness that he was her superior" (Chap. X). But her self-complacency was not really shaken until the Sunday when Felix came expressly to show her the narrowness of her values.

Noticing that Esther was reading *Réné,* Felix attacked the attitude towards life which she obviously shared with the hero—"*'Est-ce ma faute, si je trouve partout les bornes, si ce qui est fini n'a pour moi aucune valeur?'*" He accused her of being discontented with the world "because you can't get just the small things that suit your pleasure, not because it's a world where myriads of men and women are ground by wrong and misery, and tainted with pollution." She was shocked out of her self-complacency and subjectivity into a perception of a new set of values in terms of which she had been found gravely wanting. She would not admit to herself that Felix's behavior was justifiable or that she was bending to any of his criticisms; but she had a desire, nevertheless, to bring her behavior into line with his standards. She found herself "obliged, in spite of herself, to think of Felix Holt—to imagine what he would like her to be, and what sort of views he took of life so as to make it seem valuable in the absence of all elegance, luxury, gaiety, or romance." She was beginnng to lose "the sense of superiority in an awakening need for reliance on one whose vision was wider, whose nature was purer and stronger than her own" (Chap. XV).

After that Sunday afternoon interview "which had shaken her mind to the very roots" (an effect which does not seem commensurate, somehow, with its cause), Esther did not see Felix again for some time; and while her resentment gradually diminished, there grew in her a strong desire to understand his philosophy of life better and to show him that she was not so petty as he thought her. When she took the initiative and went to see him at his home, she began to wish for him as a lover:

> . . . now she had known Felix, her conception of what a happy love must be had become like a dissolving view. . . . The favourite Byronic heroes were beginning to look something like last night's decorations seen in the sober dawn. So fast does a little leaven spread within us—*so incalculable is the effect of one personality on another.* Behind all Esther's thoughts, like an unacknowledged yet constraining presence, there was the sense, that if Felix Holt were to love her, her life would be exalted into something quite new—into a sort of difficult blessedness, such as one may imagine in beings who are conscious of pain-

fully growing into the possession of higher powers. (Chap. XXII; my italics)

Felix regarded their new relation as a friendship which could not be allowed to have much effect upon his life. George Eliot informs us, however, that he was gradually falling in love with Esther. When Esther claimed that she could imagine herself choosing hardship as the better lot, Felix was tempted to believe in her; but he could not take the chance. He had too clear a vision of the way in which his purposes could be frustrated by a wife with refined and petty tastes: "I am a man who am warned by visions. Those old stories of visions and dreams guiding men have their truth: we are saved by making the future present to ourselves." He hoped that Esther too would come to have visions of the future:

> Some charm or other may be flung about you—some of your atta-of-rose fascinations—and nothing but a good strong terrible vision will save you. And if it did save you, you might be that woman I was thinking of a little while ago when I looked at your face: the woman whose beauty makes a great task easier to men instead of turning them away from it. (Chap. XXVII)

Felix was prophetic: for Esther was subjected to the temptation of ease and refinement; she was saved, in part at least, by a strong terrible vision of the future; and she did become a fitting help-mate for noble endeavor.

Her experiences with Felix had a powerful influence upon Esther's reactions to the change in worldly fortune which followed the discovery that she had the legal title to the Transome estate. On the one hand, this discovery seemed to herald the fulfillment of her dreams of luxury, ease, and refinement, and these things had not entirely lost their appeal for her. On the other hand, she had come to imagine Felix Holt's probable reactions to everything she did, and she heard him warning her to "remember what I once said to you about a vision of consequences; take care where your fortune leads you" (Chap. XXXVIII).

Esther's visit to Transome Court completed her education; for it gave her an opportunity to see how limited were the life and the lover

she had always dreamed of. She could have desired no one more refined and gentlemanly than Harold Transome; yet she found herself
mentally protesting that there was a light in which Harold was vulgar
compared with Felix. Her admiration of Felix acted as a touchstone
by which she could discern the hollowness and egotism of Harold's
nature. Harold himself was uncomfortably aware of her power of
judgment: "It is terrible," comments George Eliot, "the keen bright
eye of a woman when it has once been turned with admiration on
what is severely true; but then, the severely true rarely comes within
its range of vision. Esther had had an unusual illumination" (Chap.
XLIII).

Esther found, too, that having had a vision of life's high purpose
she could not be content in the motiveless ease of her new surroundings. It seemed to her "nothing less than a fall and a degradation" to
choose a life so devoid of the high feeling and purpose she had known
through Felix. Her perception of the barrenness of Mrs. Transome's
existence urged her "towards the life where the draughts of joy sprang
from the unchanging fountains of reverence and devout love" (Chap.
L). Esther too came to see visions:

> With a terrible prescience which a multitude of impressions during her
> stay at Transome Court had contributed to form, she saw herself in a
> silken bondage that arrested all motive, and was nothing better than
> a well-cushioned despair. To be restless amidst ease, to be languid
> among all appliances for pleasure, was a possibility that seemed to
> haunt the rooms of this house. (Chap. XLIX)

Although it was not until considerably later that Esther finally chose
to cast her lot with Felix, the climax of their relation occurred on the
day of Felix' trial. Her weeks at Transome Court had brought "that
state of disenchantment belonging to the actual presence of things
which have long dwelt in the imagination with all the factitious
charms of arbitrary arrangement" (Chap. XLIV). As she waited to
see Felix in prison, she feared that he too would be disenchanted: "It
was what the dread of the pilgrim might be who has it whispered to
him that the holy places are a delusion, or that he will see them with
a soul unstirred and unbelieving." But he was just the same—"no,

something inexpressibly better, because of the distance and separation and the half-weary novelties, which made him like the return of morning." At the trial Esther was moved by her ardor to testify to the nobility of his character: "Her clear voice sounded as it might have done if she had been making a confession of faith." "In this, at least," comments George Eliot, "her woman's lot was perfect: that the man she loved was her hero; that her woman's passion and her reverence for rarest goodness rushed together in an undivided current" (Chap. XLVI).[3]

III

The opening of *Daniel Deronda* is a master stroke of artistry. It establishes striking images, symbols, and situations—Gwendolen gambling, Gwendolen kissing her image in the glass, Gwendolen coldly selling the necklace, and Gwendolen chastened by Deronda's measuring gaze and his return of the necklace—that become recurring motifs in the novel and that grow in meaning as the novel progresses. The loss of the family fortune which she heard of at Leubronn and the moral authority which she senses in Deronda were the two forces that most significantly shaped Gwendolen's character and her destiny. The opening chapters call forth an account of Gwendolen's past, for it is only by knowing her history that we can understand the attitude towards the world that issued on the one hand in her egoistic gambling and on the other in her extreme sensitivity to the personality of Deronda.

Gwendolen's coldness and egoism were partly the result of her root-less, pampered existence.[4] Men need, George Eliot felt, "a spot where the definiteness of early memories may be inwrought with affection." With her family Gwendolen roved from one foreign watering place or Parisian apartment to another, and her lack of objects of habitual affection left her without a sense of social duty and without a desire for the good of something other than herself. Her selfishness was partly the product of her mother's indulgence. She had always been the pet and pride of the household, waited on by everyone "as if she had been a princess in exile"; and "she naturally found it difficult to think her own pleasure less important than others made it" (Chap III). Her ascendency in her family was the result not only of "her potent charm and peculiar filial position," but also of her strong determination to have what was pleasant and her readiness to hurt others when they got in her way (Chap. IV).

In her unchecked egoism, Gwendolen came to have a firm conviction that so exceptional a person as herself must have an exceptional destiny. She tended to regard the world around her as a trap of dullness into which her great soul had fallen and from which she was to be rescued by a favorable combination of circumstances (befitting her high worth and importance in the scheme of things) and by the strong exertion of her own magically potent will. Her most difficult problem was finding, even in imagination, a destiny befitting her own grandeur. Her ambition was not at all like Dorothea Brooke's; she had no desire for significant achievement, no "parching thirst for perfection." She wanted always to be thought of as a lady; "her horizon was that of the genteel romance" (Chap. VI). She wanted the romance, power, and egoistic satisfaction of being "very much sued or hopelessly sighed for"; but she abhorred the limitations and responsibilities of marriage, which she regarded as "a dreary state, in which a woman could not do what she liked" (Chap. IV). She shuddered at the loss of personal freedom which marriage entailed, and she was violently repelled by the thought of love-making. Her "fierceness of maidenhood" involved more than sexual frigidity; or, rather, her sexual frigidity was an expression of her desire for mastery and her unwillingness to give anything of herself to another. George Eliot makes it rather clear that Gwendolen felt one of the most oppressive conditions of her marriage to be her sexual subjection to Grandcourt. Ironically, one of the things that had made Grandcourt tolerable to her as a lover was the absence of ardor and eagerness in his attentions. With no real knowledge of him whatever, she constructed an image of him after her own desires and saw no obstacle to her determination to make marriage "a state of greater freedom than her girlhood"; Gwendolen "conceived that after marriage she would most probably be able to manage him thoroughly" (Chap. XIII).

With all her egoism, and to some degree because of it, Gwendolen had an extreme sensitivity to the world and to people when they did not respond to or echo her own consciousness. She was prey to fits of timidity and terror, one of which came upon her when she was startled by the picture of the dead face during her acting of charades. George Eliot interpreted this susceptibility as a "spiritual dread," a "fountain of awe" which had not yet "found its way into connection with the religion taught her or with any human relations":

> Solitude in any wide scene impressed her with an undefined feeling of immeasurable existence aloof from her, in the midst of which she was helplessly incapable of asserting herself. The little astronomy taught her at school used sometimes to set her imagination at work in a way that made her tremble: but always when some one joined her she recovered her indifference to the vastness in which she seemed an exile; she found again her usual world in which her will was of some avail. . . . With human ears and eyes about her, she had always hitherto recovered her confidence, and felt the possibility of winning empire. (Chap. VI)

Gwendolen's armor of egoism had its weakness; it was out of her susceptibility to spiritual dread and her sensitivity to the opinions of others that her moral consciousness was to develop. This helps us a good deal to understand why Deronda's measuring gaze had such a profound effect on her.

When she returned from Leubronn to Offendene her egoism was somewhat chastened:

> Gwendolyn's belief in her star, so to speak, had some bruises. . . . for the first time the conditions of this world seemed to her like a hurrying roaring crowd in which she had got astray, no more cared for and protected than a myriad of other girls, in spite of its being a peculiar hardship to her. (Chap. XXI)

She had lost some of her sense of power over the course of things, but she still looked at the world from a thoroughly subjective point of view and felt that life was conspiring against her, that she was receiving far less than her due. Her first thorough shock out of subjectivity came from Herr Klesmer's discouragement of her hope for pre-eminence as a professional singer and actress: "For the first time since her consciousness began, she was having a vision of herself on the common level."

Gwendolen could not accept the hard necessities of her new lot; and her rebellion at the disparity between "what she might have expected in her lot and what it was actually to be" threw her into a "sick motivelessness": "She had a world-nausea upon her, and saw no reason all through her life why she should wish to live." Happiness for her had always been associated with "personal pre-eminence and *éclat*" and when these things were denied her she took "life to be hardly worth the having" (Chap. XXIV). To Gwendolen in this condition the renewal of Grandcourt's attentions presented a prospect which, despite its taint, was irresistibly alluring. Grandcourt, finding much piquancy in the obvious reluctance of the destitute girl to accept so brilliant a match, "enjoyed thinking of her as his future wife, whose pride and spirit were suited to command every one but himself. . . . He meant to be master of a woman who would have liked to master him . . ." In Grandcourt the wilful Gwendolen had met more than her match. Her will, moreover, was to some extent paralyzed by the conscious guilt that she incurred in deliberately injuring Mrs. Glasher; and she experienced a dread of punishment which gave her a new sensitivity to moral issues and introduced her to a new phase of moral development. Her self-complacency was permanently shattered. She had been "accustomed to think herself blameless" and "other persons only" as faulty (Chap. XXVIII); but now "the struggle of mind attending a conscious error had wakened something like a new soul" in her (Chap. XXIX).

Gwendolen's vague feelings of guilt were given a positive shape by her second contact with Daniel Deronda. When she met him at Diplow shortly before her marriage, Deronda's "gravely penetrating" look (the kind of expression "which threatens to affect opinion—as if one's standard were somehow wrong") compelled her to an interest in what Deronda thought of her, her marriage to Grandcourt, and life in general (Chap. XXIX). The story that Deronda was Sir Hugo Mallinger's illegitimate son had special significance for her; for Grandcourt would eventually come into possession of Sir Hugo's estates, estates that might rightfully have been Deronda's inheritance. Deronda became, along with Mrs. Glasher and her four children, one of those who had been excluded from his rights by the unfairness of another.

When Deronda saw Gwendolen at the Abbey after her marriage, it seemed to him, from her behavior to the company, that there was "at work within her the same demonic force that had possessed her when she took him in her resolute glance and turned away a loser from the gaming-table" (Chap. XXXV). He inferred, correctly, that her life with Grandcourt had proven painful beyond her expectations, and he was moved to pity at the sight of her inner struggles. With Gwendolen's reading of Mrs. Glasher's letter "had begun her husband's empire of fear" (Chap. XXXV). She found herself very shortly after her marriage living in constant dread of a calamitous visitation of nemesis and in complete subjection to the imperious will of a man towards whom she had an overpowering moral (and we may guess physical) repulsion.

Gwendolen concentrated her energies upon keeping up appearances before the world, upon keeping her nerve and losing strikingly. But she had no desire to impress Deronda with her coolness; she sought, rather, to discover and live up to his standards and to escape from her moral impasse through his guidance: ". . . in some mysterious way he was becoming a part of her conscience, as one woman whose nature is an object of reverential belief may become a new conscience to a man." She wished that Deronda could know everything about her without her telling him. She wished Deronda to have the omniscience of God.

> Without the aid of sacred ceremony or costume her feelings had turned this man, only a few years older than herself, into a priest. . . . Young reverence for one who is also young is the most coercive of all: there is the same level of temptation, and the higher motive is believed in as a fuller force—not suspected to be a mere residue from weary experience. (Chap. XXXV)

In fact Gwendolen's wish that Deronda should understand her situation and feelings without her telling him was realized. Deronda had no supernatural omniscience; but after he heard the story of Mrs. Glasher he was able to reconstruct Gwendolen's plight. His understanding and sympathy prepared the way for a free discussion with Gwendolen of her problems.

During their interview on New Year's Eve, Gwendolen confessed to Deronda that she had made her gain out of another's loss in a way far worse than playing roulette; and she asked him what he would do if like her he felt wrong and miserable and full of dread. He advised her to try to care for something besides self; and Gwendolen, revealing her new capacity for self-judgment, replied: "You mean that I am selfish and ignorant." He answered firmly, "You will not go on being selfish and ignorant"; and he saw a change come over her face which indicated "the subsidence of self-assertion" (Chap. XXXVI).

Another interview took place when, on the last day of her stay at the Abbey, Gwendolen found Daniel alone in the library, in an appropriately religious atmosphere. What most concerned Gwendolen was the tendency towards violence which she felt in herself; it is possible that she had already had murderous impulses towards Grandcourt. Deronda hoped that she could make her fear a safeguard: "It is like quickness of hearing. It may make consequences passionately present to you. Try to take hold of your sensibility, and use it as if it were a faculty, like vision." But there was a depth and a precipitancy of passion in Gwendolen which could not be curbed by admonition and advice: "Yes, I know; I understand what you mean. . . . But if feelings rose—there are some feelings—hatred and anger—how can I be good when they keep rising. And if there came a moment when I felt stifled and could bear it no longer—" (Chap. XXXVI).

The nature of their relationship at this point underwent a profound alteration, Deronda becoming to Gwendolen what the suffering Christ is to the devout Christian. When he discerned that his advice "was thrown into the pallid distance of mere thought before the outburst of her habitual emotion," he felt "as if he saw her drowning while his limbs were bound" (Chap. XXXVI); and his face revealed the suffering which came from his profound sympathy. "The pained compassion" which Gwendolen saw in his features "affected her with a compunction unlike any she had felt before"; and in her distress at grieving him she promised Deronda that she would try, that his effort in her behalf would not be in vain. After this, one of her chief motivations in suppressing her destructive impulses was her knowledge of the suffering which she could cause him.

Gwendolen's misery and her violent urge to escape from the constricting power of her husband reached a new intensity during the Grandcourts' Mediterranean cruise. Her mind teemed with images of the possible ways in which her desire for Grandcourt's death might be realized. Her temptation, however, had its corresponding dread, the result of her past remorse for wrongdoing. She was also restrained by the fact that "she had learned to see all her acts through the impression they would make on Deronda"; and she could imagine no escape from his judgment, for "he seemed to her a terrible-browed angel from whom she could not think of concealing any deed so as to win an ignorant regard." It was only because of Deronda that she did not experience utter despair: "the possible remedies that lay in his mind, *nay, the remedy that lay in her feeling for him, made her only hope*" (Chap. LIV; my italics).

After Grandcourt's death, Gwendolen felt a compelling need to confess her most secret desires to Deronda: "I will tell you everything as God knows it. I will tell you . . . the exact truth. What should I do else?" As Deronda listened he experienced "one of those moments when the very anguish of passionate pity makes us ready to choose that we will know pleasure no more, and live only for the stricken and afflicted." Gwendolen, seeing his suffering on her account, was once more "pierced, as she had been by his face of sorrow at the Abbey, with a compunction less egoistic than that which urged her to confess, and she said, in a tone of loving regret—'I make you unhappy' " (Chap. LVI).

Gwendolen found in Deronda not only sympathy but also forgiving pity. When he looked at her fully for the first time after she told him that she was a guilty woman, his "full glance in its intense mournfulness seemed to say, 'I know it, but I shall all the less forsake you.' " In her case, he felt, the will to evil had led to a remorse which was "the precious sign of a recoverable nature" (Chap. LVI). "I believe," he told her, "that you may become worthier than you have ever yet been—worthy to lead a life that may be a blessing." She could not believe in a possible goodness in herself, however, unless she was sustained by a sense of his presence: "I will bear any penance. I will lead any life you tell me. But you must not forsake me. You must be near." He assured her that he could never have any impulse to forsake her; but when he left the room "she sank to her knees, in hysterical crying. The distance between them was too great. She was a banished soul—beholding a possible life which she had sinned herself away from" (Chap. LVII). Clearly, Deronda was for Gwendolen a combination of the suffering, forgiving Christ—the God who is love—and God the lawgiver and judge, from whom the sinner inevitably suffers a sense of alienation.[5]

When he next saw her, at Sir Hugo's home in London, he told her that her sorrow had not spoiled her life; rather it had prepared her for a higher existence: "You can, you will, be among the best of women, such as make others glad they were born." His words "were like the touch of a miraculous hand to Gwendolen," filling her with a strength "that seemed the beginning of a new existence": "So potent in us is the infused action of another soul, before which we bow in complete love" (Chap. LXV). But to Gwendolen the new existence seemed inseparable from Deronda's direct inspiration. Her greatest trial came when she learned of his love for Mirah and his plan, now that he had discovered his Jewish identity, to travel to the East in order to labor for the fulfillment of Mordecai's dream of a Jewish state.

Gwendolen's reliance on Deronda "had become to her imagination like the firmness of the earth, the only condition of her walking." On the first shock of hearing of his plans she felt bewildered and forsaken:

> There comes a terrible moment to many souls when the great movements of the world, the larger destinies of mankind . . . enter like an earthquake into their own lives. . . . Then it is that the submission of the soul to the Highest is tested . . . and a religion shows itself which is something else than a private consolation.
>
> That was the sort of crisis which was at this moment beginning in Gwendolen's small life: she was for the first time feeling the pressure of a vast mysterious movement. . . . here had come a shock which went deeper than personal jealousy—something spiritual and vaguely tremendous that thrust her away, and yet quelled all anger into self-humiliation. (Chap. LXIX)

Gwendolen could not rebel against the larger claims which took Deronda away from her, and her discovery of the great world which lay
aloof from herself was the beginning of her ultimate integration of
self into the world. But her immediate feeling was nevertheless one
of desolation: "I said I should be forsaken. I have been a cruel woman.
And I am forsaken." She was roused once more by Deronda's suffering: "You have been very good to me. I have deserved nothing. . . .
Don't let me be harm to *you*. It shall be the better for me—" When
he left she fell into fits of hysterical weeping, but finally fell asleep;
and when she woke in the morning light she turned to comfort her
mother who had sat by her bed all night: "Don't be unhappy. I shall
live. I shall be better" (Chap. LXIX).

It seems, at the end of the novel, that though she has yet a long,
painful process to undergo, Gwendolen will ultimately become one of
those women who make others glad that they were born. "Would her
remorse have maintained its power within her," asks George Eliot,

if it had not been for that outer conscience which was made for her
by Deronda? It is hard to say how much we could forgive ourselves
if we were secure from judgment by another whose opinion is the
breathing-medium of all our joy—who brings to us with close pressure and immediate sequence that judgment of the Invisible and Universal which self-flattery and the world's tolerance would easily melt
and disperse. In this way our brother may be in the stead of God to
us, and his opinion which has pierced even to the joints and marrow,
may be our virtue in the making. That mission of Deronda to Gwendolen had begun with what she had felt to be his judgment of her at
the gaming-table. He might easily have spoiled it:—much of our lives
is spent in marring our own influence and turning others' belief in us
into a widely concluding unbelief which they call knowledge of the
world, while it is really disappointment in you or me. Deronda had
not spoiled his mission. (Chap. LXIV)

THE RECONCILIATION OF REALISM AND MORALISM

We are now, I think, in a position to see clearly the outcome of George Eliot's quest for values in a Godless universe—the quest in which she employed her novels as experiments in life. There are two orders—the cosmic and the moral—and we approach them in two ways, objectively and subjectively. Each order must be viewed with the proper combination of objectivity and subjectivity if we are to have both truth and value. George Eliot rejected the subjective approach as a means of arriving at truth about the nature of the world, but she felt it to be the only way of comprehending the significance of human values, which have their origin, after all, in personal consciousness. But even when we deal with values, objectivity is important, for if we are to see values as having an external sanction, an existence apart from our own feelings, we must be able to relate to other men objectively, to see them as subjective objects, as they are for themselves as well as for us.

The cosmic order must be viewed objectively, scientifically, if we are to have a knowledge of it which enables us to adapt ourselves to it and it to our purposes. When the cosmic order is seen in an entirely subjective way—from the point of view of religion or metaphysics—the world is not seen truly, and the mitigation of human ills through intelligent control of nature is impossible. When man projects his own consciousness into the cosmic order, making it in this way a moral order, the result is morality without truth—illusory morality, which often embodies pernicious attitudes.

On the other hand, a completely objective view of the cosmic order, although it yields truth, provides no morality, no sense of purpose. Without objectivity there is no truth, but without subjectivity there is no value. Science is amoral, impersonal; it seeks to know the relations which objects have to each other, and in order to do this it must deliberately suppress the subjective principle, as far as possible, and ignore the effects which external conditions have upon human satisfactions. When external objects are seen only as they are related to each other, and not as they are related to the needs of the heart, they have no human meaning. Science presents an indifferent, unhuman world.

When the cosmic order is seen from a purely subjective point of view, it is a comfortable home for the human spirit. Since the subjective principle is found to be the innermost essence of reality, the whole cosmos evidences the importance of man and sanctions his thoughts, feelings, and institutions. The course of nature is governed by perfect wisdom and perfect love. The objective point of view convinces us, however, that man's desire for absolute, immediate power over the course of things can never be fulfilled. Man and the cosmos are not in harmony; there is a disparity between the inward and the outward which can never be eliminated. The cosmos becomes, for the human spirit, an alien place, devoid of meaning and love.

Objective knowledge of the cosmic order disappoints many of our hopes, but it also gives us a measure of security and allays a number of our fears. It gives us a real rather than an imagined power over the course of things. Knowledge mediates between man and the cosmos by bringing the objective within the realm of the subjective. Nothing is more alien than that which the mind cannot comprehend. To understand is, in a sense, to possess, to humanize. The cosmos is indifferent to man, but through knowledge man can envisage the cosmos and create within it a world of his own.

The cosmic order, no matter how it is viewed, cannot provide a true source or sanction of human values. Although an objective knowledge of the cosmic order enables us to serve moral ends by mitigating the painful disparity between the inward and the outward, only human feeling can determine the ends which this knowledge should be used to serve. But it is futile to *begin* our search for the moral implications of the cosmic order by addressing it from a predominantly personal point of view; for then, instead of relating to the world, we relate only to our own subjectivity hypostatized into an object.

With respect to the cosmic order, George Eliot reconciles truth and value, realism and moralism, by combining the objective and the subjective approaches to reality. Her procedure is to view the cosmos first objectively, as it is presented by science, and then, without losing sight of its true nature, to seek its moral implications by regarding it from the subjective point of view, as it affects human destiny. To be both objectively true and morally valid, doctrines founded upon the moral implications of the order of things must be both scientifically verifiable and psychologically meaningful. If a moral doctrine is based upon a mistaken conception of the external order, that doctrine is false no matter how much satisfaction it gives or how strongly we feel it to be true. If a doctrine is not corroborated by our subjective experience, that doctrine, whatever its scientific accuracy may be, is simply meaningless.

We have seen that when man views the cosmic order in a completely subjective manner he makes it into an illusory moral order. On the other hand, when the human order is viewed objectively, from an external, impersonal point of view, moral values appear to be illusory. If we regard man, either the individual or the species, in terms of cosmic space and cosmic time, he is reduced to utter insignificance. When the individual sees himself in this way, he says, like Tolstoy's Konstantin Levin, "In infinite time, in infinite matter, in infinite space, is formed a bubble-organism, and that bubble lasts a while and bursts, and that bubble is me."[1] In a letter to Mrs. Charles Bray, George Eliot spoke of the individual consciousness as "a globule of dew on a rose-leaf that at mid-day there will be no trace of" (*Letters,* II, 156).

George Eliot felt the objective view of man to be important in that it checks our egoism; thinking too highly of our own importance in the scheme of things leads to perpetual dissatisfaction and to callousness towards others. She did not, however, regard man as unimportant. The objective view of man must be tempered by the subjective view, the view which recognizes human feelings and achievements to be supremely important in their own sphere. The fact that when it is viewed in terms of cosmic time the span of a human life appears infinitesimal need not, should not, and by and large, she argued in a letter of December 1874 to Mrs. Ponsonby, does not affect man's sense of the importance of human endeavors or his sense of the value of moral ideals. What difference does the relative shortness of human existence make, she asked Mrs. Ponsonby, *"when you have to consider the value of human experience?" (Letters,* VI, 100.) The shortness of our lives does not lessen our concern that existence be as satisfying as possible. If human life is felt to be important by human beings, then to them it is important, whether the cosmos cares about man or not. There is, for George Eliot, a class of moral doctrines which have nothing to do with the cosmic order of things and which do not need to be validated by the cosmology of science. These doctrines are concerned only with that which is specifically human, with man's conception of his own dignity and with human ideals and satisfactions so far as they affect the relations between human beings. They derive their sanction only and sufficiently from the personal consciousness of human beings.

George Eliot insisted upon the importance and validity of man's subjective experience of himself. From the objective point of view the human order is seen to be a part of the mechanistic cosmic process. Man's behavior is determined by blind forces at work both within and without. The individual appears to be the helpless pawn of heredity and environment. Intellectual and emotional processes, moral impulses and satisfactions, are reduced to physiological states and sequences. George Eliot felt the objective analysis of mental and moral phenomena to be extremely useful; but she argued repeatedly that it should not prejudice our attitude towards the subjective, the felt aspects of experience. To regard human thought and feeling, pleasure and pain, as matters of little significance because of their physiological basis is, she contended, "equivalent to saying that you care no longer for colour, now you know the laws of the spectrum" (*Letters,* VI, 98).

Mrs. Ponsonby, having had all of her values called into doubt by

245

her study of science, wrote to George Eliot because George Eliot's novels had led her to feel that their author was "in possession of some secret which makes it possible for her to combine sympathy for modern scientific thought with 'approval for moral greatness and beauty and purity in the high ideals which you would set before us.' "[2] Science had made Mrs. Ponsonby feel that moral endeavor is futile by denying the traditional conception of the freedom of the will. George Eliot replied:

> As to the necessary combinations through which life is manifested, and which seem to present themselves to you as a hideous fatalism, which ought logically to petrify your volition—have they, *in fact,* any such influence on your ordinary course of action in the primary affairs of your existence as a human, social, domestic creature? And if they don't hinder you from taking measures for a bath, without which you know you cannot secure the delicate cleanliness which is your second nature, why should they hinder you from a line of resolve in a higher strain of duty to your ideal, both for yourself and others? But the consideration of molecular physics is not the direct ground of human love and moral action, any more than it is the direct means of composing a noble picture or of enjoying great music. One might as well hope to dissect one's own body and be merry in doing it, as take molecular physics (in which you must banish from your field of view what is specifically human) to be your dominant guide, your determiner of motives, in what is solely human. That every study has its bearing on every other is true; but pain and relief, love and sorrow, have their peculiar history which makes an experience and knowledge over and above the swing of atoms. (*Letters,* VI, 98–99)

A month and a half later George Eliot again cautioned Mrs. Ponsonby that

> we must not take every great physicist—or other 'ist'—for an apostle, but be ready to suspect him of some crudity concerning relations that lie outside his special studies, if his exposition strands us on results that seem to stultify the most ardent, massive experience of mankind, and hem up the best part of our feelings in stagnation. (*Letters,* VI, 120)

As Feuerbach shows, the tendency of the subjective point of view is to experience the internal as if it were external. The subjective mind projects its own conceptions, feelings, and wishes outward and then regards them as objective realities. Strongly held beliefs are thus felt to have an objective source and sanction. When this point of view characterizes society as a whole, the existing religious, social, and political orders are felt to be divinely ordained. Whatever is, is right; for whatever is has been produced and is currently sustained by something objective and superior to itself. The human order and the individuals within it are endowed with absolute purpose, meaning, and value. The objective view of man and society shows this conception of an absolute, external source and justification of the moral order to be an illusion. Individual feelings and convictions are largely the products of social conditioning. Social institutions and values are the objective embodiments of individual and racial experience. They are historically evolved, and they vary with time and place. The objective view of the moral order is distressing in that it shows human institutions, beliefs, and values to be the shifting, relative creations of human beings. Existence, thus seen, is often felt to be absurd, devoid of universally valid and intelligible purpose, without any meaning other than that which the individual arbitrarily gives to it. The human order is self-created; it rests on nothing but itself. When we go beyond it we find only unconscious brute existence, an unmitigated awareness of which makes the human world seem phantasmal and reduces the self to insignificance.

Given the fact that the moral order is not sustained by anything outside of itself, how can human values be said to have objective validity? Is there any standard of value other than personal whim, taste, or conviction? Personal values, like orthodox values, are satisfactory as long as they are not shattered by experience. But the individual has no security in the values which he assigns to his own actions and existence, for these values change with his moods and his fortunes. If the world does not please him, if he fails in his purpose, if he finds that nothing he wants for himself is worth having, he will be disillusioned and life will seem meaningless. Even if he is fortunate, there is always before him the prospect of death which annihilates his own value-giving subjectivity and makes his satisfactions appear transitory and insignificant. Man, therefore, craves something outside of himself, something which is not affected by the fluctuating pleasures and pains

247

of his own experience and which endures beyond the term of his own life, to give indubitable significance to his being.

George Eliot finds a subjective sanction of morality in the feelings of the individual and an objective sanction of morality in the feelings of other men, of humanity. Her insistence upon other men as the objective sanction of morality and upon living for others as its end is the rock, as it were, upon which her religion of humanity is built. George Eliot's morality is grounded upon human subjectivity, but it is not, therefore, entirely subjective; or it is only so, logically, when mankind is considered as a single subject. Mankind as a subject has no object to which it can meaningfully relate or from which it can derive value; but to the individual, other men are significant objects, objective sources of value. Other men are significant objects to me because they have a consciousness akin to my own. To the individual, his fellows are separate, objectively existing beings ("I am not you"), who are, at the same time, similar to him in nature ("I am like you") and responsive to his inner life. In religion man finds value by making his own subjectivity objective to himself (God is a source of value only because he is a subjective object), but the subjective object from which he derives his morality has no external reality—other, Feuerbach would add, than in the species. But other men are, to the individual, subjective objects—and therefore objective sources of value—which do exist outside of the individual consciousness.

The primal, undeniable ground of value for George Eliot is the individual's importance to himself; it is a fact that his own pleasures and pains are of great moment to him. This is the subjective basis of morality. The objective basis of morality is other men; and we become aware of it only when we regard our fellows objectively, that is, as subjects in themselves to whom we are objects. If I am important to myself, and other men have an inner life like my own, then they must be important to themselves. I evaluate the actions of my fellows in terms of the effects which they have upon me. Similarly, they must evaluate my actions by the effects which I have upon them. Other men, then, give my deeds, my life, an objective value. I can consider their feelings and judgments insignificant only if I regard my own subjectivity as unique, thereby denying the existence of a similar subjectivity in others, or if I am indifferent to my own feelings. In the latter case, nothing whatever matters; and in the former nothing matters but myself.

The moral satisfaction that we derive from living for the good of others is dependent upon our ability to project ourselves imaginatively into the consciousness of others and into the future. By living for others, we also live in others, and by envisioning the effects of our existence upon those who live after us we can experience a sense of impersonal immortality. George Eliot reminded Mrs. William Smith that although the remainder of her own life could only be "patience and resignation,"

> We are not shut up within our individual life, and it is one of the gains of advancing age that the good of young creatures becomes a more definite joy to us. With this renunciation for ourselves which age inevitably brings, we get more freedom of soul to enter into the life of others: what we can never learn they will know, and the gladness which is a departed sunlight to us is rising with the strength of morning to them. (*Letters*, V, 405–406)

Even death loses some of its sting when we live in and for others. George Eliot wrote to Mrs. Robert Lytton: "I try to delight in the sunshine that will be when I shall never see it any more. And I think it is possible for this sort of impersonal life to attain great intensity,— possible for us to gain much more independence than is usually believed, of the small bundle of facts that make our own personality" (*Letters*, V, 107).

If we live for others as well as for ourselves, we will have a sense of the indubitable worth of our lives, a worth which is independent of the course of our personal fortunes. George Eliot assured Alexander Main that "amid all the considerable trials of existence, men and women can nevertheless greatly help each other; and while we can help each other it is worth while to live" (*Letters*, V, 358). If we are very fortunate we may find personal happiness; but whether we are happy or not, George Eliot contends, we can lead meaningful lives by contributing to the happiness of others and by relieving their sufferings (see *Letters*, VI, 327). This is what Dorothea Brooke learns, this is what sustains her: "If we had lost our own chief good," she tells Will Ladislaw, "other people's good would remain and that is worth trying for. Some can be happy. I seemed to see that more clearly than ever, when I was the most wretched. I can hardly think how I could have borne the trouble, if that feeling had not come to me to make strength" (*Middlemarch,* Chap. LXXXIII). Romola, too, like many other characters in George Eliot's novels, comes to feel life's meaning in this way. In the plague-stricken village, removed from the complexities and intrigues of Florentine life which had obscured her sense of duty, Romola experiences the elemental fellowship with suffering which gives a life of service an indisputable meaning: "If everything else is doubtful, this suffering that I can help is certain: if the glory of the cross is an illusion, the sorrow is only the truer" (*Romola,* Chap. LXIX). The essence of George Eliot's moral philosophy is expressed in the concluding line of her poem, "Self and Life": "Life is justified by love."

NOTES

Chapter I

1. See Robert Gorham Davis, "The Sense of the Real in English Fiction," *Comparative Literature,* III (1951), esp. 200–203.
2. Alfred North Whitehead, *Science and the Modern World* (Mentor Book; New York, 1948), pp. 16–17.
3. Mario Praz, *The Hero in Eclipse in Victorian Fiction,* trans. Angus Davidson (London, 1956), p. 2.
4. "German Wit: Heinrich Heine," *Essays and Leaves from a Notebook* (Cabinet ed.; Edinburgh and London, 1885), pp. 72–73; hereafter cited as *Essays.*
5. *Comte's Philosophy of the Sciences* (London, 1853), pp. 5–6.
6. *A General View of Positivism,* trans. J. H. Bridges (London, 1865), Chap. I, p. 20.
7. "Literature, Science, and Democracy," *The Pacific Spectator,* VIII (1954), 335–336, 337–338.
8. *The George Eliot Letters,* ed. Gordon S. Haight (7 vols., New Haven, 1954–1955), I, 7. All quotations from George Eliot's correspondence are from this edition, which I shall cite simply as *Letters,* with the volume and page numbers parenthetically in the text.
9. She wrote, for example, to her aunt, Mrs. Samuel Evans: "I feel that my besetting sin is the one of all others most destroying, . . . Ambition, a desire insatiable for the esteem of my fellow creatures. This seems the great stumbling block in my path Zionward" (*Letters,* I, 19). See also I, 40 and 70.
10. From a letter to Maria Lewis, 17 July 1839, (*Letters,* I, 27–28); later published in *The Christian Observer,* XL (1840), 38.
11. All quotations from the novels and poems, unless otherwise indicated, are from the Cabinet ed. of *The Works of George Eliot* (20 vols., Edinburgh and London, 1878–1880); reference to novels will be by chap. and/or book; otherwise simply to *Works.*
12. For Marian Evans' unsympathetic attitude towards art see *Letters,* I, 9, 13, and 21–24.
13. Spinoza, for example, argued:

Seeing then that our mind subjectively contains in itself and partakes of the nature of God, and solely from this cause is enabled to form notions explaining natural phenomena and inculcating morality, it follows that we may rightly assert the nature of the human mind . . . to be a primary cause of Divine revelation. All that we clearly and distinctly understand is dictated to us . . . by the idea and nature of God.

In his chapter "Of the Divine Law" Spinoza clearly identifies God with nature and knowledge of nature, which is made possible by God, with knowledge of God: ". . . since without God nothing can exist or be conceived, it is evident that all natural phenomena involve and express the conception of God as far as their essence and perfection extend, so that we have greater and more perfect knowledge of God in proportion to our knowledge of natural phenomena."—*A Theologico-Political Treatise*, trans. R. H. M. Elwes, Bohn's Philosophical Library (London, 1883), pp. 14 and 59.

14. *Christian Theism* (London, 1839), Preface and pp. 19, 33, 51, 53.
15. Hennell rejected Jesus' Essene-inspired emphasis on "monastic austerity and . . . heavenly-mindedness."

There is a general depreciation of the common enjoyments of earth . . . The duty of self-denial seems to be inculcated to an extent more consistent with the spirit of monachism, than with that cheerful morality which would enlarge rather than restrict the bounds of innocent enjoyment. . . . For these reasons, it is possible that the precepts of the Gospels may not appear a complete and safe code of morality to the philanthropist or legislator who deems that the appointed chief object of human effort is the increase of happiness and improvement upon this earth.—*Christian Theism*, pp. 9–10.

16. *Letters*, I, 242, 265–266, 276, 278, 279, and 280.
17. *Leader*, V (22 April 1854), 377.
18. Pp. 9f. This notebook is in the MS vault of the Yale University Library's Rare Book Room.
19. *Fortnightly Review*, III (1866), 770–771.
20. "Notes on 'The Spanish Gypsy,'" J. W. Cross, *George Eliot's Life as Related in Her Letters and Journals*, Cabinet ed. (3 vols., Edinburgh and London, 1885), III, 35–36.

Chapter II

1. *Essays*, p. 187.
2. *Westminster Review*, LIV (1851), 179; citations in the *Westminster Review* are to the American edition.

3. *Westminster Review*, LXV (1856), 343–344.
4. *A System of Logic* (8th ed., New York, 1893), p. 236; hereafter cited as *Logic*.
5. See *The Positive Philosophy of Auguste Comte*, trans. Harriet Martineau (2 vols., New York and London, 1853), I, 7–8.
6. *The Foundations of a Creed*, First Series of *Problems of Life and Mind*, (2 vols., Boston, 1874), I, 282; hereafter cited as *PLM*.
7. "Thoughts of G. H. Lewes," p. 11.
8. For a discussion of George Eliot's use of web imagery in *Middlemarch*, see Reva Stump, *Movement and Vision in George Eliot's Novels* (Seattle, 1959), pp. 141–149.
9. *Daniel Deronda*, epigraph to Chap. XXI.
10. *Principles of Ethics* (2 vols., New York, 1910), I, Chap. I, Sec. 1.
11. "How We Come to Give Ourselves False Testimonials, and Believe in Them," in *Impressions of Theophrastus Such*.
12. For an extensive discussion of Eliot's use of imagery of vision, see Reva Stump, *Movement and Vision in George Eliot's Novels, passim*. See also Barbara Hardy, *The Novels of George Eliot* (Fair Lawn, N.J., 1959), pp. 223–226.
13. *The Principles of Success in Literature*, ed. F. N. Scott (3rd ed. Boston, 1894), pp. 37, 43–44, 47, 49, 52, 60–63, 65. The principle of vision is a constant subject in Lewes' philosophic writings. See *PLM*, I, Chap. III and "Prolegomena," the *Biographical History of Philosophy from Thales to Comte* (4th ed. 2 vols., London, 1871), I, xxxvi.
14. See *Letters*, VI, 216–217.
15. On the educative function of the omniscient narrator technique, see W. J. Harvey, *The Art of George Eliot* (New York, 1962), pp. 40–41. The whole of the second chapter is relevant.
16. See *First Principles* (5th ed. New York, 1880), Part I, Chap. V, Sec. 32.
17. *A General View of Positivism*, p. 17.
18. "Leaves from a Note-Book," *Essays*, pp. 301–303.
19. Cross, *George Eliot's Life*, III, 38–39.
20. *The Positive Philosophy of Auguste Comte*, II, 75, 76.
21. "Address to Working Men, by Felix Holt," *Essays*, pp. 268–269.
22. "A Political Molecule."
23. "O May I Join the Choir Invisible," *The Legend of Jubal and Other Poems*, p. 301.
24. "Margaret Fuller and Mary Wollstonecraft," *Leader*, VI (13 Oct. 1855), 989.
25. "The Natural History of German Life: Riehl," *Essays*, pp. 218, 220.
26. *Ibid.*, pp. 195–196, 210, 221, 223.
27. *History of Philosophy*, I, xcv.
28. *Ibid.*, I, xcv, xcviii–xcix.

Chapter III

1. *Evolution and Ethics and Other Essays* (London, 1894), pp. 1–86, esp. pp. 10, 11, 13, 26, 27, 31, 43, 53, 75, 82, 83.
2. This account is drawn from *The Principles of Sociology* (New York, 1882), Part I, Chaps. I and II; the quotations are from pp. 8, 10, and 15.
3. *Problems of Life and Mind,* Third Series: *The Study of Psychology* (Boston, 1879), pp. 71–72. See also J. S. Mill's essay, "Nature."
4. *The Study of Psychology,* pp. 80, 135, 136, 137, 139
5. *Ibid.,* pp. 144, 145.
6. *A History of Modern Philosophy* (New York, 1950), II, 454. Lewes is generally regarded as Spencer's disciple. For Spencer's theory of the parentage of mental forms and moral sentiments, see especially *The Principles of Biology* (New York, 1874), Part II, Chap. VIII, and *Principles of Psychology* (New York, 1880), Part IV, Chap. VII, Sec. 208, and Chap. VIII (also Appendix B of Vol. I); and Part VIII, Chaps. V–VIII.
7. *The Descent of Man,* Modern Library Giant ed., p. 490. Chaps. IV and V, which deal with the evolution of man's moral and intellectual faculties, are of especial interest.
8. Alexander Bain, *Mental and Moral Science* (2nd ed., London, 1868), p. 722.
9. See, e.g., *Daniel Deronda,* Chaps. XLII and LXIII, and *The Spanish Gypsy,* p. 84 and *passim.* See also "The Modern Hep! Hep! Hep!," in *Impressions of Theophrastus Such.* See my discussion in Chap. X of George Eliot's use in her fiction of Lewes' and Spencer's evolutionary explanation of moral phenomena and Chaps. IX–XII of George Willis Cooke's *George Eliot* (Boston, 1883).
10. The passages are included in Cross's *George Eliot's Life,* II, 218–219.
11. Cooke, *George Eliot,* p. 239.
12. "The Modern Hep! Hep! Hep!," in *Impressions of Theophrastus Such.*
13. *The Descent of Man,* pp. 472, 481.
14. *The Study of Psychology,* p. 150.
15. See *The Descent of Man,* Chap. IV, and Spencer, *Principles of Psychology,* Pt. VIII, Chap. V, "Sociality and Sympathy."
16. *Principles of Psychology,* Pt. VIII, Chap. VIII.
17. "Worldliness and Other-Worldliness: The Poet Young," *Essays,* pp. 45, 52, 53, 57.
18. See *The Descent of Man,* p. 472, note 5.

Chapter IV

1. George Eliot's review of *Modern Painters,* Vol. III, *Westminster Review,* LXV (1856), 343–344. For George Eliot's and the positivist's attitude towards realism and subjectivity see also Chap. I above, Sec. IV.

2. "The Future of German Philosophy," *Leader*, VI (28 July, 1855), 723–724.
3. All quotations in this paragraph are from Mill's *Autobiography*, World's Classics ed., pp. 190–191 and 232–234.
4. All quotations in this paragraph are from *The Positive Philosophy of Auguste Comte*, I, 1–2.
5. Quotations from II, 227, 228, 396 and 741.
6. *The Life and Works of Goethe*, Everyman's Library, pp. 51–54.
7. *The Positive Philosophy of Auguste Comte*, I, 2.
8. *From Hegel to Marx* (New York, 1936), p. 221.
9. *The History of Philosophy*, I, xi, xli; and xxxi–xxxv, *passim*.
10. *Leader*, VI (28 July 1855), 724.
11. *The History of Philosophy*, I, lii.
12. *Life and Works of Goethe*, p. 353.
13. *Ibid.*, p. 366.
14. See Chap. II, Sec. IV above and *Middlemarch*, Chaps. XV and XVI.
15. Review of Cousin's *Du Vraix, du beau, et du bien*, in "Contemporary Literature of France," *Westminster Review*, LX (1853), 328. Both this article and that on Gruppe demonstrate very clearly George Eliot's firm grasp of the issues of contemporary philosophy.
16. *Essays*, pp. 130–131, 163.
17. *The Life and Works of Goethe*, p. 366.
18. Some idea of the moral implications of these two points of view can be gathered from one of George Eliot's earliest published writings, a tale entitled "A Little Fable with a Great Moral" which appeared in the Coventry *Herald* in 1847. Thematically, the fable has much in common with her mature fiction. Idione and Hieria are the prototypes of the two kinds of women (the Hetty Sorrel and the Dinah Morris types) who people her novels; and her use of self-contemplation in a mirror to denote egoism is repeated with Hetty, Esther Lyon, Rosamond, and Gwendolen Harleth. See *Essays of George Eliot*, ed. Thomas Pinney (New York, 1963), pp. 21–22.
19. These and the following passages from Feuerbach are from *The Essence of Christianity*, trans. George Eliot (2nd ed., Harper Torchbook, New York, 1957), pp. 204–206, 101–110 *passim*, 122–133 *passim*.

Chapter V

1. *First Principles*, Pt. I, Chap. I, Sec. 4.
2. Charles Christian Hennell, *An Inquiry Concerning the Origin of Christianity* (2nd ed., London, 1841), pp. 322–323. There is a valuable discussion of Hennell in Basil Willey, *Nineteenth Century Studies* (New York, 1949), pp. 207–220.

3. David Friedrich Strauss, *The Life of Jesus, Critically Examined,* trans. from the 4th German ed. by George Eliot (London, 1846), Secs. 8 and 10. For discussions of Strauss, see Willey, *Nineteenth Century Studies,* pp. 220–227; Sidney Hook, *From Hegel to Marx,* pp. 78–89; Albert Schweitzer, *The Quest of the Historical Jesus* (New York, 1948), Chaps. VII, IX; and Ernst Cassirer, *The Problem of Knowledge* (New Haven, 1950), pp. 301–305.

4. All the passages from Feuerbach are from *The Essence of Christianity,* pp. xxxv, xxxviii, 2, 5, 7–8, 12, 13–14, 29–30. For other accounts of Feuerbach's thought see William H. Chamberlain, *Heaven Wasn't His Destination, The Philosophy of Ludwig Feuerbach* (London, 1941); Hook, *From Hegel to Marx,* Chap. VII; Willey, *Nineteenth Century Studies,* pp. 227–236; Karl Barth's Introduction to *The Essence of Christianity;* and Henri de Lubac, S.J., *The Drama of Atheist Humanism,* trans. Edith M. Riley (New York, 1950), pp. 7–17.

5. *The Essence of Christianity,* pp. xxxvii, xliii, 40, 63, 99, 120, 121, 135, 140, 141, 178, xliv, 21, 148.

6. John Stuart Mill, who is here in thorough agreement with Feuerbach, argues "that when we mean different things we have no right to call them by the same name. . . . Language has no meaning for the words Just, Merciful, Benevolent, save that in which we predicate them of our fellow-creatures." "I will call no being good," proclaims Mill, "who is not what I mean when I apply that epithet to my fellow-creatures; and if such a being can sentence me to hell for not so calling him, to hell I will go."—*An Examination of Sir William Hamilton's Philosophy* (6th ed., London, 1889), Chap. VII, esp. pp. 127 and 129.

7. *The Essence of Christianity,* pp. 16, 22, 97.

8. "Contemporary Literature of England," *Westminster Review,* LVII (1852), 134.

9. Cross, *George Eliot's Life,* III, 34, 35, 36.

10. "Belles Lettres," *Westminster Review,* LXIV (1855), 312.

11. *Fugitive Essays by Josiah Royce* (Cambridge, Mass., 1920), p. 281.

12. *Ibid.,* pp. 279–280.

13. *The Essence of Christianity,* p. 271.

14. *Ibid.,* pp. 64, 171.

15. *Ibid.,* p. 269.

16. *Ibid.,* pp. 34, 37, 46, 47, 50, 53, 58, 60.

17. *Ibid.,* pp. 53, 159, 160, 202, 209, 213, 214, 247, 261, 262, 266, 268, 272, 273.

18. The quotations from this essay are from *Essays,* pp. 125, 132, 140, 149, 150, 153, 156, 158, 159–162 *passim.*

19. *The Essence of Christianity,* pp. 209, 246.

20. *Ibid.,* pp. 252, 253, 261, 263.

21. *Ibid.,* p. 268

22. Quoted by Chamberlain in *Heaven Wasn't His Destination,* p. 120.

NOTES

Chapter VI

1. *George Eliot,* pp. 166, 168, 170.
2. Henry James, *Partial Portraits* (London, 1888), p. 50.
3. *George Eliot,* p. 169.
4. *Fugitive Essays by Josiah Royce,* pp. 265, 286, 286–287.
5. "The Spanish Gypsy by George Eliot," *Literary Reviews and Essays by Henry James,* ed. Albert Mordell (New York, 1957), p. 283. See also N. N. Feltes, "George Eliot and the Unified Sensibility," *PMLA,* LXXIX (1964), 130–136.
6. *The Essence of Christianity,* p. xxxv.
7. *"Middlemarch" from Notebook to Novel: A Study of George Eliot's Creative Method* (Urbana, 1960), Chap. III; the quotations are from pp. 103, 115, 119, 123.
8. Fred C. Thomson's study of Eliot's notebook for *Felix Holt*—"The Genesis of *Felix Holt,*" *PMLA,* LXXIV (1959), 576–584—has shown that that novel, too, underwent radical changes in the course of its composition. The genesis of *Felix Holt,* Mr. Thomson argues, was "in the adulterous intrigue of Mrs. Transome with Lawyer Jermyn and the bitter consequences of this transgression to herself and their son Harold. The politics, and even the role of Felix himself, were probably afterthoughts."—p. 576.
9. Cross, *George Eliot's Life,* III, 34, 35, 36.
10. *Life and Works of Goethe,* p. 354.
11. *Journal of English and Germanic Philology,* LIII (1954), p. 149, note 14. For a defense of George Eliot's determinism, see George Levine, "Determinism and Responsibility in the Works of George Eliot," *PMLA,* LXXVII (1962), 268–279. Mr. Levine and I have arrived, independently, at similar conclusions.
12. "Moral Freedom in a Determined World," *Commentary,* XXV (1958), 439.
13. "Thomas Carlyle," *Leader,* VI (1855), 1034.
14. *Ibid.*
15. *Westminster Review,* LXVIII (1852), 71.
16. See W. J. Harvey, *The Art of George Eliot,* pp. 40–41, and Chapter II ("Moral and Aesthetic Bases"), *passim;* and Richard Stang, *The Theory of the Novel in England, 1850–1870* (New York, 1959), pp. 40–43.
17. *Freud and the Crisis of our Culture* (Boston, 1955), p. 19.
18. *George Eliot,* p. 170.

Chapter VII

1. See Barbara Hardy, *The Novels of George Eliot* (Fair Lawn, N.J., 1959), Chaps. III, IV, and IX; and D. R. Carroll, "An Image of Disenchantment

in the Novels of George Eliot," *Review of English Studies,* XI (1960), 29–41.
2. See Barbara Hardy, "The Image of the Opiate in George Eliot's Novels," *Notes & Queries,* new series, IV (1957), 487–490.
3. For the text of "Erinna" see my article, "George Eliot's Unpublished Poetry," *Studies in Philology,* LVI (1959), 545–548.
4. *The Essence of Christianity,* p. 82.
5. "Looking Inward," *Impressions of Theophrastus Such.*
6. *The Legend of Jubal and Other Poems,* pp. 245–246.
7. *The Novels of George Eliot,* pp. 198–199.

Chapter VIII

1. *George Eliot* (London, 1947), p. 171. Mr. Bullett feels that Adam suffers from this unqualified approval.
2. See Joan Bennett, *George Eliot* (Cambridge, 1948), pp. 107–111; George R. Creeger, "An Interpretation of *Adam Bede,*" *ELH,* XXIII (1956), 232–234; Barbara Hardy, *The Novels of George Eliot,* Chap. II; and Reva Stump, *Movement and Vision in George Eliot's Novels,* Chaps. II–IV. Mrs. Hardy, Miss Stump, and I have arrived, independently and by different methods, at very similar conclusions about *Adam Bede.*
3. See Chap. V above for a discussion of the religious nature of interpersonal relationships in *Adam Bede.*
4. *Principles of Psychology,* Pt. VIII, Chap. VIII, Sec. 529. See also, above, Chap. III.
5. *Leader,* II (20 Sept. 1851), 898.
6. I am not arguing, however, that the ending of *Adam Bede* is a complete artistic success. For interesting discussions of the technical problems of the ending, see Reva Stump, pp. 56–66, and W. J. Harvey, *The Art of George Eliot,* pp. 179–182.
7. For a discussion of the conflict between Maggie and her environment, see my article, "Towards a Revaluation of George Eliot's *The Mill on the Floss,*" *Nineteenth Century Fiction,* XI (1956), 18–31 and Chap. X below. See also Jerome Thale, "Image and Theme: *The Mill on the Floss,*" *University of Kansas City Review,* XXIII (1957), 227–234. Mr. Thale, who deals interestingly with the river imagery in the novel, points out the recurrence of metaphors suggesting that "Maggie needs a 'wider, deeper, and fuller' channel than the narrow one offered by St. Ogg's."
8. *The Great Tradition* (London, 1948), p. 39.
9. *Ibid.,* p. 41.
10. Bullett, *George Eliot,* pp. 118, 188. Bennett, *George Eliot,* pp. 120–121, 129.
11. Claude T. Bissell, in "Social Analysis in the Novels of George Eliot," *ELH,* XVIII (1951), 221–239, argues, quite correctly, that Maggie "turns back to

face the uncomprehending wrath of society at the call of a moral principle.
. . . Maggie's action thus becomes a symbolic denial of the validity of utili-
tarian ethics." He feels, however, that since Maggie's course "can bring no
approval from the community and a troubled peace to her own conscience,"
"the dilemma is too great for Maggie Tulliver, and, one suspects, for George
Eliot. The flood waters of the Floss provide a convenient solution."—p. 234.

Chapter IX

1. There has been a good deal of disagreement about the unity of *Middlemarch.* For some of the negative reactions, see Henry James, "George Eliot's
'Middlemarch,' " *Nineteenth-Century Fiction,* VIII (1953), 161–170—re-
printed from the *Galaxy* of March, 1873; Arnold Kettle, *An Introduction to
the English Novel* (London, 1951), Vol. I, Chap. VII; and F. George
Steiner, "A Preface to 'Middlemarch,' " *Nineteenth-Century Fiction,* IX
(1955), 262–279. Gerald Bullett (*George Eliot,* pp. 220–227), Joan Bennett
(*George Eliot,* pp. 162–167), W. J. Harvey (*The Art of George Eliot,* pp.
143–148), Lord David Cecil (*Early Victorian Novelists* [New York, 1935],
p. 312), and Gordon Haight (Riverside *Middlemarch* [Cambridge, Mass.,
1956], xv) all claim for *Middlemarch* the virtues that James and Steiner
deny it. The most careful analysis of the novel's unity is David R. Carroll's
"Unity Through Analogy: An Interpretation of 'Middlemarch,' " *Victorian
Studies,* II (1959), 305–316.

I believe that the artistic unity of *Middlemarch* can be demonstrated, but
the demonstration of it is not part of my present purpose. My discussion of
the roles which the subjective and objective approaches to reality play in
shaping the behavior and the ultimate worldly and moral destinies of the
leading characters can, however, help to resolve the esthetic issue. The
unity of *Middlemarch* lies, I believe, in the fact that every character and
situation in the novel is an aspect of a single subject: the effect upon human
destiny of the subjective and objective approaches to reality, the connectedness of human lots, and the interaction between the self and its social
medium. The subject has several parts, to be sure, but it arises out of a
singleness of vision—out of a vision of life informed and made coherent by
the fundamental, interrelated principles of the cosmology and epistemology
of science.

For valuable discussions of the novel's artistry, see Barbara Hardy, *The
Novels of George Eliot, passim;* Reva Stump, *Movement and Vision in
George Eliot's Novels,* Chaps. VII and VIII; F. R. Leavis, *The Great Tra-
dition,* 61–79; Mark Schorer, "Fiction and the 'Analogical Matrix,' " in
Critiques and Essays on Modern Fiction 1920–1951, ed. John W. Aldridge
(New York, 1952), pp. 91–97; Jerome Beaty, "History by Indirection: the

Era of Reform in 'Middlemarch,' " *Victorian Studies,* I (1957), 173–179; Quentin Anderson, "George Eliot in *Middlemarch,*" in *From Dickens to Hardy,* ed. Boris Ford (Pelican Books, 1958), pp. 274–293; John Hagan, "*Middlemarch:* Narrative Unity in the Story of Dorothea Brooke," *Nineteenth-Century Fiction,* XVI (1961), 17–31; Newton P. Stallknecht, "Resolution and Independence: A Reading of *Middlemarch,*" in *Twelve Original Essays on Great English Novels,* ed. Charles Shapiro (Detroit, 1960), pp. 125–152; and Jerome Beaty, "*Middlemarch*" *from Notebook to Novel, passim.*

2. James, "George Eliot's 'Middlemarch,' " p. 165; Stephen, Preface to the Everyman *Middlemarch,* p. viii; Bullett, *George Eliot,* p. 228.

3. *George Eliot,* pp. 175–176.

Chapter X

1. "The Modern Hep! Hep! Hep!" *Impressions of Theophrastus Such;* the following quotations are also from this essay.

2. In "River Imagery in 'Daniel Deronda,' " *Nineteenth-Century Fiction,* VIII (1954), 300–306, Jerome Thale points out that Deronda's passivity is presented concretely in his aimless drifting on the river, while moral activity is associated with rowing purposefully to a destination: "As he himself realizes, he lacks purpose in life and merely drifts along with the current on the raft provided by his mother's money and the care of Sir Hugo Mallinger."—p. 301.

3. The biological explanation of Deronda's relation to Mordecai and to Judaism should modify, I think, the views of this aspect of the novel which are advanced by F. R. Leavis in *The Great Tradition* and in his Introduction to the Harper Torchbook edition of *Daniel Deronda* (New York, 1961), by Edgar Rosenberg, in *From Shylock to Svengali* (Stanford, 1960), Chap. VII, and by Robert Preyer in his article "Beyond the Liberal Imagination: Vision and Reality in 'Daniel Deronda,' " *Victorian Studies,* IV (1960), 33–54.

4. Cross, *George Eliot's Life,* pp. 35–36.

5. *Ibid.,* p. 38.

6. *The Essence of Christianity,* p. 271 and footnote. See Gordon Haight, *George Eliot and John Chapman* (New Haven, 1940), pp. 80–81; Lawrence and Elisabeth Hanson, *Marian Evans and George Eliot* (London, 1952), pp. 169–170; and Gerald Bullett, *George Eliot,* pp. 95–101.

7. In a very stimulating discussion of the novel, Carole Robinson argues that "George Eliot's praise of the life to which she has committed her heroine" is hollow, and that this hollowness, and "the hollowness of the heroine herself," comes "not from the moral intention behind the novel, but from the novelist's uncertainty of the validity of that intention."—"*Romola:* A Read-

ing of the Novel," *Victorian Studies*, VI (1962), 39. There are some excellent comments on *Romola* in Barbara Hardy, *The Novels of George Eliot*, especially on pp. 170–176.

Chapter XI

1. *The Essence of Christianity*, p. 158. See Chapter V above.
2. *Ibid.*, p. 158.
3. For discussions of other aspects of *Felix Holt* see Fred C. Thomson, *"Felix Holt* as Classic Tragedy," *Nineteenth-Century Fiction*, XVI (1961), 47–58, and David R. Carroll, *"Felix Holt:* Society as Protagonist," *Nineteenth-Century Fiction*, XVII (1962), 237–252.
4. On Gwendolen's character see F. R. Leavis, *The Great Tradition*, 79–125, and Henry James, *"Daniel Deronda:* A Conversation," published as an appendix in *The Great Tradition*. For discussions of other aspects of the novel see D. R. Carroll, "The Unity of 'Daniel Deronda,' " *Essays in Criticism*, IX (1959), 369–380; and Barbara Hardy, *The Novels of George Eliot*, Chaps. IX–XI.
5. See *The Essence of Christianity*, Chaps. III–V, and Dinah Morris' interpretation of Christ in *Adam Bede*, Chap. XXX.

Chapter XII

1. *Anna Karenina*, Modern Library ed., p. 917.
2. *Letters*, VI, 97, fn. 3. The phrase in single quotes is from Mrs. Ponsonby's letter.

BIBLIOGRAPHY

In addition to listing works cited in the text, I have included books and articles that have significantly influenced or are especially relevant to my study. For a fuller listing of George Eliot's periodical writings, see Thomas Pinney, ed., *Essays of George Eliot*, Appendix A.

I. GEORGE ELIOT

Primary Sources

Cross, J. W. *George Eliot's Life as Related in Her Letters and Journals*, Cabinet ed. 3 vols., Edinburgh and London, 1885.

Eliot, George. "The *Antigone* and Its Moral." *Leader*, VII (1856), 306.

———— "Art and Belles Lettres." *Westminster Review*, American ed. LXV (1856), 343–356.

———— "Belles Lettres." *Westminster Review*, American ed. LXIV (1855), 312–321.

———— "Contemporary Literature of England." *Westminster Review*, American ed. LVII (1852), 132–134.

———— "Contemporary Literature of France." *Westminster Review*, American ed. LX (1853), 327–330.

———— *Essays and Leaves from a Note-Book*, Cabinet ed. Edinburgh and London, 1885.

———— *Essays of George Eliot*, ed. Thomas Pinney. New York, 1963.

———— "The Future of German Philosophy." *Leader*, VI (1855), 723–724.

———— *The George Eliot Letters*, ed. Gordon S. Haight. 7 vols., New Haven, 1954–1955.

———— "Literature." *Leader*, V (1854), 377.

———— "Margaret Fuller and Mary Wollstonecraft." *Leader*, VI (1855), 988–989.

———— Review of Greg's *The Creed of Christendom*. *Leader*, II (1851), 897–899.

———— Review of Mackay's *The Progress of the Intellect. Westminster Review*, American ed. LIV (1851), 177–185.

———— "The Romantic School of Music." *Leader*, V (1854), 1027–1028.

———— "Silly Novels by Lady Novelists." *Westminster Review*, American ed. LXVI (1856), 243–254.

———— "Thomas Carlyle." *Leader*, VI (1855), 1034–1035.

———— *The Works of George Eliot*, Cabinet ed. 20 vols., Edinburgh and London, 1878–1880.

Haight, Gordon S., ed. *The George Eliot Letters.* 7 vols. New Haven, 1954–55.
Paris, Bernard J. "George Eliot's Unpublished Poetry." *Studies in Philology,* LVI (1959), 539–558.
Pinney, Thomas, ed. *Essays of George Eliot.* New York, 1963.

Secondary Works

Allott, Miriam. "George Eliot in the 1860's." *Victorian Studies,* V (1961), 93–108.
Anderson, Quentin. "George Eliot in *Middlemarch.*" *From Dickens to Hardy,* ed. Boris Ford. Baltimore, 1958.
Beaty, Jerome. "History by Indirection: The Era of Reform in *Middlemarch.*" *Victorian Studies,* I (1957), 173–179.
────── *"Middlemarch" from Notebook to Novel: A Study of George Eliot's Creative Method.* Urbana, 1960.
Beebe, Maurice. "Visions are Creators: The Unity of *Daniel Deronda.*" *Boston University Studies in English,* I (1955), 166–177.
Bennett, Joan. *George Eliot, Her Mind and Her Art.* Cambridge, 1948.
Bissell, Claude T. "Social Analysis in the Novels of George Eliot." *ELH,* XVIII (1951), 221–239.
Bullett, Gerald William. *George Eliot, Her Life and Books.* London, 1947.
Carroll, David. *"Felix Holt:* Society as Protagonist." *Nineteenth-Century Fiction,* XVII (1962), 237–252.
────── "An Image of Disenchantment in the Novels of George Eliot." *Review of English Studies,* XI (1960), 29–41.
────── "The Unity of *Daniel Deronda.*" *Essays in Criticism,* IX (1959), 369–380.
────── "Unity through Analogy: An Interpretation of *Middlemarch.*" *Victorian Studies,* II (1959), 305–316.
Cecil, Lord David. *Early Victorian Novelists.* New York, 1935.
Cooke, George Willis. *George Eliot, A Critical Study of Her Life, Writings and Philosophy.* Boston, 1883.
Creeger, George R. "An Interpretation of *Adam Bede.*" *ELH,* XXIII (1956), 218–238.
Diekhoff, John S. "The Happy Ending of *Adam Bede.*" *ELH,* III (1936), 221–227.
Hagan, John. *"Middlemarch:* Narrative Unity in the Story of Dorothea Brooke." *Nineteenth-Century Fiction,* XVI (1961), 17–31.
Haight, Gordon Sherman. *George Eliot and John Chapman, with Chapman's Diaries.* New Haven, 1940.
──────, ed. *Middlemarch.* Cambridge, Mass., 1956.
Hanson, Lawrence and Elisabeth. *Marian Evans and George Eliot.* London, 1952.

Hardy, Barbara. "The Image of the Opiate in George Eliot's Novels." *Notes and Queries,* New Series, IV (1957), 487–490.

—— *The Novels of George Eliot: A Study in Form.* Fair Lawn, N.J., 1959.

Harvey, W. J. *The Art of George Eliot.* New York, 1962.

Heilman, Robert B. "Return to Raveloe; Thirty-five Years After." *English Journal,* XLVI (1957), 1–10.

Holloway, John. *The Victorian Sage; Studies in Argument.* London, 1953.

Hough, Graham. "Novelist-Philosophers, XII. George Eliot." *Horizon,* XVII (1948), 50–62.

House, Humphrey. "Qualities of George Eliot's Unbelief." *All in Due Time.* London, 1955.

Hyde, William J. "George Eliot and the Climate of Realism." *PMLA,* LXXII (1957), 147–164.

James, Henry. "George Eliot's *Middlemarch.*" *Nineteenth-Century Fiction,* VIII (1953), 161–170.

—— *Literary Reviews and Essays,* ed. Albert Mordell. New York, 1957.

—— *Notes and Reviews.* Cambridge, Mass., 1921.

—— *Partial Portraits.* London, 1888.

—— *Views and Reviews.* Boston, 1908.

Kaminsky, Alice R. "George Eliot, George Henry Lewes, and the Novel." *PMLA,* LXX (1955), 997–1013.

Kettle, Arnold. *An Introduction to the English Novel.* 2 vols. London, 1951. Vol. I.

Kitchel, Anna Theresa. *George Lewes and George Eliot; a Review of Records.* New York, 1933.

—— *Quarry for Middlemarch.* Berkeley, 1950.

Leavis, Frank Raymond. *The Great Tradition; George Eliot, Henry James, Joseph Conrad.* London, 1948.

—— Introduction to *Daniel Deronda,* Harper Torchbook ed. New York, 1961.

Levine, George. ""Determinism and Responsibility in the Works of George Eliot." *PMLA,* LXXVII (1962), 268–279.

McKenzie, K. A. *Edith Simcox and George Eliot.* London, 1961.

Paris, Bernard J. "Towards a Revaluation of George Eliot's *The Mill on the Floss.*" *Nineteenth-Century Fiction,* XI (1956), 18–31.

Praz, Mario. *The Hero in Eclipse in Victorian Fiction,* trans. Angus Davidson. London, 1956.

Preyer, Robert. "Beyond the Liberal Imagination: Vision and Reality in *Daniel Deronda.*" *Victorian Studies,* IV (1960), 33–54.

Robinson, Carole. "*Romola:* a Reading of the Novel." *Victorian Studies,* VI (1962), 29–42.

Rosenberg, Edgar. *From Shylock to Svengali.* Stanford, Cal., 1960.

Royce, Josiah. *Fugitive Essays.* Cambridge, Mass., 1920.

Rust, James D. "The Periodical Writings of George Eliot, 1851–1857." Unpublished doctoral dissertation, Yale University, 1945.

Schorer, Mark. "Fiction and the Analogical Matrix." *Critiques and Essays on Modern Fiction, 1920–1951,* ed. John W. Aldridge. New York, 1952.

Stallknecht, Newton P. "Resolution and Independence: a Reading of *Middlemarch*." *Twelve Original Essays on Great English Novels,* ed. Charles Shapiro. Detroit, 1960.

Stang, Richard, ed. *Discussions of George Eliot. Boston,* 1960.

––––– "The Literary Criticism of George Eliot." *PMLA,* LXXII (1957), 952–961.

––––– *The Theory of the Novel in England, 1850–1870.* New York, 1959.

Steiner, F. George. "A Preface to *Middlemarch*." *Nineteenth-Century Fiction,* IX (1955), 262–279.

Steinhoff, W. R. "Intent and Fulfillment in the Ending of *The Mill on the Floss*." *Image of the Work,* ed. Bertrand Evans, Josephine Miles and William R. Steinhoff. Berkeley, 1955.

Stephen, Sir Leslie. *George Eliot,* "English Men of Letters" series. New York and London, 1902.

–––––, ed. *Middlemarch,* Everyman's Library ed. 1930.

Stump, Reva. *Movement and Vision in George Eliot's Novels.* Seattle, 1959.

Svaglic, Martin J. "Religion in the Novels of George Eliot." *Journal of English and Germanic Philology,* LIII (1954), 145–159.

Thale, Jerome. "Image and Theme: *The Mill on the Floss*." *University of Kansas City Review,* XXIII (1957), 227–234.

––––– *The Novels of George Eliot.* New York, 1959.

––––– "River Imagery in *Daniel Deronda*." *Nineteenth-Century Fiction,* VIII (1954), 300–306.

Thomson, Fred C. "*Felix Holt* as Classic Tragedy." *Nineteenth-Century Fiction,* XVI (1961), 47–58.

––––– "The Genesis of *Felix Holt*." *PMLA,* LXXIV (1959), 576–584.

Willey, Basil. *Nineteenth Century Studies: Coleridge to Matthew Arnold.* London, 1949.

Williams, Raymond. *Culture and Society, 1780–1950.* New York, 1958.

II. BACKGROUND

Primary Sources

Bain, Alexander. *Mental and Moral Science, a Compendium of Psychology and Ethics,* 2nd ed. London, 1868.

Bray, Charles. *The Philosophy of Necessity; or Law in Mind as in Matter,* 3rd ed., revised and abridged. London, 1889 [1841].*

* The dates in brackets are the dates of first publication.

Comte, Auguste. *A General View of Positivism*, trans. J. H. Bridges. London, 1908.

—— *The Catechism of Positivism; or, Summary Exposition of the Universal Religion*, trans. Richard Congreve. London, 1858.

—— *The Positive Philosophy of Auguste Comte*, trans. Harriet Martineau. 2 vols., New York and London, 1853.

—— *System of Positive Polity*, trans. not named. 4 vols. London, 1875–1877.

Darwin, Charles. *The Descent of Man*, Modern Library ed. [1871].

Feuerbach, Ludwig. *The Essence of Christianity*, trans. from 2nd German ed. by George Eliot, Harper Torchbook ed. New York, 1957 [1854].

Hennell, Charles Christian. *An Inquiry Concerning the Origin of Christianity*, 2nd ed. London, 1841 [1838].

—— *Christian Theism*. London, 1839.

Huxley, T. H. *Evolution and Ethics and Other Essays*. London, 1894.

Lewes, G. H. "Causeries." *Fortnightly Review*, III (1866), 770–771.

—— *Comte's Philosophy of the Sciences: Being an Exposition of the Principles of the Cours de Philosophie Positive of Auguste Comte*. London, 1853.

—— "Criticism in Relation to Novels." *Fortnightly Review*, III (1865), 352–361.

—— *The History of Philosophy, from Thales to Comte*, 4th ed., corrected and partly rewritten. 2 vols., London, 1871.

—— "The Lady Novelists." *Westminster Review*, American ed. LVIII (1852), 70–77.

—— *The Life and Works of Goethe*, Everyman's Library ed. [1855].

—— *Life of Maximilien Robespierre*. London, 1849.

—— *The Principles of Success in Literature*, 3rd ed., ed. Fred N. Scott. Boston, 1894.

—— *Problems of Life and Mind*, 1st series: *The Foundations of a Creed*. 2 vols., London, 1874–1875.

—— *Problems of Life and Mind*, 2nd series: *The Physical Basis of Mind*. Boston, 1877.

—— *Problems of Life and Mind*, 3rd series: *The Study of Psychology, Its Object, Scope, and Method*. Boston, 1879.

—— "Thoughts of G. H. Lewes." MS notebook, Rare Book Room, Yale University Library.

Mill, J. S. *Auguste Comte and Positivism*. London, 1865.

—— *Autobiography*, World's Classics ed. London, 1924 [1873].

——*An Examination of Sir William Hamilton's Philosophy*, 6th ed. London, 1889 [1865].

—— *A System of Logic, Ratiocinative and Inductive: Being a Connected View of the Principles of Evidence and the Methods of Scientific Investigation*, 8th ed. New York, 1879 [1843].

—— *Utilitarianism*, Everyman's Library ed. London, 1910 [1863].

Spencer, Herbert. *First Principles,* 5th ed. New York, 1880 [1862].
—— *Principles of Biology,* Vol. I. New York, 1874 [1864].
—— *Principles of Ethics,* Vol. I. New York, 1910 [1879].
—— *Principles of Psychology,* Vols. I and II. New York, 1880 [1855].
—— *Principles of Sociology,* Vol. I. New York, 1882 [1876].
Spinoza, Benedict de. *Theological-Political Tractate,* trans. R. H. M. Elwes, Bohn Philosophical Library ed. London, 1883.
Strauss, David Friedrich. *The Life of Jesus, Critically Examined,* trans. from the 4th German ed. by George Eliot. London, 1846.
Sully, James. *Pessimism, a History and a Criticism.* London, 1877.

Secondary Works

Buckley, Jerome Hamilton. *The Victorian Temper: a Study in Literary Culture.* Cambridge, Mass., 1951.
Cassirer, Ernst. *The Problem of Knowledge.* New Haven, 1950.
Chamberlain, William B. *Heaven Wasn't His Destination. The Philosophy of Ludwig Feuerbach.* London, 1941.
Davis, Robert Gorham. "The Sense of the Real in English Fiction." *Comparative Literature,* III (1951), 200–217.
Greenhut, Morris. "George Henry Lewes and the Classical Tradition in English Criticism." *Review of English Studies,* XXIV (1948), 126–137.
—— "George Henry Lewes as a Critic of the Novel." *Studies in Philology,* XLV (1948), 491–511.
Höffding, H. *A History of Modern Philosophy,* 2 vols., New York, 1950. Vol II.
Hofstadter, Richard. *Social Darwinism in American Thought, 1860–1915,* rev. ed. Boston, 1955.
Hook, Sidney. *From Hegel to Marx; Studies in the Intellectual Development of Karl Marx.* New York, 1936.
—— "Moral Freedom in a Determined World." *Commentary,* XXV (1958), 431–443.
Houghton, Walter E. *The Victorian Frame of Mind, 1830–1870.* New Haven, 1957.
Kaminsky, Jack. "The Empirical Metaphysics of George Henry Lewes." *Journal of the History of Ideas,* XIII (1952), 314–332.
Langer, Susanne K. *Philosophy in a New Key,* New American Library ed. New York, 1948.
Lubac, Henri de, S.J. *The Drama of Atheist Humanism,* trans. Edith M. Riley. New York, 1950.
Metz, Rudolf. *A Hundred Years of British Philosophy,* trans. J. W. Harvey, T. E. Jessup, and Henry Stuart. New York, 1938.
Myers, Henry. "Literature, Science, and Democracy." *The Pacific Spectator,* VIII (1954), 333–345.

Quillian, William F., Jr. *The Moral Theory of Evolutionary Naturalism.* Yale Studies in Religious Education XVII. New Haven, 1945.

Schweitzer, Albert. *The Quest of the Historical Jesus, a Critical Study of Its Progress from Reimarus to Wrede.* New York, 1948.

Trilling, Lionel. *Freud and the Crisis of Our Culture.* Boston, 1955.

Whitehead, Alfred North. *Science and the Modern World,* New American Library ed. New York, 1948.

Willey, Basil. *More Nineteenth-Century Studies.* London, 1956.

INDEX

altruism, 56, 58, 68
activity, 44–45, 175
   see also resignation and activity
aesthetic theory
   GE's, 115–127 *passim*
   Lewes on, 77
   positivism's influence upon, 25
   see also art, the novel, realism
alienation
   characters experience, 141
   from cosmos, 4, 21, 243
   treatment of, in *Silas Marner,* 138–141
   urge to overcome sense of, 3
Allbutt, Clifford, 115, 117
Anderson, Quentin, 260 n.1
a priori method, 51, 72, 73, 74, 80, 81,
   120, 182
art, 77, 136
   an instrument of knowledge, 116–120
   civilization a product of, 54
   Dorothea Brooke on, 9
   Goethe's, 78
   Marian Evans on, 9, 251 n.12
   morally educative, 121–127 *passim*
   moral purpose in GE's, 115–117, 121
   that mends Nature, 53, 135

   see also aesthetic theory, the novel,
   realism
Athens, 134–135

Bacon, Francis, 73, 75, 82
Bain, Alexander, 67, 71
   Mental and Moral Science, 254 n.8
Barth, Karl, 256 n.4
Beaty, Jerome, 119, 257 n.7, 259 n.1,
   260 n.1
Bennett, Joan, 164, 192, 258 n.10, 259 n.1
Benthamites
   Mill's and GE's objections to, 33
Bissell, Claude T., 258–259, n.11
Blackwood, John, 35, 118, 120, 138, 164
Blackwood, William, 8
Bible, 13, 90
   see also Scriptures
Bodichon, Mme. Eugène, 17, 21, 90
Bray, Charles, 11, 32, 90, 112
   The Philosophy of Necessity, 12
Bray, Mrs. Charles, 18, 227, 244
Brezzi, Joseph, 6
Bridges, J. H., 251 n.6
Browning, Oscar, 226

INDEX

novels amplify, 126–127
positivists' definition of, 50–51
religion product of, 91
source and limit of knowledge, 73, 74
transmittal by tradition, 58, 193
experience–vision–sympathy pattern, 68–71, 126–127, 128–129, 146–147, 228
in Adam Bede, 151–153
in Daniel Deronda, 204–209
in Dorothea Brooke, 186–192
in Maggie Tulliver, 163, 165–167
see also experience–vision–sympathy pattern
experiments in life
GE's novels as, 116–121, 127, 147–148, 219, 222, 242
like scientist's experiments, 38–39
Ezra, 196

feeling, 165, 166
morality product of, 57, 64, 70–71, 124, 244, 248
truth of, 61–63, 120
fellow-feeling, 66, 68, 69
moral order manifested in, 52, 121
Feltes, N. N., 257 n.5
Feuerbach, Ludwig, 6, 14, 25, 79, 84–87, 92–98, 100, 102, 103, 104–113 passim, 115, 116, 117, 129, 136, 153, 165, 171, 180, 216, 223, 225, 246, 248, 256 n.4
The Essence of Christianity, 84; 92; 255 n.19; 256 n.4, 5, 7, 13–17, 19–21; 257 n.6; 258 n.4; 260 n.6; 261 n.1, 2, 5
The Essence of Religion, 112
Fichte, Johann Gottlieb, 76, 93
Fielding, Henry, 30
forms of thought
evolved, 51, 59, 60, 254 n.6
free will, 121, 122, 124, 126, 246
see also inheritance of acquired characteristics
gambling, 130, 131, 170, 175, 225, 233

God, 56, 168, 170, 237, 239, 240, 248
as a moral influence, 111–112

Bulstrode's relation to, 171–172
Dr. Cumming's, 110–112
Feuerbach's analyses of, 93–97, 105–108, 153
ideal of a human goodness, 57
other men influence our idea of, 223–224, 241
pantheistic conception of, 12–13, 251–252 n.13
relinquishment of, 46
Silas Marner's relation to, 139–141
Goethe, Johann Wolfgang von, 77–78, 80–81, 84, 120, 147
"Experiment as the Mediator between the Object and the Subject," 83
Greece, 195
Greeks
religion of, 91
Greg, William Rathbone
The Creed of Christendom, 153–154
Gruppe, O. F., 73–74, 77, 80
Gegenwart und Zukunft der Philosophie in Deutschland, 73
Haeckel, Ernst Heinrich, 114
Hagan, John, 260 n.1
Haight, Gordon S., 251 n.8; 259 n.1; 260 n.6
Hanson, Lawrence and Elisabeth, 260 n.6
Hardy, Barbara, vii, viii, 4, 147, 253 n.12, 257 n.1, 258 n.2, 259 n.1, 261 n.7
Harrison, Frederick, 57, 119
Hartley, David, 76
Harvey, W. J., vii, viii, 353 n.15, 257 n.16, 258 n.6, 259 n.1
heart, needs of, 1, 3, 4, 24, 243
Hegel, Georg Wilhelm Friedrich, 76, 92, 93
Hennell, Charles Christian, 90
influence upon GE, 11–13, 91–93
interpretation of Christ, 11, 92
pantheism of, 12–13
Christian Theism, 12; 252 n.14, 15
Inquiry Concerning the Origin of Christianity, 12, 255 n.2
Hennell, Sara, 10, 16, 22, 44, 90, 92, 93, 138, 186
Christianity and Infidelity, 90
Thoughts in Aid of Faith, 61

275

Higher Criticism, 11–13, 90–92
see also Hennell, Strauss, Spinoza
Höffding, Harald, 59, 254 n.6
Hook, Sidney, 4, 79; 123; 255 n.8; 256 n.3
Hornung, Joseph, 125
Houghton, Mrs. Henry, 44
Hume, David, 59, 74, 76
Huxley, T. H.
on cosmic vs. ethical processes, 53–55
"Evolution and Ethics," 53, 254 n.1

Idealism, 4, 56, 59, 76, 77–78, 80, 93
see also metaphysics
identity
racial, 64, 193–198, 206–209, 210–214
social, 217
imagination, 222, 249
GE's theory of, 34–42 *passim,* 118
historic, 41–42
immortality experienced through, 46
moral, 67, 70
same for artist and scientist, 35–36
see also vision
immortality, 68, 69
GE's objections to doctrine of, 112
impersonal, 46, 102, 116, 249
individual
impersonal immortality of, 46
importance of, 45–46
relation to society of, viii, 42–49 *passim,* 193–204, 209–210, 216–217, 223
inheritance of acquired characteristics, 48; 51; 59–61; 71; 193; 196; 207–208; 210–211; 254 n.6, 7, 9; 260 n.3
see also evolution, forms of thought, moral order
innate ideas
rejected by positivists, 50, 72-B
intelligence
necessary for vision, 55, 68
interaction
between individual and society, 42–43, 47–48, 71, 259 n.1
central to positivistic cosmology, 27–30

knowledge derived from, 50
of character and circumstance, 49–50
see also change

Jackson, Martha, 10, 13
James, Henry, 115, 191, 259 n.1, 260 n.2, 261 n.4
Literary Reviews and Essays, 257 n.5
Partial Portraits, 257 n.1
Jews, Jewish life, 64, 65, 125–126, 141, 195–197, 207–209, 240
Johnson, Dr. Samuel, 7

Kant, Immanuel, 58, 59, 76, 93
Kempis, Thomas À., 62–63, 100, 163
The Imitation of Christ, 62–63, 160–161, 204, 224
Kepler, Johann, 120
Kettle, Arnold, 259 n.1
Kingsley, Charles, 125
knowledge
derived from experience, 50–51
difficulty of, 43
gives power, 243–244
intuitive, 50–51, 72–73, 74, 76
novel an instrument of, 116–120
problem of, 72
relativity of, 73, 76, 94–95
see also epistemology, experience, vision

Laennec, Réné, 175
Langer, Suzanne, 3
laws of nature, 75
positivistic conception of, 28–30
Leavis, F. R., vii, viii, 156–157, 259 n.1, 260 n.3, 261 n.4
Lecky, W. E. H.
History of Rationalism, 25
Leibnitz, Gottfried Wilhelm, 29
Levin, Konstantin, 244
Levine, George, 257 n.11
Lewes, G. H., 3, 14, 25, 30, 42, 61, 119, 216, 254 n.6
epistemology of, 75–81 *passim,* 120
cosmic evolution, 29
Dorothea, 8
experience, 50–51
Goethe, 77–78, 80–81, 83

The manuscript was edited by Alexander Brede. The book was designed by Peter Nothstein. The type face is Linotype Granjon, designed in 1924 by George W. Jones based on a face originally cut by Claude Garamond in the 16th Century.

The book is printed on Warren's Olde Style Antique and bound in Interlaken Vellum Deluxe. Manufactured in the United States of America.